BUYING A HOME IN PORTUGAL

by

David Hampshire

SURVIVAL BOOKS • LONDON • ENGLAND

First published 1998
Second Edition 2002

Survival Books Limited, 1st Floor, 60 St James's Street
London SW1A 1ZN, United Kingdom
☎ +44 (0)20-7493 4244, 🖹 +44 (0)20-7491 0605
✉ info@survivalbooks.net
🖥 www.survivalbooks.net

British Library Cataloguing in Publication Data.
A CIP record for this book is available from the British Library.
ISBN 1 901130 52 5

Printed and bound in Finland by WS Bookwell Ltd

ACKNOWLEDGEMENTS

My sincere thanks to all those who contributed to the second edition of this book, in particular Joanna Styles, who researched and updated this edition, and Joe and Kerry Laredo (proof-reading and desktop publishing). I would also like to thank Maria de Jesus E. Pina, Frances Belo, Michael Clarke and Soren Hojbjerg for their help and everyone else who contributed in any way whom I have omitted to mention. Finally a special thank you to Jim Watson for the superb cover, cartoons and maps.

What Readers and Reviewers

When you buy a model plane for your child, a video recorder, or some new computer gizmo, you get with it a leaflet or booklet pleading 'Read Me First', or bearing large friendly letters or bold type saying 'IMPORTANT – follow the instructions carefully'. This book should be similarly supplied to all those entering France with anything more durable than a 5-day return ticket. It is worth reading even if you are just visiting briefly, or if you have lived here for years and feel totally knowledgeable and secure. But if you need to find out how France works then it is indispensable. Native French people probably have a less thorough understanding of how their country functions. – Where it is most essential, the book is most up to the minute.

Living France

We would like to congratulate you on this work: it is really super! We hand it out to our expatriates and they read it with great interest and pleasure.

ICI (Switzerland) AG

Rarely has a 'survival guide' contained such useful advice. This book dispels doubts for first-time travellers, yet is also useful for seasoned globetrotters – In a word, if you're planning to move to the USA or go there for a long-term stay, then buy this book both for general reading and as a ready-reference.

American Citizens Abroad

It is everything you always wanted to ask but didn't for fear of the contemptuous put down – The best English-language guide – Its pages are stuffed with practical information on everyday subjects and are designed to complement the traditional guidebook.

Swiss News

A complete revelation to me – I found it both enlightening and interesting, not to mention amusing.

Carole Clark

Let's say it at once. David Hampshire's *Living and Working in France* is the best handbook ever produced for visitors and foreign residents in this country; indeed, my discussion with locals showed that it has much to teach even those born and bred in l'Hexagone. – It is Hampshire's meticulous detail which lifts his work way beyond the range of other books with similar titles. Often you think of a supplementary question and search for the answer in vain. With Hampshire this is rarely the case. – He writes with great clarity (and gives French equivalents of all key terms), a touch of humour and a ready eye for the odd (and often illuminating) fact. – This book is absolutely indispensable.

The Riviera Reporter

Have Said About Survival Books

What a great work, wealth of useful information, well-balanced wording and accuracy in details. My compliments!

Thomas Müller

This handbook has all the practical information one needs to set up home in the UK – The sheer volume of information is almost daunting – Highly recommended for anyone moving to the UK.

American Citizens Abroad

A very good book which has answered so many questions and even some I hadn't thought of – I would certainly recommend it.

Brian Fairman

A mine of information – I may have avoided some embarrassments and frights if I had read it prior to my first Swiss encounters – Deserves an honoured place on any newcomer's bookshelf.

English Teachers Association, Switzerland

Covers just about all the things you want to know on the subject – In answer to the desert island question about the one how-to book on France, this book would be it – Almost 500 pages of solid accurate reading – This book is about enjoyment as much as survival.

The Recorder

it's so funny – I love it and definitely need a copy of my own – Thanks very much for having written such a humorous and helpful book.

Heidi Guiliani

A must for all foreigners coming to Switzerland.

Antoinette O'Donoghue

A comprehensive guide to all things French, written in a highly readable and amusing style, for anyone planning to live, work or retire in France.

The Times

A concise, thorough account of the DOs and DON'Ts for a foreigner in Switzerland – Crammed with useful information and lightened with humorous quips which make the facts more readable.
American Citizens Abroad

Covers every conceivable question that may be asked concerning everyday life – I know of no other book that could take the place of this one.

France in Print

Hats off to *Living and Working in Switzerland*!

Ronnie Almeida

R. Minho

Valença

Bragança

Chaves

Braga

Vila Real

Porto

R. Douro

Atlantic

Ocean

R. Vougo

Aveiro

Guarda

Covilhã

R. Mondego

Coimbra

Serra da Estrela
Nature Park

Figueira
da Foz

Castelo
Branco

SPAIN

Batalha

Tomar

Alcobaça

Portalegre

Obidos

Santarém

R. Tagus

Sintra

Estremoz

Elvas

Lisbon

Estoril

Setúbal

Évora

R. Sado

Beja

R. Guadiana

Sines

Lagos

Albufeira

Faro

Sagres

CONTENTS

APPENDICES 217

INDEX 247

ORDER FORMS 254

IMPORTANT NOTE

Readers should note that the laws and regulations for buying property in Portugal <u>aren't</u> the same as in other countries and are also liable to change periodically. **I cannot recommend too strongly that you check with an official and reliable source (not always the same) and take expert legal advice before paying any money or signing any legal documents. Don't however, believe everything you're told or read, even, dare say it, herein!**

To help you obtain further information and verify data with official sources, useful addresses and references to other sources of information have been included in all chapters and in appendices A to C. Important points have been emphasised throughout the book in **bold** print, some of which it would be expensive and foolish to disregard. **Ignore them at your peril or cost.** Unless specifically stated, the reference to any company, organisation, product or publication in this book doesn't constitute an endorsement or recommendation.

AUTHOR'S NOTES

- Costs and prices should be taken as estimates only, although they were mostly correct at the time of publication.

- His/he/him also means her/she/her (please forgive me ladies). This is done to make life easier for both the reader and (in particular) the author, and isn't intended to be sexist.

- Spelling is (mostly) English and not American.

- Warnings and important points are shown in **bold** type.

- The following symbols are used in this book: ☎ (telephone), 🖹 (fax), 🖳 (Internet) and ✉ (e-mail).

- Lists of **Useful Addresses**, **Further Reading** and **Useful Websites** are contained in **Appendices A, B and C** respectively.

- For those unfamiliar with the Metric system of weights and measures, imperial conversion tables are included in **Appendix D**.

- The Portuguese translation of many key words and phrases is shown in brackets in *italics*. A list of property, mortgage and other terms used in this book is included in a Glossary in **Appendix E**.

- Maps of Portugal showing the regions and provinces are included in **Appendix F**. A map of Portugal showing the major cities and geographical features is shown on page 6.

INTRODUCTION

If you're planning to buy a home in Portugal or even just thinking about it – this is the book for you! Whether you want a villa, farmhouse, townhouse or an apartment, a holiday or a permanent home, this book will help make your dreams come true. The purpose of *Buying a Home in Portugal* is to provide you with the information necessary to help you choose the most favourable location and the most appropriate home to satisfy your individual requirements. Most importantly, it will help you avoid the pitfalls and risks associated with buying a home in Portugal, which for most people is one of the largest financial transactions they will undertake during their lifetimes.

You may already own a home in your home country, however, buying a home in Portugal (or in any foreign country) is a different matter altogether. One of the most common mistakes people make when buying a home in Portugal is to assume that the laws and purchase procedures are the same as in their home country. This is almost certainly not the case! Buying property in Portugal is generally safe, although if you don't follow the rules provided for your protection, a purchase can result in serious financial losses, as some people have discovered to their cost.

Before buying a home in Portugal you need to ask yourself exactly why you want to buy a home there. Is your primary concern a good long-term investment or do you wish to work or retire there? Where and what can you afford to buy? Do you plan to let (rent) your home to offset the running costs? What about property, capital gains and inheritance taxes? *Buying a Home in Portugal* will help you answer these and many other questions. It won't, however, tell you where to live and what to buy, or whether having made your decision you will be happy – that part is up to you!

For many people, buying a home in Portugal has previously been a case of pot luck. However, with a copy of *Buying a Home in Portugal* to hand you'll have a wealth of priceless information at your fingertips – information derived from a variety of sources, both official and unofficial; not least the hard won personal experiences of the author, his friends, colleagues and acquaintances. This book doesn't, however, contain all the answers (most of us don't even know the right questions to ask). What it will do is reduce the risk of making an expensive mistake that you will bitterly regret later and help you make informed decisions and calculated judgements, instead of costly mistakes and uneducated guesses (forewarned is forearmed!). **Most importantly of all, it will help you save money and will repay your investment many times over.**

The world-wide recession in the early 1990s caused an upheaval in world property markets, during which many 'gilt-edged' property investments went to the wall. However, property remains one of the best long-term investments and it's certainly one of the most pleasurable. Buying a home in Portugal is a wonderful way to make new friends, broaden your horizons and revitalise your life – and it provides a welcome bolt-hole to recuperate from the stresses and strains of modern life. I trust this book will help you avoid the pitfalls and smooth your way to many happy years in your new home in Portugal, secure in the knowledge that you have made the right decision.

Good luck!

David Hampshire
May 2002

1.

WHY PORTUGAL?

If you want guaranteed year-round sunshine, kilometres of beautiful white sandy beaches, excellent food (particularly seafood), a wide selection of entertainment and an abundant choice of quality homes at affordable prices, then Portugal may be just what you're looking for. Although the vast majority of holidaymakers (and residents) come to Portugal to soak up the sun, there's much more to the country than beaches and swimming pools. Portugal has something for everyone including magnificent beaches for sun-worshippers; spectacular unspoilt countryside for greens; a surfeit of mountains and waters for sports fans; a lively night-life for the jet set; elegant and sophisticated manageable cities for 'townies'; good wine and cuisine for gourmets; a wealth of outstanding historic buildings and monuments, museums and galleries for art lovers; numerous festivals and fiestas for inveterate party-goers; and tranquillity for the stressed. When buying a home in Portugal you aren't simply buying a home, but a lifestyle, and as a location for a holiday, retirement or permanent home, it has few equals.

There are many excellent reasons for buying a home in Portugal, although it's important not to be under any illusions regarding what you can expect from a home there. The first and most important question you need to ask yourself is exactly why you want to buy a home in Portugal. For example, are you seeking a holiday or a retirement home? If you're seeking a second home, will it be mainly used for long weekends or for lengthier stays? Do you plan to let it to offset the mortgage and running costs? If so, how important is the property income? Are you primarily looking for a sound investment or do you plan to work or start a business in Portugal? Often buyers have a variety of reasons for buying a home abroad; for example many people buy a holiday home with a view to living there permanently or semi-permanently when they retire. If this is the case there are many more factors to take into account than if you're 'simply' buying a holiday home which you will occupy for just a few weeks a year (when it's usually wiser not to buy at all!). If, on the other hand, you plan to work or start a business in Portugal, you will be faced with a whole different set of criteria.

Can you really afford to buy a home in Portugal? What of the future? Is your income secure and protected against inflation and currency fluctuations? In the late 1980s many foreigners purchased holiday homes in Portugal by taking out second mortgages on their family homes abroad and stretching their financial resources to the limits. Not surprisingly, when the recession struck in the early 1990s many people had their homes repossessed or were forced to sell at a huge loss when they were unable to maintain the payments. Buying a home abroad can be a good long-term investment, although in recent years many people have had their fingers burnt in the volatile property market in many countries, including Portugal.

Property values in Portugal increase at an average of around 5 per cent a year or in line with inflation (with little or no increase in real terms), although in some fashionable resorts and developments prices rise faster than average, which is usually reflected in much higher purchase prices. There's a stable property market in most of Portugal (barring recessions), which acts as a discouragement to speculators wishing to make a fast buck, particularly when you consider that capital gains tax can wipe out much of the profit made on the sale of a second home. You also need to recover the costs associated with buying a home in Portugal when you sell. **You shouldn't expect to make a quick profit when buying property in Portugal, but should look upon it as an investment in your family's future happiness, rather than merely in financial terms.**

There are both advantages and disadvantages to buying a home in Portugal, although for most people the benefits outweigh the drawbacks. Among the many advantages are guaranteed sunshine and mild winters (particularly in the Algarve); one of the best climates and least spoilt regions in Europe (most of Portugal is a sleepy, laid-back place more in tune with the 19th or mid-20th century than the new millennium); good value for money; relatively inexpensive to get to from most western European countries; good rental possibilities (in most areas); an abundance of local craftsmen and home services (particularly in resort areas); excellent sports facilities, particularly for water sports, golf and tennis; fine food and wine at reasonable prices; a slower, relaxed pace of life and a healthy lifestyle; the friendliness and warmth of the Portuguese people; the beauty and tranquillity of Portugal on your doorstep; stable democratic government and membership of the European Union (EU); and, last but not least, the superb quality of life.

Among the disadvantages of buying a home in Portugal are the relatively high costs associated with buying; possible unexpected renovation and restoration costs (if you don't do your homework); the dangers of buying a property with debts and other problems (if you don't take legal advice); a high rate of burglary and housebreaking in some areas; overcrowding in popular tourist areas during the peak summer season; high traffic congestion in most towns and cities; poor roads and infrastructure in most rural areas; periodic water shortages in some regions (particularly during the summer); and the expense of getting to and from Portugal if you own a holiday home there and don't live in a nearby country (or a country with good air connections).

Unless you know exactly what you're looking for and where, it's best to rent a property for a period until you're more familiar with an area. As when making all major financial decisions, it's never wise to be too hasty. Many people make expensive (even catastrophic) errors when buying a home abroad, usually because they do insufficient research and are in too much of a hurry, often setting themselves ridiculous deadlines such as buying a home during a long weekend break or a week's holiday. Not surprisingly, most people wouldn't dream of acting so rashly when buying a property in their home country! It isn't uncommon for buyers to regret their decision after some time and wish they had purchased a different property in a different region (or even in a different country!).

Before deciding to buy a home in Portugal, it's best to do extensive research and read as much as you can about Portugal and what it's like to live (or work) there. It also helps to study specialist property magazines such as World of Property and Homes Overseas (see Appendix A for a list), and to visit overseas property exhibitions such as those organised by World of Property in Britain. **Bear in mind that the cost of investing in a few books or magazines (and other research) is tiny compared with the expense of making a big mistake.** Don't, however, believe everything you read!

This chapter provides information about permits and visas, retirement, working, starting a business, communications, getting to Portugal and getting around (particularly with regard to driving).

DO YOU NEED A PERMIT OR VISA?

Before making any plans to buy a home in Portugal, you must check whether you will need a visa or residence card (see page 209) and ensure that you will be permitted to use the property when you wish and for whatever purpose you have in mind. While foreigners are freely permitted to buy property in Portugal, visitors aren't allowed to remain longer than 60 or 90 days at a time (depending on nationality) without obtaining an extension or a residence permit. If there's a possibility that you or a family member may wish to live permanently or work in Portugal, you should enquire whether it will be possible before making any plans to buy a home there.

All foreigners need a residence card (*autorização de residência*) to live permanently in Portugal and non-EU nationals may need a visa to enter Portugal, either as a visitor or for any other purpose. Citizens of non-EU countries may need to obtain a visa (*visto para residência*) from a Portuguese consulate in their home country before coming to Portugal to work, study or live. All foreigners need a residence card (*autorização de residência*) to live permanently in Portugal, including EU nationals. Applications must be made at the nearest Foreigners' Department (*Serviço de Estrangeiros e Fronteiras/SEF*) of the Portuguese Ministry of Internal Affairs (there are offices in most major cities). Non-EU nationals planning to reside permanently in Portugal must obtain a 'residence visa' before entering the country. Proof of income is required for both residence and work permits. After obtaining a residence card you must then obtain a Portuguese (blue) identity card (*bilhete de indentidade*).

When in Portugal you should always carry your foreign or Portuguese identity card or passport. You can be asked to produce your identification papers at any time by the Portuguese police or other officials, and if you don't have them with you, you can be fined (although this is unlikely). **Permit** infringements are taken seriously by the Portuguese authorities and if you're discovered living illegally in Portugal there are severe penalties, including fines and even deportation for flagrant abuses (which will mean being excluded from Portugal for a number of years).

RETIREMENT

Most foreigners planning to retire in Portugal no longer require a residence visa (*visto para residência*) from a Portuguese consulate before arriving in Portugal. EU nationals can come to Portugal as visitors and remain for up to 180 days, although after 90 days they must apply for an extension to remain as a visitor for a further 90 days or apply for a residence card (*autorização de residência*). Non-EU nationals who arrive by air must complete a form (half of which is in effect a residence visa) allowing them to stay for up to 60 days and which can be extended twice (60 days each time) up to a maximum of 180 days. Before 180 days have expired they must apply for a residence card if they wish to remain longer.

All non-employed residents must provide proof that they have an adequate income or financial resources to live in Portugal without working. A Portuguese bank statement showing a balance of around €3,000 generally suffices or a letter from a Portuguese bank manager stating that you regularly import money. Non-EU nationals require copies of their bank statements and, if married, a statement from the husband certifying that he is supporting his wife (or from the wife is she's the main breadwinner). The minimum income necessary for EU nationals is roughly equivalent (there's no official figure) to the Portuguese statutory minimum wage, which was €348.01 per month in 2001, or the amount Portugal provides to its citizens on social security programmes. Hopefully your income will be far greater than this, otherwise you will find it impossible to survive! If your income is fixed, you should be aware that it could be outstripped by rises in the cost of living (see **Cost of Living** on page 115).

EU nationals receiving a state pension from an EU country are entitled to subsidised health treatment in Portugal including free emergency treatment. If you're in receipt of a state pension, you must show that you've transferred your state pension to Portugal and produce form E121 when registering with the regional office of Portuguese social security (*Centro Regional de Segurança Social*). If you aren't in receipt of a state pension or are a non-EU national, private health insurance is necessary.

WORKING

If there's a possibility that you or any family members may wish to work in Portugal, you must ensure that it will be possible before buying a home. If you don't qualify to live and work in Portugal by birthright, family relationship or as a national of an EU country (or a European Economic Area country), obtaining a work permit may be difficult or even impossible. If you're an EU national, you don't require official approval to live or work in Portugal, although you still require a residence card (*autorização de residência*). If you visit Portugal to look for work, you have 180 days in which to find employment or establish a business and apply for a residence card.

EU nationals who come to Portugal to work for a period of less than three months and seasonal workers whose work duration doesn't exceed eight months, don't require a residence card. Employees whose work period will last more than three months and less than 12 months require a temporary residence permit valid for the duration of their employment contract. If the contract is extended, but the total (cumulative) period doesn't exceed one year, the residence card will be extended for a period equal to the work extension. If the cumulative work period exceeds one year, the renewed residence card will automatically be valid for five years.

Before moving to Portugal to work, you should dispassionately examine your motives and credentials. What kind of work can you realistically expect to do in Portugal? What are your qualifications and experience? Are they recognised in Portugal? How good is your Portuguese? Unless it's fluent, you won't be competing on equal terms with the Portuguese (you won't anyway, but that's a different matter!). Most Portuguese employers aren't interested in employing anyone without at least a working knowledge of Portuguese. Are there any jobs in your profession or trade in the area where you wish to live? The answers to these and many other questions can be disheartening, but it's better to ask them before moving to Portugal than afterwards. Note that salaries in Portugal are generally low and the Portuguese are among the poorest paid workers in the EU. Exceptional skills and qualifications are required to get a decent job in most industries, plus language proficiency.

Many people turn to self-employment or start a business (see below) to make a living, although this path is strewn with pitfalls for the newcomer. **Most foreigners don't do sufficient homework before moving to Portugal.** While hoping for the best, you should plan for the worst case scenario and have a contingency plan and sufficient funds to last until you're established (this also applies to employees). If you're planning to start a business in Portugal, you must also do battle with the notoriously obstructive bureaucracy (good luck/*¡boa sorte!*). **Note that it's difficult for non-EU nationals to obtain a residence permit to be self-employed in Portugal.**

Self-employment

If you're an EU-national or a permanent resident with a residence card (*autorização de residência*), you can work as a self-employed person or as a sole trader in Portugal. If you want to be self-employed in a profession or trade in Portugal, you must meet certain legal requirements and register with the appropriate organisation, as applicable. Under Portuguese law a self-employed person may require an official status and it may be illegal to simply hang up a sign and start business. Members of some professions and trades must possess professional qualifications and certificates recognised in Portugal and are usually required to sit a written examination in Portuguese. In certain professions, such as the law, it's unusual to be permitted to practise in Portugal without Portuguese qualifications.

As a self-employed person you don't have the protection of a limited company should your business fail, although there are certain tax advantages. It may be advantageous to operate as a limited company such as a *Sociedade por Quotas (Lda)*.

Obtain professional advice before deciding whether to operate as a sole trader or form a company in Portugal, as it has far-reaching social security, tax and other consequences. All self-employed persons must register for income tax, social security and VAT (IVA), and anyone with an income in Portugal requires a foreigner's identification number (*numero de contribuinte*), obtainable from your local tax office (*finanças*).

Starting a Business

Most foreigners find Portugal a frustrating country in which to do business. The bureaucracy associated with starting a business there is staggering and ranks among the most pernicious in the western world (even worse than France and Spain). For foreigners the red tape is almost impenetrable, especially if you don't speak Portuguese, as you will be inundated with official documents and must be able to understand them. It's only when you come up against the full force of Portuguese bureaucracy that you understand what it <u>really</u> means to be a foreigner in Portugal! It's difficult not to believe that the authorities' sole purpose in life is to obstruct business (in fact it's to protect their own jobs).

Patience and tolerance are the watchwords when dealing with Portuguese bureaucrats (and will do wonders for your blood pressure). Although many foreigners find it hard to believe, things have improved considerably in recent years and the regulations and procedures have become less onerous since Portugal joined the EU. Despite the red tape, Portugal is traditionally a country of small companies and sole traders, and there are hundreds of thousands of family-run businesses (of all sizes) employing the vast majority of the working population. Among the best sources of help and information are your local chamber of commerce (*câmara de comércio*) and town hall (*câmara*).

Prospects: Many small businesses in Portugal exist on a shoestring, with owners living from hand to mouth, and certainly aren't what could be considered thriving enterprises. Self-employed businessmen usually work extremely long hours, particularly those running bars or restaurants (days off are almost impossible in the high season), often for little financial reward. As in most countries, many people choose to be self-employed for the lifestyle and freedom it affords (no clocks or bosses), rather than the money. It's important to keep your plans small and manageable and work well within your budget, rather than undertake a grandiose scheme. You should be prepared to spend some years getting established, during which time you may be lucky to meet your expenses (therefore it's important to have sufficient capital to tide you over), particularly if you're paying rent (or a mortgage) on both your home and business premises.

Location: Choosing the location for a business is even more important than the location for a home. Depending on the type of business, you may need access to motorway and rail links or to be located in a popular tourist area or near local attractions. Local plans regarding communications, industry and major building developments, e.g. housing developments and new shopping centres, may also be important. Plans regarding new motorways and rail links are normally available from local town halls.

Experience: Generally speaking you shouldn't consider running a business in Portugal in a field in which you don't have previous experience (excluding 'businesses' such as bed and breakfast or self-catering accommodation, where experience isn't usually necessary). It's often wise to work for someone else in the same line of business to gain experience, rather than jump in at the deep end. Thoroughly investigate an existing or proposed business before investing any money. **As any expert (and many failed entrepreneurs) will tell you, Portugal isn't a country for amateurs, particularly amateurs who don't speak fluent Portuguese.** It isn't always necessary to speak Portuguese if your customers will be exclusively foreigners, although it's important that at least one partner or employee speaks fluent Portuguese. Otherwise you will need to pay a secretary, business agent or *despachante* (see below) to do simple tasks that you could easily do yourself.

Employees: Hiring employees shouldn't be taken lightly in Portugal and must be taken into account <u>before</u> starting a business. You must enter into a contract under Portuguese labour law and employees enjoy extensive rights. It's also <u>very</u> expensive to hire employees, as in addition to salaries you must usually pay social security contributions plus 14 months' salary a year, five weeks' paid annual holiday and around 14 paid public holidays.

Type of Business: The most common businesses operated by foreigners in Portugal include holiday accommodation, e.g. bed & breakfast and self-catering accommodation; caravan and camping sites; farming; catering (e.g. bars, cafés and restaurants); hotels; shops; franchises; estate agencies; translation and interpretation; language schools; and holiday and sports centres (e.g. gymnasiums, tennis, golf, squash, water sports and horse-riding).

The majority of businesses established by foreigners are linked to the leisure and catering industries, followed by property investment and development.

Tourism-based Businesses: If you're planning to buy or start a mainly seasonal business based on tourism, check carefully whether the potential income will be sufficient to provide you with a living wage. This also applies to most bars and restaurants in resort areas, particularly those run by foreigners, many of which open and close within one season. Don't overestimate the length of the season or the potential income and, most importantly, don't believe everything a person selling you a business tells you (although every word may be true). Nobody sells a good business for a bargain price, least of all one making huge profits. In resort areas, trade falls off dramatically outside the main tourist season (June to September) and many businesses must survive for a whole year on the income earned in the summer months. The rest of the year you may be lucky to cover your costs. A vendor may tell you that the official books show only a fraction of the actual turnover, although you should take such claims with a pinch of salt unless they're backed by irrefutable documentary evidence (which is highly unlikely).

Buying an Existing Business: It's much easier to buy an existing business in Portugal rather than start a new one and it's also less of a risk. The paperwork for taking over an existing business is also simpler, although still complex. Note, however, that buying a business that's a going concern is difficult as the Portuguese aren't in the habit of buying and selling viable businesses, which are usually passed down from generation to generation. If you plan to buy a business, obtain an independent valuation (or two) and employ an accountant to audit the books. **Never sign anything you don't understand 110 per cent and even if you think you understand it, you should still obtain unbiased professional advice, e.g. from local experts such as banks and accountants.** In fact it's best not to start a business until you have the infrastructure established, including an accountant, lawyer and banking facilities. There are various ways to set up a small business in Portugal and it's essential to obtain professional advice regarding the best method of establishing and registering a business, which can dramatically affect your tax position. It's also important to employ an accountant to do your books (but keep a close eye on the fees).

Starting a New Business: Most people are far too optimistic about the prospects of a new business in Portugal and over-estimate income levels (it often takes years to make a profit). Be realistic or even pessimistic when estimating your income and overestimate the costs and underestimate the revenue (then reduce it by 50 per cent!). While hoping for the best, you should plan for the worst and have sufficient funds to last until you're established. New projects are rarely, if ever, completed within budget and you need to ensure that you have sufficient working capital and can survive until a business takes off. Portuguese banks are wary of lending to new businesses, especially businesses run by foreigners. If you wish to borrow money to buy property or for a business venture in Portugal, you should carefully consider where and in what currency to raise the necessary finance.

Legal Advice: Before establishing a business or undertaking any business transactions in Portugal, it's important to obtain legal advice to ensure that you're operating within the law. There are severe penalties for anyone who ignores the regulations and legal requirements. Expert legal advice is also necessary to make the most of any favourable tax and business breaks, and to make sense of the myriad of rules and regulations. It's imperative to ensure that contracts are clearly defined and water-tight before making an investment, as if you become involved in a legal dispute it's likely to take years to resolve. Before starting a business in Portugal you should obtain advice from a lawyer (*advogado*) and an accountant (*contabilista*). Many foreigners also employ an intermediary, called a *despachante*, to act as a middleman between them and the bureaucracy. This speaks volumes for the stifling and tortuous Portuguese bureaucracy, which is so complicated and cumbersome that it's necessary for citizens to employ a special official simply to do business with the government! Many Portuguese lawyers, accountants and agents speak English and other languages, particularly in resort areas.

Avoiding the Crooks: In addition to problems with the Portuguese authorities, assorted crooks and swindlers are unfortunately fairly common in Portugal, particularly in resort areas. You should always have a healthy suspicion regarding the motives of anyone you do business with in Portugal (unless it's your mum or spouse), particularly your fellow countrymen. It's generally best to avoid partnerships as they rarely work and can be a disaster. In general, you should trust nobody and shouldn't sign anything or pay any money before having a contract checked by a lawyer. It's a sad fact of life that foreigners who prey on their fellow countrymen are common in Portugal. In most cases you're better off dealing with a long-established Portuguese company with roots in the local community (and therefore a good reputation to protect), rather than your compatriots. Note that if things go wrong you may be unprotected by Portuguese law, the wheels of which grind extremely slowly (when they haven't fallen off completely!).

Research: <u>Beware</u>! For many foreigners, starting a business in Portugal is one of the quickest routes to bankruptcy known to mankind. In fact, the majority of foreigners who open businesses in Portugal would be better off investing in lottery tickets, when they would at least have a chance of getting a return on their investment! Many would-be entrepreneurs leave Portugal with literally only their shirts on their backs, having learnt the facts of Portuguese business life the hard way. **If you aren't prepared to thoroughly research the market and obtain expert business and legal advice, then you shouldn't even think about starting a business in Portugal (or anywhere else for that matter).**

The key to starting or buying a successful business in Portugal is exhaustive research, research and yet more research (plus innovation, value for money and service). It's an absolute must to check out the level of competition in a given area. Note that even when competition is light, there may be insufficient business to sustain another competitor. A saturation of trades and services is common in Portugal, particularly in resort areas where there's a glut of bars, cafés, restaurants and retail outlets catering to tourists. **Your chances of making a living from a bar, restaurant or retail outlet in a resort area are practically zero, as there's simply too much competition and too few customers to go around.**

Some foreigners (e.g. bar and restaurant owners) will do almost anything to lure their competitors' customers, even reducing prices to below cost. In winter you may be lucky to take eurosymbol100 a day in a bar and it often isn't worth opening your doors! The Portuguese survive because they invariably own their business premises, have low overheads and live inexpensively. If you're convinced that you have what it takes, don't burn your bridges and sell up abroad, but rent a home in Portugal and spend some time doing research before taking the plunge. You should also lease your business premises (at least initially), rather than buying them outright. However, before doing so it's imperative to ensure that you fully understand your rights regarding possible future rent increases and the renewal and termination of a lease.

Many foreigners start businesses in Portugal on a whim and a prayer with little business acumen or money and no understanding of Portuguese. They're simply asking for trouble. **It's pitiful (but all too common) to see newcomers working all the hours under the sun struggling to make a living from a business that's doomed to failure.** Bear in mind that when a couple operate a business together, it can put an intolerable strain on their relationship and many marriages fail under the pressures.

Further Information: Most international accountants have offices in Lisbon and are an invaluable source of information (in English and other languages) on subjects such as forming a company, company law, taxation and social security. Price Waterhouse publishes a useful booklet, *Doing Business in Portugal*, which costs around US$40 and can be ordered online (⌨ www.pwcglobal.com).

Wealth Warning: Whatever people may tell you, working for yourself isn't easy and it requires a lot of hard work (self-employed people generally work much longer hours than employees); a sizeable investment and sufficient operating funds (under-funding is the major cause of business failures); good organisation (e.g. bookkeeping and planning); excellent customer relations; and a measure of luck (although generally the harder you work, the more 'luck' you will have). Don't be seduced by the relaxed way of life in Portugal – if you want to be a success in business you cannot play at it.

Nevertheless, although there are numerous failures for every success story, many foreigners <u>do</u> run successful businesses in Portugal. Those who make a go of it do so as a result of extensive market research, wise investments, excellent customer relations and most important of all, a lot of hard work.

KEEPING IN TOUCH

Although Portuguese technology isn't the best in the world, its communications services (both domestic and international) have improved considerably in the last decade. The country now enjoys good telephone (including mobile phones), fax, mail (although extremely variable) and courier services.

Telephone

The Portuguese telephone service used to be operated exclusively by Telecom Portugal, which was a state-owned monopoly. However, in 2000 the telecommunications market was fully liberalised and numerous providers now operate in the Portuguese market, which because of competition has opened up considerably and become much more competitive with welcome reductions in the price of calls. Although there are many providers, a substantial number provide telephone services for companies only and Telecom Portugal is still the market leader with Novis and Oni the main competitors in the domestic call market. All operators have comprehensive websites, parts of which are available in English, where you can consult charges etc.: Telecom Portugal (🖳 www.telecom.pt), Novis (🖳 www.ip.pt) and Oni (🖳 www.onisolutions.pt).

Until fairly recently, the Portuguese telephone system was antiquated and unreliable, but it has undergone extensive modernisation and is now much improved with most of the network having digital switching and 'state of the art' technology. Telephone usage tends to rate below that of most other western European countries, although recently it has increased significantly because of cheaper call charges and the use of mobile phones. Mobile phones are extremely popular in Portugal (some estimates calculate that 90 per cent of the adult population has a mobile phone!), although they tend to be more expensive than in many other countries and call costs are also high (mobile phones can also be rented). Mobile phone networks in Portugal are operated mainly by Optimus (🖳 www.optimus.pt), TMN (🖳 www.tmn.pt) and the European giant, Vodafone (🖳 www.vodafone.pt). All mobile phone numbers start with 91, 93 or 96. Mobile phones operate on the GSM 900/1800 digital system and foreign mobile phones generally work in Portugal.

Further information about telecommunications in Portugal can be obtained from the communications watchdog, ANACOM (*Autoridade Nacional de*

Comunicações), who run an informative website, much of which is available inEnglish (🖥 www.icp.pt). The website also includes regulations and information on how to make a complaint about a provider's service.

Installation: When moving into a new home in Portugal with a telephone line, you must have the account transferred to your name. If you're planning to move into a property without an existing telephone line, you will need to have one installed (although it isn't compulsory!). To have a telephone installed or reconnected, you must visit the local office of Telecom Portugal with a copy of your property's deeds (*escritura*) or a rental contract and your passport or residence card. Note that staff don't usually speak English unless you live in an area that's popular with foreign residents. If you're taking over a property from the previous occupants, you should arrange for the telephone account to be transferred to your name from the day you take possession. Before buying a property check that previous telephone bills have been paid, otherwise you may find yourself liable for them. It used to take many months or even years to get a telephone line installed in Portugal, although nowadays it usually takes a few weeks in most urban areas (it can take much longer in rural areas). The cost of having a private telephone line connected in a property that's already wired for a telephone (e.g. by the builder) is around €9 plus a monthly rental of €1.05.

Using the Telephone: Private and business telephone numbers in Portugal all now have nine digits. The first digit is always '2' followed by the town or regional code, which may be one or two digits, e.g. 1 is Lisbon, 2 is Porto and 89 is Faro. Note, however, that you always dial the nine digits from wherever you are in the country even for local calls. The country code for Portugal is 351. The emergency number for ambulance, fire and police is 112 (this is a multilingual service available in Portuguese, English and French). Numbers with the prefix 800 are freephone numbers. Dial 118 for enquiries or directory assistance, for which there's a charge, although you can look up a number free online (🖥 www.118.pt).

Payphones: Most payphones accept Credifone phonecards (*cartãoes telefónicos*) valid for 50, 100 and 150 units, which are available from post offices, telephone offices, news stands, tobacconists, supermarkets and other retail outlets. In Lisbon and Porto a separate Telecom (*Telefones de Lisboa e Porto/TLP*) phonecard system is in operation (along with Credifone) which uses 'patch' (non-strip) cards which are incompatible with Credifone cards. There are also payphones that accept coins, although these are rare and are more likely to be out of order than card payphones. To make an international call from a payphone you need a lot of coins and must usually insert at least €2. Most coin payphones accept 5, 10, 20, 50 and 1 euro coins and employ the old-fashioned coin drop system, whereby unused coins are displayed and drop down as they're used. A warning tone sounds and a light over the dial is illuminated when more coins are required.

It's also possible to make calls in towns and cities from booths (*cabines*), at main post offices and Telecom Portugal offices (*loja de Telecom*), where you pay for your call afterwards. Telecom offices in Lisbon and Porto are open late in the evening. Using a private telephone office is a bit more expensive (e.g. 15 per cent) than using a payphone, but it's more convenient and Telecom Portugal offices may accept credit cards. There are payphones with counters (*contadors*) in bars, cafés, tourist offices and news stands, which may be indicated by the sign of a red horse in a white circle with a green background and the words *Correio de Portugal - Telefone*. Note that the cost of calls from bars and cafés vary as the proprietor sets his own rate, which is usually posted, e.g. €0.30 for a local call. You should avoid making calls from hotels, which can be expensive.

Costs: Call and line rental charges in Portugal are among the highest in Europe, although this is changing now that the telecommunications market is fully liberalised. You can choose to make calls through any number of providers (note that Telecom Portugal is the only line provider at the moment) either indirectly by marking the four-digit code for the provider before the number you wish to call or by pre-selection when your phone automatically dials via the provider. There are numerous tariffs and time bands for both domestic and international calls, and it pays to shop around to find the cheapest rates, particularly for international calls. Some customers use several providers according to the nature of the calls they make. Many providers also offer special deals with discounts for frequently dialled numbers etc. With Telecom Portugal the cheapest rate for international calls is from 9pm until 9am Monday to Friday and on public holidays and any time at weekends. Telephone bills are issued monthly and are itemised. Many expatriates use a callback service (such as Dial International Telecom/DIT) where subscribers 'call' a number in Britain or the USA and can make international calls over leased lines at up to 75 per cent below standard rates. Callback companies advertise in English-language publications in Portugal. Marconi, a subsidiary of Portugal Telecom, also provides cheaper international calls. Note that resident pensioners and senior citizens whose monthly income is below the statutory minimum salary are entitled to substantial discounts on line rental and call charges with Telecom Portugal.

International Calls: International Direct Dialling (IDD) calls can be made from Portugal to most countries, from both private and public telephones. A full list of IDD country codes and area codes for main cities and tariffs is shown in the information pages of telephone directories. To make an international call you must first dial 00 to obtain an international line and then the country code (e.g. 44 for Britain), the area code <u>without</u> the first zero (e.g. 20 for London) and the subscriber's number. For example, to call the central London number 7654 3210 from Portugal you would dial 00 44 20-7654 3210. To make a call to a country without IDD you must dial the international operator: 177 (this number also provides operator assistance). Note that there's a high surcharge for operator connected international calls, the tariffs for which are shown in telephone directories. International directory enquiries are available by dialling 179.

Portugal subscribes to a Home Direct service that allows you to call a number giving you direct and free access to an operator in the country you're calling, e.g. 800-800 440 to the UK and 800-800 to the USA followed by the number for your preferred phone company (AT&T 128, MCI 123, Sprint 187 and TRT 188). The operator will connect you to the number required and will also accept credit card calls. Most countries have a home direct service including Australia, Belgium, Brazil, Canada, Chile, Denmark, Finland, France, Germany, Guatemala, Hong Kong, Indonesia, Ireland, Japan, South Korea, Norway, the Netherlands, Spain, Sweden, the United Kingdom, Uruguay and the USA.

Internet 'Telephone' Services: The success of the Internet is built on the ability to gather information from computers around the world by connecting to a nearby service for the cost of a local telephone call. If you have correspondents or friends who are connected to the Internet, you can make international 'calls' for the price of a local telephone call to an Internet provider. Once on the Internet there are no other charges, no matter how much distance is covered or time is spent on-line. Internet users can buy software that effectively turns their personal computer into a voice-based telephone (both parties must have compatible computer software). You also need a sound card, speakers, a microphone and a modem, and access to a local Internet provider. While the quality of communication isn't as good as using a telephone (it's similar to using a CB radio) and you need to arrange call times in advance, making international 'calls' costs virtually nothing. The Internet is also useful for sending and receiving electronic mail (e-mail).

The Internet has really taken off in recent years in Portugal, although private usage is still much below that in most western European countries mainly because few Portuguese own computers. Many companies have websites and e-mail, and many have pages in English. There are several Internet Service Providers (ISPs) particularly around Lisbon and on the Algarve, and some offer flat rates or 'pay-as-you-surf' rates with free Internet access. There are also subscription ISPs. In 2002 the large ISP Telepac was named as the 'Best Internet Provider in Portugal' for the second year running. Internet cafés are growing in popularity and most large towns have at least one. Post offices in main towns also provide Internet access.

Fax

There has been a huge increase in the use of fax (facsimile) machines in Portugal during the last decade, helped by lower prices and the unreliability of the Portuguese postal service. Before taking a fax machine to Portugal, check that it will work there (i.e. is compatible) or that it can be modified. Note, however, that getting an imported fax machine repaired in Portugal may be impossible unless the same machine is sold there. Post offices in major cities and towns provide a fax service (Corfax) where you can send or receive a fax, which is charged according to the destination and the length of the call. Note, however, that the procedure for sending faxes from a post office is lengthy and many people prefer to use private business offices, such as travel agencies or stationery shops. Hotels also offer a fax service. Faxes sent from private businesses are more expensive than those sent via the post office and cost around €4 per page for Europe and around €5 per page for North America.

Postal Services

There's a post office (*correio/agência do correio*) in most towns in Portugal. In addition to the usual post office services, a limited range of other services are provided including telegrams, fax and telex transmissions, and domestic and international giro money orders. Telephones aren't provided in most Portuguese post offices. Unlike many other western European post offices, the Portuguese post office produces few leaflets and brochures and you may even have difficulty obtaining a tariff of postal charges, although most information is now available online (🖳 www.ctt.pt). You shouldn't expect post office staff to speak English or other foreign languages. Business hours at main post offices are usually from 8.30am or 9am to 7pm in major cities and large towns, and from 9am to 12.30pm and 2pm to 6pm in small towns. In large towns and cities, post offices don't close for lunch and are also open on Saturday mornings, e.g. 9am to 12.30pm. In major cities such as Lisbon, some post offices have extended opening hours. There are mobile post offices in rural areas.

The Portuguese postal service has improved considerably in the last decade, although it's still poor compared with many other western European countries. Delivery times in Europe vary considerably according to the countries concerned and where letters are posted in Portugal (possibly even according to the post box used), and letters may arrive quicker when posted at a main post office (but don't count on it). Letters to European destinations usually take 4 to 6 days to be delivered and 7 to 14 days to North America. It's recommended to use registered mail (*registo*) or a courier service for important mail. When sending parcels to or from Portugal, always ensure that they're securely wrapped and sealed, otherwise they're likely to arrive in tatters. Portugal employs a four-digit post code (*código postal*) before the town, which should always be used.

In addition to ordinary and express domestic mail services, the post office also provides a national and international courier service (EMS) and an economy (*económico*) international service which combines surface mail in Portugal with airmail (*via aérea/por avião*) outside Portugal (however, it's only marginally cheaper than normal mail, so is hardly worth using). There's also an international surface (*superfície*) mail service which is very slow and can take months to North America or Australia. In towns there are red post boxes for ordinary mail (*correio normal*) and blue post boxes for express mail (*correio azul*). Many people who live in rural areas must collect their mail from the nearest post office or alternatively rent a post office box (*apartado*).

International letter rates depend on the destination; postcards (*catãos*) cost the same as letters (*cartas*). Postcards and letters sent by normal (air) mail weighing up to 20g cost €0.28 in Portugal, €0.46 to Spain, €0.54 to other EU countries and the rest of Europe, and €0.70 to the rest of the world. Stamps (*selos*) are sold at post offices and at other outlets (e.g. news kiosks) with the sign of a red horse in a white circle with a green background (as seen on telephone boxes) and the words *Correio de Portugal – Selos/CTT Selos*. There are also stamp machines located outside post offices and in city centres.

Courier Services

The only guaranteed way to send something urgently is by courier (*mensageiro*) or to send letters by fax or e-mail. Express mail and courier services are provided by the post office, Portuguese railways and airlines, and international (e.g. DHL and UPS) and domestic courier companies. One of the most economical ways to send urgent international parcels is via the post office's EMS service serving around 160 countries. Within Portugal, EMS packages up to 25kg (55lb) are guaranteed to arrive at their destination within 24 hours, while mail sent to EU countries is guaranteed delivery within 24 or 48 hours (depending on the country) and mail to New York is guaranteed to arrive within 48 hours. The maximum delivery time to any country is three or four days.

GETTING THERE

Although it isn't so important if you're planning to live permanently in Portugal and stay put, one of the major considerations when buying a holiday home there is the cost of getting to Portugal from your home abroad. How long will it take to get to a home in Portugal, taking into account journeys to and from airports, ports and railway stations? How frequent are flights, ferries or trains at the time(s) of year when you plan to travel? Are direct flights or trains available? Is it feasible to travel by car? What is the cost of travel from your home country to the region where you're planning to buy a home in Portugal? Are off-season discounts or inexpensive charter flights available? Are costs likely to rise or fall in the future? If a long journey is involved, you should bear in mind that it may take you a day or two to recover, e.g. from jet lag after a long flight. Obviously the travelling time and cost of travel to a home in Portugal will be more important if you're planning to spend frequent long weekends there, rather than a few long stays each year.

Airline Services: Many major international airlines provide scheduled services to Lisbon and many also fly to Porto. The Portuguese state-owned national airline, TAP (Air Portugal), is Portugal's major international carrier. Although it isn't rated as one of the world's best airlines, TAP has a good safety record and its standard of service has improved considerably in recent years. Its fares have also become more competitive. Portugal has a departure tax for international flights, which is generally included in the price of a ticket for all flights.

There are international airports in Lisbon (Portela), Porto (Francisco Sá Carneiro), Faro, Funchal (Madeira) and São Miguel (Azores), and regional airports at Bragança, Chaves, Coimbra, Covilhã, Portimão, Vila Real and Viseu. Air taxis are available at regional airports. The main airlines servicing all three of Portugal's international airports are TAP, Portugália (Portugal's main domestic airline which operates international flights on some European routes), British Airways, GB Airways, Lufthansa, Luzair and Air Liberté. Other airlines serving Lisbon and Porto include Air Inter Europe, Alitalia, Iberia, KLM, Swiss, Varig and Viasa. Lisbon is also served by Aeroflot, Air France, Air Malta, Condor, Delta, Lauda Air, Royal Air Maroc, SAS, TAAG (Angola Airlines), Transavia, Tunis Air and TWA. Madeira (Funchal) is served by TAP, British Airways, Condor, SATA and Transavia, while the Azores (Ponta Delgada) are served by TAP and SATA.

Scheduled Flights: There are scheduled flights from many European and international destinations to both Lisbon and Porto and a number of major airlines also serve Faro. From Britain TAP operates daily scheduled flights from London (Heathrow) to Lisbon, Porto and Faro, and twice weekly scheduled flights to Funchal (💻 www.tap.pt). British Airways has flights from London (Heathrow) to Lisbon and GB Airways flies from London (Gatwick) to Faro, Lisbon and Porto (💻 www.britishairways.com). TAP offers various discounted fares including APEX and super APEX, infant and child, senior citizen, youth, excursion and various promotional fares. The scheduled economy return fare from London to Faro starts at around £140.

From North America there are direct TAP flights from Newark (New Jersey) and New York (JFK) to Lisbon (TAP has a code sharing agreement with Delta Airlines for connecting flights to and from the USA). You can also fly to Madrid from Los Angeles, Miami, New York or Montréal with Iberia and get an inexpensive add-on flight from there to your destination in Portugal. Many other national airlines fly from North America to Portugal with a change of plane in Europe (usually in the airline's home country). There are also charter flights to Portugal from North America (e.g. Boston, New York and

Toronto) during the high season. A scheduled flight from New York to Lisbon costs from around $US700 in the low season up to $US1,000 in the high season. If you're unable to get a direct flight to Portugal from North America or Asia or want to save money, it's usually best to fly via London, from where there are many inexpensive charter flights to Portugal. Fares on scheduled flights to and from Portugal have fallen in recent years due to increased competition, although they're still high compared with charter fares.

Charter Flights: Inexpensive charter flights to Portugal are common from many European countries, particularly Britain and Germany. There are charter flights from Britain to Lisbon, Porto and Faro from London, Manchester, Birmingham, Newcastle, Glasgow and Edinburgh, plus charter flights to Faro from many UK regional airports. Note that travelling to Faro by charter and taking the train or bus to Lisbon or Porto may be the cheapest way to get there. It's often cheaper for North Americans and others travelling on intercontinental flights to fly to London and get a charter flight from there, particularly outside the summer season. Charter fares vary considerably with the season, the most expensive being the high season from June to August. September-October and April-May are a little cheaper, but the best deals are available in the low season from November to March. Fares from London to Faro are usually between £50 and £120 return, although they're higher at peak periods such as Christmas, Easter, high summer (July/August) and school holiday periods. Shop around and check the advertisements in the travel sections in the Saturday and Sunday editions of national newspapers, e.g. the Saturday *Daily Telegraph* and the *Sunday Times* in Britain (plus the weekly London *Time Out* magazine) and the *Los Angeles Times* and *New York Times* in the USA. STA Travel (🖳 www.statravel.com) offers some of the best flight deals in a number of countries.

Train Services: There are international trains to Portugal (Lisbon) from Paris and a number of other European cities, although a change of train is necessary at the Spanish border (Irún) or in Madrid. If you're travelling from Britain, you can take the Eurostar service from London to Paris. From Paris you take the TGV to Irún in Spain and change to the Rápido Sud-Expresso across Spain via San Sebastian, Vilar Formoso, Guarda, Pampilhosa (where you can change for Porto) and south to Lisbon. An alternative is to travel from Paris to Madrid where you change to the Talgo Lusitânia Comboio Hotel via Cáceres to Marvão-Beirã, Abrantes and Entroncamento (connection to Coimbra and Porto), and on to Lisbon. There are frequent connections from Lisbon to the Algarve. The journey from Paris to Lisbon takes around 18 hours and Madrid to Lisbon around eight hours.

Paris to Lisbon in tourist class costs around €152 return, which can be more expensive than the cost of a charter flight as well as considerably longer. Train buffs may be interested in the Thomas Cook *European Timetable*, which is much more than a collection of train times and contains information on shipping services, customs regulations, visa requirements and town plans. It's available direct from Thomas Cook Publishing, PO Box 227, Peterborough PE3 8XX, UK (☎ 01733-413477, 💻 www.thomascooktimetables.com).

Ferries: There are no direct international ferries to Portugal, although if you're travelling from Britain, Brittany Ferries and P&O operate ferry services between Britain and northern Spain (from where it's around 800km/500mi to Porto, 1,000km/620mi to Lisbon and 1,300km/800mi to Faro) or you can travel via the Channel ports of France from where it's around 1,800km/1,120mi to Porto, 1,900km/1,180mi to Lisbon and 2,200km/1,370mi to Faro. Both Brittany Ferries and P&O offer comparable standards of comfort, services and fares, and ships provide a variety of facilities and services including a choice of bars and restaurants; swimming pool; Jacuzzi; sauna; cinemas; shops; hairdressing salon; photographic studio; medical service; children's playroom; and evening entertainment including a night-club, casino, discotheque and musical entertainment.

Both Brittany Ferries and P&O have a number of fare tariffs (depending on the time of the year) and offer a choice of single and return fares (plus mini-breaks and saver returns). Children aged under four travel free and those aged from 4 to 14 travel for half fare. It's wise to book well ahead when travelling during peak periods and at any time when you require a luxury cabin. If possible it's best to avoid travelling during peak times, when ships can be uncomfortably crowded. Travelling by ferry from Britain to Spain will save you around 1,200km/750mi of driving when compared with travelling via the Channel ports through France. Ferries can also be a cheaper way to travel, particularly for families with children and a car, as you don't pay expensive air fares for children or car rental at your destination. Travelling from Britain to southern Portugal by road (via France) entails spending three full days driving and at least two nights in an hotel en route, plus meals and petrol costs, although it can work out cheaper than the ferry. Note that the sea can be rough between Spain and Britain (the Bay of Biscay is famous for its storms) and travel isn't recommended during bad weather if you're a bad sailor. When seas are rough, there's absolutely no respite from seasickness and the journey will be a nightmare (keep a good supply of seasickness pills handy!). Check the weather report and be prepared to travel via France or fly.

Brittany Ferries operate a twice-weekly service from mid March to mid-November between Plymouth in Britain and the Spanish port of Santander. The journey time is around 24 hours with one night spent on board. The cost in 2002 for a vehicle up to 5m in length including the driver was from €251 to €496 (depending on the season) for a standard return. The cost of a cabin isn't included in the fare and is from €32 to €42 per person sharing a four-berth cabin, and from €92 to €125 for a two-berth private cabin (which is well worth the extra cost). Reclining seats are also available at a cost of €6. Additional adult car and foot passengers pay from €40 to €149 for a standard return. Food and drink is quite expensive, particularly bar drinks and snacks. Reservations can be made by telephone (UK only) 0870-536 0360 or online (🖳 www.brittanyferries.co.uk). Brittany Ferries operate a Travel & Property Owners' Club for frequent travellers, offering savings of up to one-third off standard fares, depending on the time of year (for information contact Brittany Ferries, Millbay, Plymouth PL1 3EW, UK).

P&O Ferries operate a year-round, twice-weekly service between Portsmouth in Britain and the Spanish port of Bilbao (the ferry port is actually at Santutzi, around 13km/8mi to the north-west of the city centre). The route is served by the P&O ferry *Pride of Bilbao*, the largest cruise ferry operating out of Britain (capacity 2,500 passengers, 600 cars). Departures from Portsmouth are at 8pm on Tuesdays and Saturdays, arriving in Bilbao at 8am on Thursdays and Mondays respectively. Departures from Bilbao are 12.30pm on Mondays and Thursdays, arriving in Portsmouth at 4.30pm on Tuesdays and Fridays respectively. The journey time is 35 hours from Portsmouth and 30 hours from Bilbao. Ferries operate throughout the year.

In 2002 the cost of a standard return for the smallest vehicle (up to 5m in length and under 1.5m high) was from €476 to €1,000 (depending on the time of year) including the driver. The cost of a cabin isn't included in the fare and is from €128 sharing a four-berth cabin, and from €197 for a two to four-berth private cabin, which is well worth the extra cost. A luxury cabin provides a double bed, two easy chairs, writing desk, TV, shower, toilet, washbasin, two large windows and room service. Reservations can be made by telephone (UK only ☎ 0870-242 4999) or online (🖳 www.poport smouth.com). One of the best travel deals around is offered by P&O, whose preference shareholders (owning at least 600 shares) receive discounts of up to 50 per cent on all P&O sailings.

Note that due to the high cost of ferry and road travel and the long travelling times between the UK and Portugal, you may be better off flying and hiring a car on arrival, or even leaving a car at your Portuguese home if you visit Portugal frequently or spend long periods there.

International Buses: There are regular international bus services to Portugal's major cities from a number of European countries. For example Eurolines (🖳 www.eurolines.co.uk) operates year-round coach services from Britain to Lisbon (39 hours) and Faro (43 hours). However, fares can be more expensive than charter flights, e.g. around £80 single and £130 return. Unless you have a fear of flying or a love of coach travel, you may find nearly two days on a bus an absolute nightmare. Buses are, however, comfortable and air-conditioned, and are equipped with toilets and video entertainment.

Allow plenty of time to get to and from airports, ports and bus and railway stations, particularly when travelling during peak hours when traffic congestion can be horrendous.

GETTING AROUND BY PUBLIC TRANSPORT

Public transport services in Portugal vary considerably according to where you live, although they have been improved in recent years. Public transport is good in Lisbon and Porto, both of which have extensive bus and tram networks (Lisbon also has a four-line metro system, whose recent refurbishment includes contemporary art works at all stations). There are also funiculars and elevators (*elevadores*) in Lisbon which link the lower city with the hilly residential areas. Lisbon travel passes for trams, buses and funiculars are available for around €2.50 a day and 1 or 3-day Lisbon Cards valid for all transport and museums in the city cost around €11 and €24 respectively. Passes and cards can be bought from kiosks and tourist offices around the city.

Portugal has comprehensive inter-city bus and domestic airline services and is also served by international coaches, trains and excellent air links. It's a small country and it's relatively easy and inexpensive to get around by bus and train. However, outside the main towns and cities public transport is usually sparse (with the exception of the Algarve which is served by local trains and has a good bus service) and most people find it necessary to have their own transport. Taxis are common in resort areas and cities and are relatively inexpensive by European standards and good value for short journeys, particularly when the cost is shared between a number of people. Information about public transport can be obtained from local tourist offices in Portugal and Portuguese National Tourist Offices abroad.

Bus: Buses are the most common form of public transport in Portugal, particularly in rural areas. There are mainly three types of buses in Portugal: *expressos*, which are fast, comfortable, direct buses between major cities; *rápidas* which are fast regional services; and *regional* or *carreiras* (CR) which stop everywhere and are very slow.

Most bus services in Portugal are operated by private regional companies (after the privatisation of the government-owned company Rodoviaria National) such as Avic, Cabanelas, Empresa, Malfrense, Solexpresso and Stagecoach. *Rede Nacional de Expressos* operate a comprehensive national bus service (💻 www.rede-expressos.pt). There are express regional services in most areas, e.g. the Faro-based Eva Transportes company, which offers a luxury coach service called *alta qualidade* (💻 www.eva-bus.com).

Express buses are usually the cheapest way to get around the country and you can usually book on the spot for the same day, although it's wise to reserve a ticket in advance for long-distance routes, particularly during the summer. Lisbon-Faro takes just over four hours and costs around €28 return for the luxury Eva express. Lisbon-Porto takes around 3.5 hours and costs around €25 return. Bus services in cities such as Lisbon and Porto are excellent and operate on a zone system, where you buy a ticket for the number of zones you need to cross. In country areas, services are often infrequent by day and may be non-existent at night and at weekends. Local services may also leave early in the morning to accommodate school and market hours. Unlike train stations, bus stations are usually located in the centre of town.

Rail: The Portuguese rail service is operated by Caminhos de Ferro Portugueses (CP) and trains are clean, comfortable, inexpensive and punctual. The network covers over 3,500km/2,175mi, although many country areas aren't served by trains at all. CP employs mainly electric and diesel trains, of which there are various classes including *rápido* and *intercidade* (*IC*) express services between major towns and cities; *interregional* (*IR*) trains which are reasonably fast but make quite a few stops; and *suburbano* or *regional* (*R*) trains which stop everywhere. An *alfa pendular* (*AP*) class train is a special *rápido* fast service (slightly faster than an *IC* train) operating between major cities such as Lisbon and Porto. Travel on express services such as *intercidades* and *alfa pendular* trains is more expensive (up to double the cost of slow *regional* trains) and it's necessary (e.g. on *alfa pendulars*) to reserve a seat. Car trains and sleeping berths are available on long-distance (Faro-Lisbon-Porto) and overnight international (marked IN on timetables) services, e.g. to Madrid. There are narrow-gauge mountain railways in the north of the country, although many of these have been closed and replaced by buses.

Inter-city and regional trains have both first and second-class carriages, while local and suburban trains have just one class. Trains are generally slower than long-distance buses, but cheaper and more comfortable for long journeys (sit back and enjoy the scenery). It's worth paying extra for first class, which has comfortable reclining seats and air-conditioning. Tickets must be purchased before boarding a train and cannot usually be obtained on board. Tickets can be bought at stations, travel agents or by telephone (☎ 808-208 208 (open from 7am to 11pm)). Reservations for *AP* and *IC* trains can be made online (🖥 www.cp.pt) and tickets for these services only can also be obtained from ATMs up to 21 days before departure. There's a fine for travelling without a ticket, although if the ticket office was closed where you boarded you can pay the conductor. Note that some stations are located well outside towns and there may be no connecting bus service.

Lisbon serves as a hub for Portugal's main rail lines and is directly connected to around 20 major towns. Changing trains in Lisbon can be confusing as there are four main train stations (*estação*) each serving a different region: Rossio serves Sintra and points west; Santa Apolónia serves the international, northern and eastern lines; Cais do Sodré serves Estoril and Cascais; and Barreiro (across the Rio Tejo) serves southern lines to the Costa Azul and the Algarve (to reach it you need to take a ferry from the Terreiro do Paço dock). A local (slow) train service runs along the Algarve coastline from Vila Real de Santo António to Lagos.

Children aged under four and not occupying a seat travel free and those aged between 4 and 11 travel for half fare. Families can obtain a free family card (*cartão de família*) and receive a discount when travelling together for distances over 150km. Those aged between 12 and 26 can obtain a youth card (*cartão jovem*) and receive discounts of up to 30 per cent on long journeys at certain times. Pensioners aged over 65 can obtain a golden card (*cartão dourado*) and receive a discount of 30 per cent off normal fares and a discount of up to 50 per cent during off-peak hours. Tourist passes (*bilhetes turísticos*) are available for 7, 14 or 21 days. There are also special return tickets on 'blue days' (most days except Friday and Sunday afternoons, Monday mornings, public holidays and the day before a public holiday) for trips over 100km/60mi.

Air: There are a number of airlines offering domestic services in Portugal including TAP-Air Portugal (🖥 www.tap.pt); Portugália – TAP's main competitor (🖥 www.pga.pt); SATA Air Azores (🖥 www.sata.pt) and Air Luxor (🖥 www.airluxor.com). Flight times on popular routes are Lisbon-Faro (40mins), Lisbon-Porto (45mins), Lisbon-Funchal (Madeira – 1hr, 40mins), Lisbon-Ponta Delgada (Azores, 2hrs, 20mins). Note that direct flights between Porto and Faro are virtually non-existent. Domestic flights within Portugal are relatively expensive and aren't generally worth considering unless you're in a hurry (or someone else is paying). Lisbon-Faro or Lisbon-Porto flights cost around €100 for an economy fare. The return fare from Lisbon to Madeira is around €200 for an economy fare. A domestic departure tax is included in the ticket price for all domestic flights, the amount of which depends on your destination. Those aged under 26 can obtain an 'under-26' card and receive a 50 per cent discount with Portugália and limited discounts with TAP. Private aircraft and helicopters can be rented from many airports in Portugal.

DRIVING IN PORTUGAL

Motoring in Portugal has changed out of all recognition in the last few decades, during which the number of cars has increased dramatically. Like all Latins, the Portuguese personality changes the minute they get behind the wheel of a car, when even the most tolerant and patient people can become motoring anarchists. Many Portuguese rush around at breakneck speed (totally out of character with their usual *amanhã* attitude) in their haste to reach their destination or the next life (although it should be noted that not all Portuguese drivers are bad). When driving in Portugal you should regard all drivers as totally unpredictable and drive defensively.

Among the local drivers' many idiosyncrasies are a total lack of lane discipline (lane markings are treated as optional); overtaking with reckless abandon on blind bends; failure to use indicators or mirrors; driving through red lights and the wrong way up one-way streets; and parking anywhere it's illegal. The Portuguese drive on both the right <u>and</u> left sides of the road (when they aren't driving in the middle!). When driving at night, watch out for bicycles, motorcycles, donkeys, horses and ox carts without lights. Maniacs on ear-splitting motorcycles and mopeds are a menace in towns. Motorists should also keep a wary eye out for pedestrians, particularly elderly people, who often cross the road without looking.

On the rare occasions when they aren't overtaking, some Portuguese drivers sit a few centimetres from your bumper trying to push you along irrespective of traffic density, road and weather conditions, or the speed limit. There's no solution, short of moving out of the way or stopping, which may be impossible. Try to leave a large gap between your vehicle and the one in front in order to give the tailgater behind you more time to stop.

Anyone who has driven in Portugal won't be surprised to learn that it has the worst accident record in western Europe (Portugal had no written Highway Code until 1994!). Road accidents are responsible for around 35 deaths per 100,000 of population each year, compared with eight in the UK and 17 in France. The condition of roads and the standards of driving are generally much worse than in northern European and North American countries (the Portuguese are mostly first-generation drivers lacking experience and parental influence). Many drivers seem unaware of the danger and recklessly speed in poor road and weather conditions. Eccentric and impatient drivers, *machismo*, drunken and drugged motorists and pedestrians, stray animals, vehicles without lights, badly marked roads, and sharp bends without warning signs or crash barriers; all contribute to the hazards of driving in Portugal. Portuguese drivers are supposed to be tested for their mental competence to drive, although how many of them get through this test is a mystery (bribing examiners is allegedly commonplace).

Adding to the confusion and hazards on Portuguese roads are thousands of tourists and retirees, whose driving habits vary from exemplary to suicidal (including many, such as the British, who don't even know which side of the road to drive on!). However, don't be too discouraged by the maniacs and tailgaters. Driving in Portugal can be a pleasant experience, particularly in country areas, which are relatively traffic-free most of the time. If you come from a country where traffic drives on the left, you will quickly get used to driving on the 'wrong' side of the road. Just take it easy at first and bear in mind that there are other motorists around just as confused as you are!

Roads

Many Portuguese roads have been (or are being) upgraded, thanks largely to EU funds. There are now long stretches of motorway including toll roads (such as the A-1 between Lisbon and Porto, and the IP1 along the Algarve). Toll roads are the quickest and safest way to cover long distances as they aren't used much by local drivers due to the high cost. Main roads are generally in good condition, but minor country roads and roads in towns and villages may be full of potholes and in terrible condition (a four-wheel drive vehicle is useful in rural areas). In rural areas narrow twisting roads with dangerous bends are commonplace and there are usually no crash barriers to stop you falling into the valley below. Road lighting is often poor in towns and built-up areas and parking in Portuguese cities and large towns is virtually non-existent and among the worst in Europe (which is saying something!).

The coastal roads of the Algarve and the Lisbon-Cascais axis are among the most dangerous. Driving in large towns and cities is chaotic and to be avoided if at all possible (especially Lisbon and Porto) and many small towns have narrow streets where manoeuvring can be almost impossible. Some two-way roads (i.e. roads with just one lane in each direction) have a hard shoulder, which acts as a second lane in each direction and which is useful to move out of the way of overtaking vehicles travelling in the opposite direction, or to allow space for faster cars to overtake.

Importing a Car

Before planning to import a car into Portugal, check the latest regulations. For many years Portugal levied punitive taxes on all imported vehicles, which depended on the new price, age and engine size. Previously the tax on luxury cars with large engines could be more than the car cost new ten years earlier! However, in accordance with EU law there's now no tax on a car imported from another EU country that has been owned for at least six months (although there's still official obstruction to registering imported vehicles). If you import a vehicle, the associated paperwork can be completed by a customs agent (*despachante*) and is well worth the fee (the Automóvel Clube de Portugal (ACP) will also handle the importation for members).

Once you obtain a Portuguese residence card you aren't permitted to drive a vehicle with foreign registration, although a period of grace is permitted (e.g. six months) while awaiting your Portuguese registration. Note that if you own a Portuguese-registered car, any other person who drives it (including a spouse or other family member) requires an official declaration (*declaração*). Non-residents can keep and use a foreign registered car in Portugal for up to six months a year (although many leave a foreign-registered car at their Portuguese homes and use them when they visit). Note that Portugal is one of the most expensive countries in the EU in which to purchase a new car (although some models are more reasonably priced than others). Portuguese number plates show the year and month of a vehicle's first registration.

Driving Licences

It's no longer necessary for EU residents to exchange their pink EU licence for a Portuguese licence (*carta de conduçao*), although the Portuguese authorities may tell you otherwise. Non-EU nationals must apply for a Portuguese driving licence as soon as they become residents. Non-residents don't require a Portuguese driving licence to buy or operate a Portuguese-registered car and may drive in Portugal for a maximum of six months a year with a foreign or international driving permit (IDP). An IDP isn't usually required for Portugal, although it's sometimes worthwhile obtaining one, particularly if you plan to spend an extended period there. Your licence must be carried at all times when driving in Portugal, along with your vehicle registration (proof of ownership) and insurance certificate. Failure to carry documentation in your car usually attracts a fine of up to €100.

Car Insurance

All motor vehicles plus trailers and semi-trailers must be insured for third party liability when entering Portugal. However, it isn't mandatory for cars insured in most European countries to have an international insurance 'green' card (see below). Motorists insured in an EU country, the Czech Republic, Hungary, Liechtenstein, Norway, Slovakia and Switzerland are automatically covered for third party liability in Portugal. The categories of car insurance available in Portugal include third party, which is the minimum required by law; third party fire and theft (also called part comprehensive in some countries); fully comprehensive (total loss); and unlimited cover. Note that fully comprehensive insurance doesn't provide the same cover as in many other countries and doesn't include injuries to passengers or cover outside Portugal (apart from third party) unless specified. If you have fully comprehensive insurance and plan to drive outside Portugal, you should obtain a green card from your insurance company.

Car Crime

Most European countries have a problem with car crime, i.e. thefts of and from cars, and Portugal is no exception. Foreign-registered vehicles are popular targets. If you drive anything other than a worthless heap you should have theft insurance, which includes your car stereo and personal belongings. If you drive a new or valuable car, it's wise to have it fitted with an alarm, an engine immobiliser (the best system) or another anti-theft device, plus a visible deterrent, such as a steering or gear stick lock. It's particularly important to protect your car if you own a model that's desirable to professional car thieves, e.g. most new sports and executive models, which are often stolen by crooks to order.

Few cars are fitted with deadlocks and most can be broken into in seconds by a competent thief. However, even the best security system won't usually prevent someone from breaking into your car and may not stop your car being stolen, but it will at least make it more difficult and may persuade a thief to look for an easier target. Radios and tape and CD players attract thieves like bees to a honey jar in Portuguese cities and resort towns. If you buy an expensive stereo system, you should buy one with a removable unit or with a removable (face-off) control panel that you can pop into a pocket or bag. However, never forget to remove it (and your mobile telephone), even when parking for a few minutes. Some manufacturers provide stereo systems that won't work when they're removed from their original vehicles or are inoperable without a security code.

When leaving your car unattended, store any valuables (including clothes) in the boot (trunk). Note, however, that storing valuables in the boot isn't foolproof, as when a car is empty a thief may be tempted to force open the boot with a crowbar. Many people leave the boot of their car unlocked (and empty) to avoid having it broken open, as it can be expensive to repair. It's never wise to leave your original car papers in your car (which may help a thief dispose of it). When parking overnight or when it's dark, it's best to park in a secure overnight car park or garage, or at least in a well-lit area. If possible, avoid parking in insecure long-term car parks, as they're favourite hunting grounds for car thieves.

General Road Rules

The following general road rules may help you to adjust to driving in Portugal. Don't, however, expect other motorists to adhere to them (many Portuguese drivers make up their own 'rules', which are infinitely variable). The All Travel Portugal website in the section on driving includes a very useful page where all Portuguese road signs are shown together with their meanings (🖳 www.alltravelportugal.com).

● You may have already noticed that the Portuguese drive on the right hand side of the road. It saves confusion if you do likewise! If you aren't used to driving on the right, take it easy until you're accustomed to it. Be particularly alert when leaving lay-bys, T-junctions, one-way streets and filling stations, as it's easy to lapse into driving on the left. It's helpful to have a reminder (e.g. 'think right!') on your car's dashboard.

● The wearing of seat belts in Portugal is compulsory on all roads at all times and includes passengers in rear seats where seat belts are fitted. Children aged under 12 must travel in the back seats of cars unless the front seat is fitted with an approved child seat (although these shouldn't be used when an air bag is fitted unless it's deactivated). Failure to wear a seat belt can result in an on-the-spot fine and subsequent offences may mean increased fines or the loss of your licence. If you're wise you will not only use your seat belt at all times, but will also buy a car fitted with an air bag. If you have an accident and aren't wearing your seat belt, your insurance company can refuse to pay a claim for personal injury. **Note, however, that rear seat lap belts without a shoulder strap (such as are fitted in the rear seats of some cars) can cause serious internal and back injuries, and should be avoided if at all possible (by children as well as adults).**

● All motorists must carry a red warning triangle and a first-aid kit. If you hire a car, make sure you ask to be shown where the triangle is kept before you leave the depot; if you are stopped by the police you're supposed to be able to show them the triangle immediately! You must also have a spare wheel and the tools for changing a wheel. It's best but not mandatory to carry a fire extinguisher and to take some spares with you, particularly if you drive an 'exotic' foreign car (e.g. any British car). Note that spare parts can be astronomically expensive in Portugal (they can be ordered by courier from other European countries at greatly reduced prices).

● In towns you may be faced with a bewildering array of signs, traffic lights and road markings. If you're ever in doubt about who has priority, give way to trams, buses and all traffic coming from your <u>right</u>. Emergency (ambulance, fire, police) and public utility vehicles attending an emergency have priority on all roads.

● Most main roads are designated priority roads, indicated by one of two signs. The most common priority sign is a yellow diamond on a white background, in use throughout most of continental Europe. The end of priority is shown by the same sign with a black diagonal line through it. The other sign is triangular and displays a broad vertical arrow with a thinner horizontal line through it or a road entering the main road from the left or right. On secondary roads <u>without</u> priority signs and in built-up areas, you must give way to vehicles coming from your <u>right</u>. **Failure to observe the priority rule is the cause of many accidents.**

● On roundabouts (traffic circles), you must give way to traffic approaching from your left unless there's a give way sign. Traffic flows anti-clockwise round roundabouts and not clockwise as in Britain and other countries driving on the left. Although the British think roundabouts are marvellous (we spend most of our time going round in circles), they aren't so popular on the continent of Europe, although they have become more common in recent years.

● Don't drive in bus, taxi or cycle lanes unless it's necessary to avoid a stationary vehicle or an obstruction. Bus drivers get irate if you drive in their lanes, identified by a continuous yellow line parallel to the kerb (you can be fined for doing so). Be sure to keep clear of tram lines and keep outside the restricted area, delineated by a line.

● The use of horns is forbidden at night in towns, except in emergencies.

- Headlamps must be used when driving at night, when driving in poor visibility during daylight and in tunnels at any time (you're reminded by a sign). Your main beam must be dipped at night when following a vehicle or when a vehicle is approaching from the opposite direction. Failure to dip your lights can result in a fine. Note that headlight flashing has a different meaning in different countries. In some countries it means 'after you' and in others, 'get out of my way' (almost always the case in Portugal). It may also mean 'I am driving a new car and haven't yet worked out what all the switches are for!' Portuguese drivers sometimes warn motorists of police radar traps and roadblocks (although this is illegal) and cause accidents by flashing their headlights. A vehicle's hazard warning lights may be used to warn other drivers of an obstruction, e.g. an accident or a traffic jam.

- Most traffic lights are situated on posts at the side of the road, although they may also be suspended above the road. The sequence of Portuguese traffic lights (*sinal*) is usually red, green, amber (yellow) and back to red. Amber means stop at the stop line; you may proceed only if the amber light appears after you've crossed the stop line or when stopping may cause an accident. However, take care before stopping at an amber light when a vehicle is close behind you, as Portuguese drivers routinely drive through amber lights and may be taken by surprise if you stop (and ram you). An amber or green filter light (possibly flashing) with a direction arrow may be shown in addition to the main signal. This means that you may drive in the direction shown by the arrow, but must give priority to pedestrians or other traffic. Flashing amber lights are a warning to proceed with caution and may indicate that you must give way to pedestrians.

- White lines mark the delineation of traffic lanes (not that these mean anything to many Portuguese drivers). A solid single line or two solid lines means no overtaking in either direction. A solid line to the right of the centre line, i.e. on your side of the road, means that overtaking is prohibited in your direction. You may overtake only when there's a single broken line in the middle of the road or double lines with a broken line on your side of the road. No overtaking is also shown by the international sign of two cars side by side (one red and one black). If you drive a right-hand drive car, take extra care when overtaking - the most dangerous manoeuvre in motoring. It's recommended that you have a special 'overtaking mirror' fitted to your car. Note that you're forbidden to overtake a stationary tram when passengers are boarding or alighting.

- Speed limits in Portugal are 60kph in towns, 90kph on country roads, 100kph on dual carriageways and 120kph on motorways (*auto-estradas*). The 60kph and 90kph speed limits are reduced during bad weather and cars with trailers, trucks and coaches are limited to 70kph outside built-up areas and to 80kph on motorways. There's also a minimum speed limit of 40kph on motorways. Note that if you've held a driving licence for less than one year, you're restricted to a maximum of 90kph on all roads and must display a '90' sticker on your car (this also applies to foreign motorists). Speeding is widespread, as tickets are rare because there are few radar systems in operation.

● Take care when approaching a railway crossing. You must take particular care at crossings without barriers, which can be <u>very</u> dangerous. Approach a railway level crossing slowly and **stop**:

    – as soon as the barrier or half-barrier starts to fall;

    – as soon as the red warning lights are illuminated or flashing or a warning bell rings;

    – when a train approaches!

Your new car may be built like a tank but it won't look so smart after a scrap with a locomotive.

● Be particularly wary of moped (*moto*) riders and cyclists. It isn't always easy to see them, particularly when they're hidden by the blind spots of a car or are riding at night without lights. Many young moped riders seem to have a death wish and tragically many lose their lives each year in Portugal. They're constantly pulling out into traffic or turning without looking or signalling. **Follow the example set by Portuguese motorists, who, when overtaking mopeds and cyclists, <u>always</u> give them a wide....<u>wide</u> berth!** If you knock them off their bikes you may have a difficult time convincing the police that it wasn't your fault. Far better to avoid them (and the police). It's also common to encounter tractors, ox carts, horses, donkeys, sheep and goats in rural areas. Keep an eye out for them and give them a wide berth.

● Parking is restricted in all towns, although free parking may be located on the outskirts of towns. In some cites (e.g. Lisbon) a blue zone system is in operation, where free limited parking is provided (parking discs are available from police stations and motoring organisations). Parking 'touts' abound in tourist areas and will try to obtain €0.50 or €1 for 'finding' you a parking space (there's no need to pay but it may prevent your car being damaged). Parked vehicles must face the same way as the direction of moving traffic and illegally parked vehicles may be clamped or towed away. In resort towns and cities most parking is pay and display (*parquímetro*), usually costing around €0.50 to €1 an hour. Parking garages are common in towns and cost around €1 an hour, but aren't always open 24 hours a day. Parking is usually free at shopping centres and hypermarkets.

- If you break down, you can obtain help from the Automóvel Clube de Portugal (ACP) (☎ 228-340 001 in the north and ☎ 219-429 103 in the south, 🖳 www.acp.pt), which has reciprocal arrangements with most foreign automobile clubs. There are orange emergency phones at regular intervals on motorways and major highways.

- Motorcyclists and their passengers must wear crash helmets at all times (although many don't or don't bother to secure them!).

- Police can (and do) impose on-the-spot fines on foreigners and drivers of vehicles that aren't registered in Portugal. Fines can be as high as €200 and only cash is accepted. Residents don't pay on-the-spot fines but are given 15 days to pay a fine at a tax office (*finanças*) after reporting to a police station (*posto da GNR*).

- The maximum legal blood alcohol level is 50mg per 100ml (0.5 grammes per litre). Drivers who are over the limit are jailed overnight and must go before a judge the following morning. There are high fines and driving bans for anyone convicted of drunken driving and anyone with more than 120mg per 100ml is liable to receive a prison sentence.

- Small petrol stations open from around 7 or 8am until 7pm Monday to Friday and 9am to 1pm on Saturday, although there are also many large self-service stations open 24 hours a day, seven days a week. Petrol (*gasolina*) costs in mid 2002 were from around €0.85 a litre for unleaded (*sem chumbo*) and around €0.65 a litre for diesel (*gasóleo*). **Take care when filling your car that you use the correct pump!** The price of petrol is controlled by the government and is therefore similar throughout the country. Note that not all petrol stations accept credit cards and those that do may levy a surcharge of €0.50. Petrol stations aren't so frequent in remote country areas, where it's wise to keep your tank topped up.

- Obtain a current map, as new road construction has been widespread in recent years. The best road maps include Michelin's *Portugal* (1:400,000) number 440 and the *Mapa das Estradas* (1:350,000) published by the Automóvel Club de Portugal.

- Pedestrians should be aware of vehicles wherever they walk, even on pedestrian crossings in towns. Cycling is also dangerous in Portugal.

Car Rental

Car rental (*aluguel de carro*) companies such as Avis, Budget, Europcar, Hertz and National have offices or agents in most cities and at major airports in Portugal. However, small local rental companies are often cheaper and are listed in the yellow pages (leaflets can also be picked up from local tourist offices). If you're a visitor, it's best to reserve a rental car before arriving in

Portugal, particularly during peak holiday periods. Fly-drive deals are available from most airlines and travel agents. When booking in advance, remember to specify an automatic model if you're unused to a manual (stick-shift) gearbox, as most rental cars are manual.

Car rental in Portugal is among the cheapest in Europe, particularly during off-peak periods. The rates of major international companies vary little, although you may get a better deal by booking in advance. One of the advantages of renting from a national company is that you can rent a car in one town and drop it off in another, although you should check the cost of this service (some companies don't charge a drop-off fee when a car is left in another major city). Although cheaper, small local companies require you to return a car to the office you got it from or to the local airport. When comparing rates, check that prices are fully inclusive of insurance and taxes (IVA at 19 per cent), that insurance cover (including personal accident) is adequate and that there are no hidden costs. Note that car rentals are restricted to Portugal unless you arrange international insurance with the rental company.

Expect to pay from around €100 per week in the low season for the smallest car (e.g. Nissan Micra/Opel Corsa), €160 or more per week in the high season. Advertised rates should include VAT, unlimited km and collision damage waiver (CDW) insurance. Optional insurance is usually available for theft and personal accident. There's an airport tax (around €12) for rental cars picked up at Lisbon airport and there are usually additional fees for roof racks, baby seats, air-conditioning and additional drivers. Most companies have low rates for weekend rentals, e.g. from 4pm on Friday until noon on Monday, and for rentals of 14 days or longer. If you book and pay in advance from North America you can usually save up to around 40 per cent on local rates. Auto Europe (☎ 1-888 223 5555 in the USA and Canada, 🖥 www.autoeurope. com) have contracts with all the major car rental companies and claim that they will beat any written offer.

When choosing a rental car, ensure that you have sufficient power for mountain driving, e.g. at least a 1.6 litre engine for two people and their luggage. If you're going to be doing a lot of driving in summer, air-conditioning is a must. Check the car (e.g. for body damage and to ensure that everything works) and the contract carefully before setting out.

To rent a car in Portugal, you must usually be aged at least 23 and must have held a full driving licence for at least one year. Note that many companies also have an upper age limit, e.g. 65. Drivers must produce a valid licence (a copy isn't acceptable) and some drivers need an international driving permit. If more than one person will be driving, all the drivers' names must be entered on the rental agreement. If a credit card isn't used, there's usually a high cash deposit and possibly the whole rental cost must be paid in advance. **When paying by credit card, carefully check your bill and your statement, as unauthorised charges aren't unknown.**

2.

FURTHER
CONSIDERATIONS

This chapter contains important considerations for most people planning to buy a home in Portugal, particularly those who are intending to live there permanently or semi-permanently. It includes information about the climate, geography, health, insurance, shopping, pets, TV, radio and learning Portuguese.

CLIMATE

Hardly surprisingly, the overwhelming attraction of Portugal for most foreigners is its excellent climate. The country has one of the most pleasant year-round climates in Europe (similar to California) and its southern Algarve coast (along with Spain's Costa del Sol) is the warmest region of Europe in winter. Portugal is noted for its generally moderate climate with mild winters (the national average winter temperature is a mild 11°C/52°F) and warm summers, with the notable exception of the north-east which has long, cold winters and hot summers. Summers are long, hot and dry everywhere, and the Algarve, Alentejo and the upper Douro valley in particular, can get very hot in the summer, although in coastal areas the heat is tempered by cooling sea breezes. There are huge temperature variations in inland regions, particularly in the north of the country. As in all southern European countries, spring and autumn are the most pleasant seasons, when it's warm and sunny but rarely too hot. Most rain falls in winter, particularly from November to March, with the heaviest rain in the north-west.

Northern Portugal has an Atlantic climate influenced by the Gulf Stream. Lisbon and Porto are only a few degrees cooler than the Algarve for most of the year and Lisbon has surprisingly mild winters with an average January temperature of 12°C (57°F). The average summer temperature is 24°C (75°F), when the heat is freshened by Atlantic breezes. In the Douro valley and Alentejo, summer temperatures can reach 40°C (104°F) and there can be relatively long periods without rain. The northern region of Portugal enjoys around ten hours of sunshine a day in summer and some four hours a day in winter. Mountainous areas such as the Serra de Estrêla and Peneda-Gerês ranges and much of the Minho and Trás-os-Montes, tend to be quite showery in summer and very cold and wet in winter. As much as 2,000mm (78in) of rain a year can fall in Minho, compared with just 300mm (12in) in the interior of the Algarve, around 700mm (27in) in Lisbon and a national average of 1,100mm (43in). The further north you go, the colder the sea becomes and the larger the waves. It snows in winter in the Serra de Estrêla region in northern Portugal, where skiing is popular from January to March.

The southern region of the Algarve enjoys one of the best year-round climates in Europe. It has a mild, Mediterranean-style climate, with mild temperate winters and hot summers. The highest average temperature in the Algarve is around 28°C (82°F) in summer, although 40°C (104°F) has been recorded here. The Algarve has an average of 12 hours sunshine a day in the summer and six hours in the winter (a total of around 3,000 hours a year). The region doesn't have a winter as such (certainly not by northern European standards) and spring starts as early as January or February. Average temperatures in the Algarve are 12°C (54°F) in winter in January and they can fall to as low as 5°C (41°F), although it's never below freezing. Rainfall averages between 350 and 600mm a year and is higher on the mountainous hinterland than on the coast (November is generally the wettest month). The Algarve suffers from a constant lack of water and experiences periodic droughts, along with most of the southern half of Iberia. Sea temperatures on the Algarve range from around 22°C (72°F) in summer to 15°C (59°F) in winter. The sea is around 2°C cooler in the western Algarve than in the east, where the warmer Mediterranean exerts its influence.

Madeira is sub-tropical with wet winters and hot summers. The average temperature is around 16°C (61°F) in winter in January and 22°C (72°F) in summer in July/August. Madeira has its high season in winter and is a popular winter holiday destination. The island enjoys a mild, year-round, sub-tropical climate and averages 2,000 hours of sunshine annually. The rainy season is from October to March, although showers are possible all year round. The temperature in Madeira hovers around 15°C (59°F) in winter and 25°C (77°F) in summer. The Azores have a surprisingly mild climate considering they're located in the Atlantic Ocean.

Approximate average daily maximum/minimum temperatures for some of Portugal's major cities are shown below in Centigrade and Fahrenheit (in brackets):

Location	Spring	Summer	Autumn	Winter
Bragança	16/5 (61/41)	28/13 (82/55)	18/7 (64/45)	8/0 (46/32)
Coimbra	21/9 (70/48)	29/15 (84/59)	23/12 (73/54)	14/5 (57/41)
Évora	19/10 (66/50)	30/16 (86/61)	22/13 (72/55)	12/6 (54/43)
Faro	20/13 (68/55)	28/20 (82/68)	22/16 (72/61)	15/9 (59/48)
Lisbon	20/12 (68/54)	27/17 (81/63)	22/14 (72/57)	14/8 (57/46)
Porto	18/9 (64/48)	25/15 (77/59)	21/11 (70/52)	13/5 (55/41)

Frequent weather forecasts (*pronósticos* or *o tempo*) are given on TV, radio and in daily newspapers. A quick way to make a rough conversion from Centigrade to Fahrenheit is to multiply by 2 and add 30.

GEOGRAPHY

Portugal is situated in the extreme south-west corner of Europe, occupying around one sixth of the Iberian peninsula (92,390km^2/35,675mi^2) with an

Atlantic coastline of over 830km (515mi). The country extends just 560km (347mi) from north to south and 220km (136mi) east to west and is one of Europe's smallest countries (around the same size as Austria and Ireland) with a population of around 10.1m. Somewhat surprisingly, Portugal was the first country on the European continent to establish its borders; it's bounded on the south and west by the Atlantic Ocean and on the north and east by Spain.

Portugal is one of the most geographically diverse countries in Europe and offers everything from majestic mountain ranges and lush green valleys in the north, to flat dry plains and rolling hills in the south. It also has a plethora of sandy beaches and vast forests (over a quarter of the country is forested). Portugal has four main rivers: the Minho in the north, which denotes the border with Spain; the Douro (also in the north), the banks of which are famous for its port wine vineyards; the Tejo (or Tagus) which flows into the Atlantic at Lisbon and roughly divides the country in half; and the Guadiana in the south-east, part of which forms the eastern frontier with Spain.

North of the river Tejo are most of Portugal's mountains, where some 90 per cent of the land is 400m (1,312ft) above sea level (although little is more than 700m (2,296ft) above sea level). This region is the source of three of Portugal's most important rivers (the Douro, Guadiana and Tejo). Further south the high Beira plains are *serra* country and feature several major mountain ranges (notably the Serra de Estrêla) which are an extension of Spain's central sierras. The highest point is the Torre peak (1,993m/6,538ft) in the Serra de Estrêla range. The mountains extend southwards, where the Serra do Açor and Serra da Lousã contain some of the most beautiful and dramatic landscapes in the country. The southern half of the country is largely flat and over 60 per cent of the land that's below 400m (1,312ft) is located here. The Algarve contains semi-tropical landscapes and enjoys a Mediterranean climate protected by the serras of Caleirão and Monchique, which act as a buffer against the harsher northern climate.

The Portuguese autonomous islands of Madeira (and its neighbouring island of Porto Santo) and the Azores are incongruously referred to as the Adjacent Isles (*adjucente*). Madeira is situated off the east coast of Africa north of the Canary Islands around 1,000km (620mi) south-west of Lisbon and is 57km (35mi) in length and 22km (14mi) wide with a population of some 300,000. Like the Azores it has volcanic origins and is green and mountainous with few beaches. The Azores are situated some 1,450km (900mi) west of Lisbon and comprise nine islands covering an area of 2,350km^2 (907mi^2) with a population of around 250,000. Portugal used to administer the colony of Macau on the Chinese mainland, which was returned to Chinese rule in 1999.

Portugal is divided into regions and provinces, shown on the maps in **Appendix F**. A map of Portugal showing the major cities and geographical features is on page 6.

HEALTH

One of the most important aspects of living in Portugal (or anywhere else for that matter) is maintaining good health. The quality of health care and health care facilities in Portugal are generally good (although variable) and have improved considerably in recent years, although they aren't up to the high standard taken for granted in North America and northern Europe. There are many English-speaking and foreign doctors in resort areas and major cities, although hospital facilities are limited in some rural areas. Nursing care and post-hospital assistance are below what most northern Europeans and North Americans take for granted, and spending on preventive medicine is relatively low. Health care costs per head in Portugal are lower than average in the European Union (EU) and the country spends a relatively small percentage of its GDP on health, although this has improved in recent years (7.8 per cent in 2000, higher than Britain). Public and private medicine operate alongside each other in Portugal and complement one another, although public health facilities are limited in some areas.

Portugal has a public health system, providing free or low cost health care for those who contribute to Portuguese social security (*segurança social*), plus their families and retirees (including those from other EU countries). There are subsidised prescriptions for members aged over 65 and charges of from 40 to 100 per cent for non-essential medicines plus substantial contributions for many services including spectacles, dentures, dental and spa treatment, and other treatment. If you don't qualify for health care under the public health system, it's essential to have private health insurance (in fact, you won't usually get a residence card without it). This is often recommended in any case if you can afford it, due to the inadequacy of public health services (which like most, are strapped for cash) and long waiting lists for specialist appointments and non-urgent operations in many areas. Visitors to Portugal should have holiday health insurance (see page 64) if they aren't covered by a reciprocal arrangement (see page 60).

There are state health centres (*centros de saúde*) in most areas (typically open from 8am to 8pm) which treat minor health problems and where it's easier to get prompt emergency treatment than at a public hospital. There are 24-hour emergency hospitals in major towns and private hospitals and clinics in major towns and resort areas (including small British hospitals in Lisbon and Porto). English-speaking Portuguese doctors and English and other foreign doctors practise in resort areas and major cities, many of who advertise in the local expatriate press. You can obtain free advice for minor ailments from pharmacies (*farmácias*), open from 9am to 1pm and 3 to 7pm Monday to Friday and from 9am to 1pm on Saturdays. There's normally a duty pharmacy (*farmácia de serviço*) open outside usual business hours. A list of duty pharmacies is posted in pharmacy windows and announced in the local press (you can also telephone 118 and ask for the name of your local duty pharmacy).

The Portuguese are among the world's healthiest people and have one of the highest life expectancies in the European Union. However, the country also once had one of the highest infant mortality rates in western Europe, although it's fallen considerably in recent years as medical services have improved. The incidence of heart disease in Portugal is among the lowest in the world, a fact officially contributed in large part to their diet (which includes lots of garlic, olive oil and red wine), as is the incidence of cancers. However, the country has a high incidence of smoking-related health problems (the percentage of smokers is among the highest in the EU).

Among expatriates, common health problems include sunburn and sunstroke, stomach and bowel problems (due to the change of diet and more often, water, but they can also be caused by poor hygiene), and various problems caused by excess alcohol (including a high incidence of alcoholism). Other health problems are caused by the high level of airborne pollen in spring in some areas (which particularly affects asthma and hay fever sufferers) and noise and traffic pollution, particularly in Portugal's major cities. If you aren't used to Portugal's hot sun, you should limit your exposure and avoid it altogether during the hottest part of the day, wear protective clothing (including a hat) and use a sun block. Too much sun and too little protection will dry your skin and cause premature ageing, to say nothing of the risks of skin cancer. Care should also be taken to replace the natural oils lost from too many hours in the sun and the elderly should take particular care not to exert themselves during hot weather.

Portugal's mild climate is therapeutic, particularly for sufferers of rheumatism and arthritis and those who are prone to bronchitis, colds and pneumonia. Portugal's slower pace of life is also beneficial for those who are prone to stress (it's difficult to remain up-tight while napping in the sun), although it takes many foreigners some time to adjust. The climate and lifestyle in any country has a noticeable affect on mental health and people who live in hot climes are generally happier and more relaxed than those who live in cold, wet climates (such as northern Europe). When you've had a surfeit of Portugal's good life, a variety of health cures are available at spas and health 'farms'.

Health (and health insurance) is an important issue for anyone retiring to Portugal. Many people are ill-prepared for old age and the possibility of health problems. There's a shortage of welfare and home-nursing services for the elderly in Portugal, either state or private, and foreigners who are no longer able to care for themselves are often forced to return to their home countries. There are few state residential nursing homes in Portugal or hospices for the terminally ill, although there are a number of private, purpose-built, retirement developments (see page 157). Portugal's provision for handicapped travellers is also poor, and wheelchair access to buildings and public transport is well below the average in western Europe.

Pre-Departure Check: If you're planning to take up residence in Portugal, even for part of the year only, it's wise to have a health check (medical or screening, eyes, teeth, etc.) before your arrival, particularly if you have a record of poor health or are elderly. If you're already taking regular medication, you should note that the brand names of drugs and medicines vary from country to country, and should ask your doctor for the generic name. If you wish to match medication prescribed abroad, you will need a current prescription with the medication's trade name, the manufacturer's name, the chemical name and the dosage. Most drugs have an equivalent in other countries, although particular brands may be difficult or impossible to obtain in Portugal.

It's possible to have medication sent from abroad, when no import duty or value added tax is usually payable. If you're visiting a holiday home in Portugal for a limited period, you should take sufficient medication to cover your stay. In an emergency a local doctor will write a prescription which can be filled at a local pharmacy or a hospital may refill a prescription from its own pharmacy. It's also wise to take some of your favourite non-prescription drugs (e.g. aspirins, cold and flu remedies, lotions, etc.) with you, as they may be difficult or impossible to obtain in Portugal or may be much more expensive. If applicable, take a spare pair of spectacles or contact lenses, dentures or a hearing aid with you.

There are no special health risks in Portugal and no immunisations are required unless you arrive from an area infected with yellow fever. You can safely drink the water, although it sometimes tastes awful and many people prefer bottled water – when not drinking red wine (which isn't only tastier, but may even be beneficial to your health – **when consumed in moderation!**) and various other alcoholic beverages. *¡Saúde!*

INSURANCE

An important aspect of owning a home in Portugal is insurance, not only for your home and its contents, but also health insurance for your family when visiting Portugal. If you live in Portugal permanently you will require additional insurance. It's unnecessary to spend half your income insuring yourself against every eventuality from the common cold to being sued for your last euro, although it's important to insure against any event that could precipitate a major financial disaster, such as a serious accident or your house being demolished by a storm. **The cost of being uninsured or under-insured can be astronomical.**

As with anything connected with finance, it's important to shop around when buying insurance. Simply collecting a few brochures from insurance agents or making a few telephone calls can save you a lot of money. Note, however, that not all insurance companies are equally reliable or have the same financial stability, and it may be better to insure with a large international company with a good reputation rather than with a small (e.g. Portuguese) company, even if this means paying higher premiums. Read all insurance contracts carefully and make sure that you understand the terms and the cover provided before signing them. Some insurance companies will do almost anything to avoid paying out on claims and will use any available legal loophole, therefore it pays to deal with reputable companies only (not that this provides a foolproof guarantee).

In all matters regarding insurance, you're responsible for ensuring that you and your family are legally insured in Portugal. Regrettably you cannot insure yourself against being uninsured or sue your insurance agent for giving you bad advice! Bear in mind that if you wish to make a claim on an insurance policy, you may be required to report an incident to the police within 24 hours (which may also be a legal requirement). The law in Portugal may differ considerably from that in your home country or your previous country of residence and you should never assume that it's the same. If you're unsure of your rights, it's best to obtain legal advice for anything other than a minor claim. Under EU rules an insurance company registered in an EU member country can sell its policies in any other EU country.

This section contains information about health insurance, household insurance, and holiday and travel insurance.

Health Insurance

If you're visiting, living or working in Portugal, it's extremely risky not to have health insurance for your family, as if you're uninsured (or under-insured) you could be faced with some very high medical bills. When deciding on the type and extent of health insurance, make sure that it covers all your family's present and future health requirements in Portugal **before you receive a large bill.** A health insurance policy should cover you for all essential health care whatever the reason, including accidents (e.g. sports accidents) and injuries, whether they occur in your home, at your place of work or while travelling. **Don't take anything for granted, but check in advance.** If you're planning to live permanently in Portugal and will be contributing to Portuguese social security, you and your family will be entitled to subsidised or free medical and dental treatment. However, many Portuguese and most foreign residents who can afford to, take out private health insurance, which offers a wider choice of medical practitioners and hospitals, and more importantly, frees them from public health waiting lists. If you aren't covered by Portuguese social security, it's important that you have private health insurance (unless you have a very large bank balance).

The policies offered by Portuguese and foreign companies generally differ considerably in the extent of cover, limitations and restrictions, premiums, and the choice of doctors, specialists and hospitals. Note that the private health care system in Portugal is as yet still in its infancy and you should check the cover offered by policies very carefully.

Proof of health insurance must usually be provided when applying for a visa or residence card (*autorização de residência*). Note that some foreign insurance companies may not provide sufficient cover to satisfy Portuguese regulations and therefore you should check the minimum cover necessary with a Portuguese consulate in your country of residence. Long stay visitors should have travel or long stay health insurance or an international health policy (see **Health Insurance for Visitors** on page 59). If your stay in Portugal is limited, you may be covered by a reciprocal agreement between your home country and Portugal (see page 60). When travelling in Portugal you should always carry proof of your health insurance with you.

Health Insurance for Residents

If you contribute to Portuguese social security, you and your family are entitled to free or subsidised medical and dental treatment. Benefits include general and specialist care, hospitalisation, laboratory services, discounted drugs and medicines, basic dental care, maternity care, appliances and transportation. Most Portuguese are covered by Portugal's public health scheme, including retired EU residents (with a residence card) receiving a state pension. If you aren't entitled to public health benefits through payment of Portuguese social security (*segurança social*) or receiving a state pension from another EU country, you must usually have private health insurance and must present proof of your insurance when applying for a residence card. If you're an EU national of retirement age, who isn't in receipt of a pension, you may be entitled to public health benefits if you can show that you cannot afford private health insurance.

Anyone who has paid regular social security contributions in another EU country for two full years prior to coming to Portugal (e.g. to look for a job) is entitled to public health cover for a limited period from the date of the last social security contribution made in their home country. Social security form E106 must be obtained from the social security authorities in your home country and given to your local social security office in Portugal. Similarly, pensioners and those in receipt of invalidity benefits must obtain form E121 from their home country's social security administration.

You will be registered as a member of social security and will be given a social security card, a list of local medical practitioners and hospitals, and general information about services and charges. If you're receiving an invalidity pension or other social security benefits on the grounds of ill-health, you should establish exactly how living in Portugal will affect those benefits. In some countries there are reciprocal agreements regarding invalidity rights (see page 60), but you must confirm that they apply in your case. Citizens of EU countries and European Economic Area (EEA) countries (Iceland, Liechtenstein and Norway) are able to make payments in their home country entitling them to use public health services in Portugal and other EU and EEA countries.

The Portuguese health system places the emphasis on cure rather than prevention and treats sickness rather than promoting good health. There's little preventive medicine, although this has changed in recent years and there are now regular health checks for children and older people, and a full immunisation programme for children. The public health service has limited resources for out-patient treatment, nursing and post-operative care, geriatric assistance, terminal illnesses and psychiatric treatment. In the past the Portuguese health system was criticised mainly for perfunctory treatment due to staff shortages, long waiting lists as a result of a shortage of hospital facilities, and a general dehumanisation of patients. Many of these problems were related to crippling bureaucracy and bad management. Although many of these problems still exist, the situation has generally improved greatly in recent years and the health system has become much more 'transparent'. Among other things, patients now have a list of rights they can expect from the health service. However, it's generally considered that the Portuguese health system is badly in need of a general over-haul (which has been promised by successive governments but has yet to materialise).

The department of social security in Portugal has a free telephone hotline (*linha verde*) for information and enquiries operating Monday to Friday from 9am to 7pm (☎ 800-290 029) and a comprehensive website (in Portuguese only), which includes downloadable documents and forms (💻 www.seg-social.pt).

Private Insurance: If you aren't covered by Portuguese social security you should take out private health insurance. It's advantageous to be insured with a company that will pay large medical bills directly. Most private health insurance policies don't pay family doctors' fees or pay for medication that isn't provided in a hospital or there's an 'excess', e.g. the equivalent of around €75, which often exceeds the cost of treatment. Most will, however, pay for 100 per cent of specialists' fees and hospital treatment in the best Portuguese hospitals. The cost of comprehensive private insurance with a Portuguese company varies considerably and can be very expensive, although young families generally get comprehensive coverage at very competitive rates. Note that Portuguese companies usually only provide health insurance for those under 55. If you are older you will have to consider health insurance from a foreign company. Generally, the higher the premium, the more choice you have regarding doctors, specialists and hospitals. You should avoid a company that reserves the right to cancel a policy when you reach a certain age, e.g. 65 or 70, or which increases premiums sharply as you get older, as to take out a new policy at the age of 65 or older at a reasonable premium is difficult. If you already have private health insurance in another country, you may be able to extend it to cover you in Portugal.

Changing Employers or Insurance Companies: When changing employers or leaving Portugal, you should ensure that you have continuous health insurance. If you and your family are covered by a company health plan, your insurance will probably cease after your last official day of employment. **If you're planning to change your health insurance company, you should ensure that important benefits aren't lost, e.g. existing medical conditions won't usually be covered by a new insurer.** When changing health insurance companies, it's wise to inform your old company if you have any outstanding bills for which they're liable.

Health Insurance for Visitors

Visitors spending short periods in Portugal (e.g. up to a month) should have a travel health insurance policy (see page 64), unless they're covered by an international health policy. If you plan to spend up to six months a year in Portugal you should take out either a travel, special long stay or international health policy, which should cover you in your home country and when travelling in other countries. Note that premiums vary considerably and it's important to shop around. Most international health policies include repatriation or evacuation (although it may be optional), which may also include shipment (by air) of the body of a person who dies abroad to his home country for burial. Note that an international policy also usually allows you to choose to have non-urgent medical treatment in the country of your choice.

Most international insurance companies offer health policies for different areas, e.g. Europe, world-wide excluding North America, and world-wide including North America. Most companies also offer different levels of cover, for example basic, standard, comprehensive and prestige. There's always an annual limit on the total medical costs, which should be at least €350,000 (although many provide cover of up to €1.1m or more) and some companies also limit the charges for specific treatment or care such as specialists' fees, operations and hospital accommodation. A medical examination isn't usually required for international health policies, although pre-existing health problems are excluded for a period, e.g. one or two years.

Claims are usually settled in all major currencies and large claims are usually settled directly by insurance companies (although your choice of hospitals may be limited). Check whether an insurance company will settle large medical bills directly, as if you're required to pay bills and claim reimbursement from an insurance company it can take several months before you receive your money (some companies are slow to pay). It isn't usually necessary to translate bills into English or another language, although you should check a company's policy. Most international health insurance companies provide emergency telephone assistance.

The cost of international health insurance varies considerably with your age and the extent of cover. Note that with most international insurance policies, you must enrol before you reach a certain age, e.g. between 60 and 80 depending on the company, to be guaranteed continuous cover in your old age. Premiums can sometimes be paid monthly, quarterly or annually, although some companies insist on payment annually in advance. When comparing policies, carefully check the extent of cover and exactly what's included and excluded from a policy (often indicated only in the very small print), in addition to premiums and excess charges.

In some countries, premium increases are limited by law, although this may apply only to residents in the country where a company is registered and not to overseas policy holders. Although there may be significant differences in premiums, generally you get what you pay for and can tailor premiums to your requirements. The most important questions to ask yourself are: does the policy provide the cover required and is it good value for money? If you're in good health and are able to pay for your own out-patient treatment, such as visits to a family doctor and prescriptions, then the best value is a policy covering specialist and hospital treatment only.

Reciprocal Health Agreements: If you're entitled to social security health benefits in another EU country or in a country with a reciprocal health agreement with Portugal, you will receive free or reduced cost medical treatment in Portugal. EU residents should apply for a certificate of entitlement to treatment (form E111) from their local social security office at least three weeks before they plan to travel to Portugal. **The form E111 can be used for a stay of three months' duration only.** If you use the E111 in Portugal, you must apply for reimbursement to Portuguese social security (instructions are provided with the form), which can take a number of months. **However, you can still receive a large bill from a Portuguese hospital, as your local health authority assumes a percentage of the cost only.** Note that a form E111 issued abroad (i.e. not in Portugal) isn't valid in Portugal if you're a Portuguese resident.

Participating countries include all EU member states and most other European countries, excluding Albania, Switzerland and Turkey. The USA doesn't have a reciprocal health agreement with Portugal and therefore Americans who aren't covered by Portuguese social security must have private health insurance in Portugal. British visitors and those planning to live in Portugal can obtain information about reciprocal health treatment from the Department of Social Security, Overseas Branch, Newcastle-upon-Tyne, NE98 1YX, UK.

Household Insurance

Household insurance (*seguro de bens domésticos*) in Portugal generally includes the building, its contents and third party liability, all of which are contained in a multi-risk household insurance policy. Policies are offered by both Portuguese and foreign insurance companies and premiums are similar, although foreign companies may provide more comprehensive cover.

Building: Although it isn't compulsory, it's best for owners to take out property insurance that covers damage to a building due to fire, smoke, water, explosion, storm, freezing, snow, theft, vandalism, malicious damage, acts of terrorism, impact, broken windows and natural catastrophes (such as falling trees). Insurance should include glass, external buildings, aerials and satellite dishes, gardens and garden ornaments. Bear in mind that although earthquakes are extremely rare in Portugal, the country lies in an earthquake zone (an earthquake in 1755 destroyed buildings from Faro to Lisbon), so you may wish to ensure that damage from earthquakes is included. Cover for earthquakes, lightning damage and subsidence usually aren't included in a standard policy, so check exactly what is excluded and what it will cost to include it.

Note that if a claim is the result of a defect in building or design, the insurance company won't pay up (another reason why it's wise to have a survey before buying a home). Property insurance is based on the cost of rebuilding your home and should be increased each year in line with inflation. **Make sure that you insure your property for the true cost of rebuilding.** It's particularly important to have insurance for storm damage in Portugal, which can be severe in some areas. If floods are one of your concerns, make sure you're covered for water coming in from ground level, not just for water seeping in through the roof. Always read the small print of contracts. If you own a home in an area that has been hit by a succession of natural disasters (such as floods), your household insurance may be cancelled.

Contents: Contents are usually insured for the same risks as a building (see above) and are insured for their replacement value (new for old), with a reduction for wear and tear for clothes and linen. Valuable objects are covered for their actual declared (and authenticated) value. Most policies include automatic indexation of the insured sum in line with inflation. Contents insurance may include accidental damage to sanitary installations, theft, money, replacement of locks following damage or loss of keys, frozen food, alternative accommodation cover, and property belonging to third parties stored in your home. Some items are usually optional, e.g. credit cards, frozen foods, emergency assistance (plumber, glazier, electrician, etc.), redecoration, garaged cars, replacement pipes, loss of rent, and the cost of travel to Portugal for holiday homeowners. Many policies include personal third party or legal liability (*responsibilidade civil*), e.g. up to €400,000, although this may be an option.

Items of high value must usually be itemised and photographs and documentation (e.g. a valuation) provided. Some companies even recommend or insist on a video film of belongings. When claiming for contents, you should produce the original bills if possible (always keep bills for expensive items) and bear in mind that replacing imported items in Portugal may be more expensive than buying them abroad. Contents' policies always contain security clauses and if you don't adhere to them a claim won't be considered. If you're planning to let a property, you may be required to inform your insurer. Note that a building must be secure with iron bars on ground-floor windows and patio-doors, shutters and secure locks. Most companies give a discount if properties have steel reinforced doors, high security locks and alarms (particularly alarms connected to a monitoring station). An insurance company may send someone to inspect your property and advise on security measures. Policies pay out for theft only when there are signs of forcible entry and you aren't covered for thefts by a tenant (but you may be covered for thefts by domestic personnel). All-risks policies offering a world-wide extension to a household policy covering jewellery, cameras and other items aren't usually available from Portuguese insurance companies, but are available from a number of foreign companies.

Community Properties: If you own a property that's part of a community development (see page 153), the building will be insured by the community (although you should always ensure that it's comprehensively insured). You must, however, be insured for third party risks in the event that you cause damage to neighbouring properties, e.g. through flood or fire. Household insurance policies in Portugal usually include third party liability up to a maximum amount, e.g. €400,000.

Holiday Homes: Premiums are generally higher for holiday homes than permanent homes due to their higher vulnerability, particularly to burglaries. Premiums are usually based on the number of days a year a property is inhabited, the interval between periods of occupancy, its location and how far it is from its nearest neighbour. Cover for theft, storm, flood and malicious damage may be suspended when a property is left empty for an extended period, e.g. longer than 30 days. You're required to turn off the water supply at the mains when vacating a building for more than 72 hours. It's possible to negotiate cover for periods of absence for a hefty surcharge, although valuable items are usually excluded (unless you have a safe). If you're absent from your property for long periods, e.g. longer than 30 days a year, you may be required to pay an excess on a claim arising from an occurrence that takes place during your absence (and theft may be excluded). **Note that (where applicable) it's important to ensure that a policy specifies a holiday home and not a principal home.** In areas with a high risk of theft (e.g. major cities and most resort areas), an insurance company may insist on extra security measures. It's unwise to leave valuable or irreplaceable items in a holiday home or a property that will be vacant for long periods. Some insurance companies will do their utmost to find a loophole which makes you negligent and relieves them of liability. You should ensure that the details listed on a policy are correct, otherwise your policy could be void.

Premiums: Premiums are usually calculated on the size (constructed area in square metres) of a property, its age, the value of the contents and the security protection, e.g. window protection at ground level, the number of entrance doors and their construction. As a rough guide, an average villa with a valuation of around €400,000 would cost around €400 per year to insure including insurance for contents valued at €15,000. Insurance is generally higher for a detached villa than an apartment and detached, older and more remote properties cost more to insure than apartments and new properties (particularly when located in towns), due to the higher risk of theft. Premiums are also higher in certain high risk areas. As in most countries, prices vary greatly from one company to another so it's best to shop around.

Claims: If you wish to make a claim, you must usually inform your insurance company in writing (by registered letter) within two to seven days of an incident or 24 hours in the case of theft. Thefts should also be reported to the local police within 24 hours, as the police report (*relatório*), of which you receive a copy (*certidão*) for your insurance company, constitutes irrefutable evidence of your claim. Check whether you're covered for damage or thefts that occur while you're away from your property and are therefore unable to inform the insurance company immediately.

Take care that you don't under-insure your house contents and that you periodically reassess their value and adjust your insurance premium accordingly. You can arrange to have your insurance cover automatically increased annually by a fixed percentage or amount by your insurance company. If you make a claim and the assessor discovers that you're under-insured, the amount due will be reduced by the percentage by which you're under-insured. For example, if you're insured for €6,000 and you're found to be under-insured by 50 per cent, your claim for €1,000 will be reduced by 50 per cent to €500. You must usually pay an excess for each claim.

Insuring Abroad: It's possible and legal to take out building and contents insurance in another country for a property in Portugal (some foreign insurance companies offer special policies for holiday homeowners), although you must ensure that a policy is valid under Portuguese law. The advantage is that you will have a policy you can understand and you will be able to handle claims in your own language. This may seem like a good option for a holiday home in Portugal, although it can be more expensive than insuring with a Portuguese company and can lead to conflicts if, for example, the building is insured with a Portuguese-registered company and the contents with a foreign based company. Most experts advise that you insure a Portuguese home and its contents with a Portuguese insurance company through a local agent.

Holiday & Travel Insurance

Holiday and travel insurance (*seguro de viagem*) is recommended for all who don't wish to risk having their holiday or travel ruined by financial problems or to arrive home broke. As you probably know, anything can and often does go wrong with a holiday, sometimes before you even get started (particularly when you don't have insurance). The following information applies equally to both residents and non-residents, whether they're travelling to or from Portugal or within Portugal. **Nobody should visit Portugal without travel (and health) insurance!**

Travel insurance is available from many sources including travel agents, insurance companies and agents, banks, automobile clubs and transport companies (airline, rail and bus). Package holiday companies and tour operators also offer insurance policies, some of which are compulsory, too expensive **and don't provide adequate cover.** You can also buy 24-hour accident and flight insurance at major airports, although it's expensive and doesn't offer the best cover. Before taking out travel insurance, carefully consider the range and level of cover you require and compare policies. Short-term holiday and travel insurance policies should include cover for holiday cancellation or interruption; missed flights; departure delay at both the start and end of a holiday (a common occurrence); delayed, lost or damaged baggage; personal effects and money; medical expenses and accidents (including evacuation home); flight insurance; personal liability and legal expenses; and default or bankruptcy insurance, e.g. against a tour operator or airline going bust.

Health Cover: Medical expenses are an important aspect of travel insurance and you shouldn't rely on insurance provided by reciprocal health arrangements (see page 60), charge and credit card companies, household policies or private medical insurance (unless it's an international policy), none of which usually provide adequate cover (although you should take advantage of what they offer). The minimum medical insurance recommended by experts is around €400,000 in Portugal and the rest of Europe, and €1.5m for the rest of the world (many policies have limits of between €2m and €3m). If applicable, check whether pregnancy related claims are covered and whether there are any restrictions for those over a certain age, e.g. 65 or 70 (travel insurance is becoming increasingly more expensive for those aged over 65).

Check any exclusion clauses in contracts by obtaining a copy of the full policy document, as all relevant information isn't included in an insurance leaflet. High risk sports and pursuits should be specifically covered and listed in a policy (there's usually an additional premium). Special winter sports policies are available and are more expensive than normal holiday insurance ('dangerous' sports are excluded from most standard policies). Third party liability cover should be around €3 million in North America and €1.5 million in the rest of the world. **Note that this doesn't cover you when you're using a car or other mechanically propelled vehicle.**

Cost: The cost of travel insurance varies considerably according to where you buy it, how long you intend to stay in Portugal and your age. Generally the longer the period covered, the cheaper the daily cost, although the maximum period covered is usually limited, e.g. six months. With some policies an excess must be paid for each claim. As a rough guide, travel insurance for Portugal (and most other European countries) costs from around €35 for one week, €50 for two weeks and €90 for a month for a family of four (two adults and two children under 16). Premiums may be higher for those aged over 65 or 70.

Annual Policies: For people who travel abroad frequently, whether on business or pleasure, an annual travel policy usually provides the best value, but carefully check exactly what it includes. Many insurance companies offer annual travel policies for a premium of around €200 for an individual (the equivalent of around three months' insurance with a standard travel insurance policy), which are excellent value for frequent travellers. Some insurance companies also offer an 'emergency travel policy' for holiday homeowners who need to travel abroad at short notice to inspect a property, e.g. after storm damage. The cost of an annual policy may depend on the area covered, e.g. Europe, world-wide (excluding North America) and world-wide (including North America), although it doesn't usually cover travel within your country of residence. There's also a limit on the number of trips a year and the duration of each trip, e.g. 90 or 120 days. An annual policy is usually a good choice for owners of a holiday home in Portugal who travel there frequently for relatively short periods. **However, carefully check exactly what is covered (or omitted) as an annual policy may not provide adequate cover.**

Claims: If you need to make a claim, you should provide as much documentary evidence as possible to support it. Travel insurance companies gladly take your money, but they aren't always so keen to pay claims and you may need to persevere before they pay up. Be persistent and make a claim <u>irrespective</u> of any small print, as this may be unreasonable and therefore invalid in law. Insurance companies usually require you to obtain a written report and report a loss (or any incident for which you intend to make a claim) to the local police or transport companies (e.g. an airline) within 24 hours. Failure to do so may mean that a claim won't be considered.

SHOPPING

Portugal isn't one of Europe's great shopping countries, either for quality or bargains, with the exception of handmade arts and crafts which are widely available at reasonable prices. However, the variety of shops and goods has improved greatly over the last few years and new motorways mean that

Lisbon and Seville, both of which have excellent shopping facilities, are within easy reach of resorts on the Algarve. Prices of many consumer goods such as TVs and stereo systems, computers, cameras, electrical apparatus and household appliances have fallen considerably in recent years, although they're generally higher than in most other EU countries due to the restricted competition. Clothes aren't particularly good value in Portugal and good quality clothing can be expensive, although there are now several retail chain stores offering good value fashion. If you're fortunate enough to be paid in a currency that has risen in value against the euro in recent years, you may be pleasantly surprised how far your money will stretch. However, Portugal is no longer an inexpensive country and the cost of living (see page 115) has risen considerably in the last decade.

Small family-run stores still constitute over half of Portugal's retailers, although the shopping scene has been transformed in the last few decades with the opening of huge shopping centres and hypermarkets. Following the trend in most European countries, there has been a drift away from town centres by retailers to out-of-town shopping centres (malls) and hypermarket complexes, which has left some town centres run down and abandoned. Hypermarkets are particularly popular and include Continente, Feira Nova, Jumbo, Lidl, Modelo and Pingo Doce. Large DIY and homeware stores, such as Metre Maco and Max Mat, are also popular. Foreign shops include Intermarche, El Corte Inglés department stores, Zara and Casa as well as many designer label boutiques. The biggest drawback to shopping in cities and towns is parking, which can be a nightmare. With the exception of street markets, where haggling over the price is part of the enjoyment, retail prices are fixed in Portugal.

Shops in Portugal usually open from 9 (or 10am) until 1pm and from 3 to 7pm (possibly 8pm) Mondays to Fridays, and from 9am to 1pm on Saturdays. Most shops are closed on Sundays except for small supermarkets and some shops in tourist areas. Some large out-of-town shopping centres remain open seven days a week, from 10am until as late as midnight. It's important to shop around and compare prices in Portugal as they can vary considerably, not only between small shops and hypermarkets, but also among supermarkets and hypermarkets in the same town. Note, however, that price differences often reflect different quality, so ensure that you're comparing similar products. The best time to have a shopping spree is during the winter and summer sales (*saldos*) in January-February and July-August respectively, when bargains abound and prices are often slashed by 50 per cent or more.

Among the best buys in Portugal are the diverse handicrafts which include needlepoint, embroidery, tapestries, hand-woven fabrics, wood carvings, wicker basketwork, textiles, carpets, ceramics, porcelain, china, tiles, pottery, bedspreads, jewellery (gold and silver, particularly filigree), lace, linen, leather goods, antiques, cork products, woollen garments, crystal, rugs, contemporary art and metalwork (e.g. wrought-iron). Items from throughout Portugal and its islands are available in Lisbon and Porto, but are usually cheaper when purchased in the province where they're made. Although the number of local artisans has fallen in the last few decades, arts and crafts have survived the 20th century better in Portugal than in most other western European countries and many foreign artists live and work there.

In major cities and tourist areas you <u>must</u> be wary of pickpockets and bag-snatchers, particularly in markets and other crowded places. <u>Never</u> tempt fate with an exposed wallet or purse or by flashing your money around. The Portuguese generally pay cash when shopping, although credit and debit cards are widely accepted in major stores and stores frequented by tourists (although some accept only Portuguese credit cards such as Multibanco). However, personal cheques (even local ones) aren't usually accepted.

Markets

Markets (*mercados*) are a common sight in towns and villages throughout Portugal and are an essential part of Portuguese life, largely unaffected by competition from supermarkets and hypermarkets. They're colourful, entertaining and fun, and an experience not to be missed, even if you don't plan to buy anything (you find the real Portugal in a market). Some towns have markets on one or two days a week only, while others have markets on every day of the year except Christmas Day. In rural and coastal areas, market days are varied in local towns so that they don't clash.

There are different kinds of markets in Portugal including indoor markets, permanent street markets and travelling street markets (*feiras*) that move from neighbourhood to neighbourhood on different days of the week or month. Prices are generally lower than in shops, although much depends on your bargaining skills (haggling is expected for expensive items or when buying in bulk). There's often a large central market (*mercado central*) in cities, and many towns and neighbourhoods of large cities have indoor or covered markets. Markets usually operate from around 8am until 1pm, although in cities and some towns they're open all day.

A variety of goods are commonly sold in markets including food, flowers, plants, clothes (markets are best for inexpensive clothes), shoes, ironmongery, crockery, hardware, cookware, linen, handicrafts, ceramics, tapestries, pottery, cassettes/CDs, arts and crafts, household wares, furniture, antiques, carpets, jewellery, watches and leather goods. Specialist markets in Lisbon and other cities sell antiques, books, clothes, stamps, postcards, medals, coins, flowers, birds and pets. **You should beware of bargain-priced branded goods in markets, such as watches, perfume and clothes, as they're invariably fakes.**

Food markets (often covered) remain highly popular, despite the proliferation of supermarkets and hypermarkets. There are also fish markets in some coastal towns. Food is invariably beautifully presented and includes fruit and vegetables (including many exotic varieties), fish, meat, live poultry, dairy products, bread and cakes, and pickled vegetables, herbs, olives and olive oil. Food is usually cheaper and fresher in markets than in supermarkets, particularly if you buy what's in season and grown locally. You should arrive early in the morning for the best choice, although bargains can often be found when stall-holders are packing up for the day.

All produce is clearly marked with its price per piece or per kilogram. There's no haggling over food prices, although at the end of the day an offer may be accepted. When shopping for food in markets, vendors may object to customers handling the fruit and vegetables, although you needn't be shy about asking to taste a piece of cheese or fruit. It's best to take a bag when buying fruit and vegetables as carrier bags aren't usually provided. When buying fruit and vegetables in markets check that the quality of produce you're given is the same as that displayed, which isn't always the case. Queues are a good sign.

Antique and flea markets are common throughout Portugal, although you shouldn't expect to find many (or any) bargains in the major cities, where anything worth buying is snapped up by dealers. However, in small towns you may turn up some real bargains. You should never assume that because something is sold in a market it will be a bargain, particularly when buying antiques (*antiguidades*), which aren't always authentic. In many cases local shops are cheaper, particularly those selling to local residents rather than tourists. Always haggle over the price of expensive items. To find out when local markets are held, enquire at your local tourist office or town hall.

Furniture & Furnishings

The kind of furniture (*móveis*) you buy for your Portuguese home will depend on a number of factors including its style and size, whether it's a permanent or holiday home, your budget, the local climate, and not least, your taste. Holiday homes are often sold furnished, particularly apartments, although furniture may be of poor quality and not to your taste. However, buying a furnished property can represent a real bargain, as the cost of the furnishings often isn't reflected in the price. If you're buying a new property as an investment for letting, most developers or agents will arrange to furnish it for you.

If you plan to furnish a holiday home with antiques or expensive modern furniture, bear in mind that you will need adequate security and insurance. If you own a holiday home in Portugal, it's usually worthwhile shipping surplus items of furniture you have in your home abroad. If you intend to live permanently in Portugal in the future and already have a house full of good furniture abroad, there's little point in buying expensive furniture in Portugal. However, many foreigners who decide to live permanently in Portugal find that they prefer to sell their furniture abroad rather than bring it to Portugal, as it often isn't suitable for Portugal's climate and house styles (antique furniture in particular often doesn't stand the heat well).

Portuguese furniture and furnishing stores often offer design services (which may be free) and stock a wide range of fabrics and materials in patterns and colours ideally suited to the Portuguese climate and conditions. A wide range of modern and traditional furniture is available in Portugal at reasonable prices. Modern furniture is popular and is often sold in huge stores in commercial centres and from large hypermarkets. Pine and cane furniture is inexpensive and widely available. Department stores also sell a wide range of (mostly up-market) furniture. There are factory shops selling both furniture and furnishings in the north of Portugal where you can choose everything on the spot, although the savings may be only nominal.

If you're spending a lot of money, don't be reluctant to ask for a reduction, as most stores will give you a discount. The best time to buy furniture and furnishings is during sales (particularly in winter), when prices of many items are slashed. Most furniture stores also offer special deals on complete furniture packages for a complete room or home. It's possible for residents to pay for furniture (and large household appliances) interest-free over one year or with interest over a longer period, e.g. five years. It may also be worthwhile comparing the cost of furniture in Spain or another European country with that in Portugal, although it usually doesn't pay to buy new furniture abroad to furnish a Portuguese home (particularly as you must add shipping costs).

If you're looking for antique furniture at affordable prices, you may find a few bargains at antique and flea markets in rural areas, although generally antiques are expensive and difficult to find. If you do come across anything worthwhile you must usually drive a hard bargain, as the asking prices are often ridiculous, particularly in tourist areas during the summer. There's a reasonable market for second-hand furniture in Portugal and many sellers and dealers advertise in the expatriate press. There are do-it-yourself hypermarkets in some areas such as Metre Maco and Max Mat, selling everything for the home including DIY supplies, furniture, bathrooms, kitchens, decorating and lighting, plus services such as tool rental and wood cutting. Note, however, that many DIY supplies and materials aren't as easy to find in Portugal as in many other European countries and are more expensive, therefore you may prefer to import them.

Household Goods

Household goods are generally of high quality in Portugal, and although the choice isn't as wide as in some other European countries, it has improved considerably in recent years. Electrical goods have traditionally been more expensive in Portugal than in most northern European countries, although the gap has narrowed and prices are now comparable (particularly in hypermarkets). However, Portuguese-made appliances, electrical apparatus and consumer goods aren't always the most reliable and they're sometimes of eccentric design, although a wide range of imported brands are also available.

Bear in mind when importing household goods that aren't sold in Portugal, that it may be difficult or impossible to have them repaired or serviced locally. If you import appliances, don't forget to bring a supply of spares and consumables such as bulbs for a refrigerator or sewing machine, and spare bags for a vacuum cleaner (unless you have a Dyson). Note that the standard size of kitchen appliances and cupboard units in Portugal isn't the same as in other countries and it may be difficult to fit an imported dishwasher or washing machine into a Portuguese kitchen. Check the size and the latest Portuguese safety regulations before shipping these items to Portugal or buying them abroad, as they may need expensive modifications. Portuguese washing machines take in cold water only and heat it in the machine, which makes machines that take in hot water (such as those sold in the USA) obsolete in Portugal.

If you already own small household appliances it's worthwhile bringing them to Portugal, as usually all that's required is a change of plug. However, if you're coming from a country with a 110/115V electricity supply such as the USA, you will need a lot of expensive transformers (see page 183) and it's usually better to buy new appliances in Portugal. Small appliances such as vacuum cleaners, grills, toasters and irons aren't expensive in Portugal and are of good quality. Don't bring a TV or video recorder without checking its compatibility first, as TVs made for other countries often don't work in Portugal without modification. If you need kitchen measuring equipment and cannot cope with decimal measures, you will need to bring your own measuring scales, jugs, cups and thermometers. Foreign pillow sizes (e.g. American and British) aren't the same as in Portugal, although various sizes are available. Portuguese textiles are generally of excellent quality and are considerably less expensive than in many other European countries.

SHOPPING ABROAD

Shopping abroad includes day trips to Spain (and possibly Gibraltar) as well as shopping excursions further afield. Seville, which can be reached in around two hours from the Algarve, is a particularly popular shopping destination. A day trip abroad makes an interesting day out for the family and can save you money, depending on what and where you buy. Don't forget your passports or identity cards, car papers, children, dog's vaccination papers and foreign currency. Whatever you're looking for, compare prices and quality before buying. Bear in mind that if you buy goods that are faulty or need repairing, you will probably need to return them to the place of purchase.

From 1st January 1993 there have been no cross-border shopping restrictions within the EU for goods purchased duty and tax paid, provided that all goods are for personal consumption or use and not for resale. Although there are no restrictions, there are 'indicative' levels for goods such as spirits, wine, beer and tobacco products, above which goods may be classified as commercial quantities. For example, persons entering Portugal aged 17 or over may import the following amounts of alcohol and tobacco without question:

- 10 litres of spirits (over 22° proof);

- 20 litres of fortified wine such as port or sherry (under 22° proof);

- 90 litres of wine (or 120 x 0.75 litre bottles/10 cases) of which a maximum of 60 litres may be sparkling wine;

- 110 litres of beer;

- 800 cigarettes or 400 cigarillos or 200 cigars or 1kg/2.2lb of smoking tobacco.

There's no limit on perfume or toilet water. If you exceed the above amounts you may need to convince the customs authorities that you aren't planning to sell the goods. There are fines for anyone who sells duty-paid alcohol and tobacco, which is classed as smuggling.

Spain: Among the best buys in Spain are the diverse handicrafts which include antiques, cultured pearls, shawls, pottery, ceramics, damascene, embroidery, fans, glassware, hats, ironwork, jewellery, knives, lace, suede and leather, paintings, porcelain, rugs, trinkets and carved woodwork. A wide range of foodstuffs (e.g. ham, olive oil and cheese) and alcohol (e.g. wine, sherry and cava) are also available at reasonable prices. Shopping for furniture (including antiques), household goods and electrical apparatus in Spain can also yield considerable savings, and Spain is also better value than Portugal for most consumer goods and quality clothes, including excellent children's clothes. Shopping hours in Spain are similar to Portugal's.

Gibraltar: Considerable savings can be made on cigarettes, petrol, foodstuffs, luxury goods (e.g. perfumes) and various consumer goods in Gibraltar. However, there are often long delays for vehicles at the border crossing into Spain as Spanish customs' officers allegedly check them for drugs and tobacco (it's mostly just obstruction related to Spain's long-running dispute with Britain over Gibraltar's ownership). It's often wise to park on the Spanish side of the border and get a bus or taxi (or walk) into Gibraltar. **However, make sure that you lock and secure your car against theft, as cars are sometimes stolen while their owners are shopping in Gibraltar!**

Shopping hours are usually from 9am until 7pm Monday to Friday and 9am to 1pm on Saturdays (most shops close on Sundays).

Never attempt to import illegal goods into Portugal and don't agree to bring a parcel into Portugal or deliver a parcel to another country without knowing exactly what it contains. A popular confidence trick is to ask someone to post a parcel abroad (usually to a post restante address) or to leave a parcel at a railway station or restaurant abroad. **The parcel usually contains drugs!** Many truck drivers are languishing in foreign jails having been the unwitting victims of drug traffickers (who conceal drugs in shipments of goods).

DUTY-FREE ALLOWANCES

Under EU rules, duty-free (*livre de impostos*) shopping within the EU ended on 30th June 1999, although duty-free shopping still exists from non-EU journeys. Duty-free allowances are the same whether or not passengers are travelling within the EU or from a country outside the EU. Since 1st January 1993, for each journey to another EU member state, travellers aged 17 or over (unless otherwise stated below) have been entitled to import the following duty-free goods:

● 1 litre of spirits (over 22° proof) or 2 litres of fortified wine, sparkling wine or other liqueurs (under 22° proof);

● 2 litres of still table wine;

● 200 cigarettes or 100 cigarillos or 50 cigars or 250g of tobacco;

● 60cc/ml of perfume;

● 250cc/ml of toilet water;

● other goods including gifts and souvenirs to the value of around €150.

Duty-free allowances apply on both outward and return journeys, even if both are made on the same day, and the combined total (i.e. double the above limits) can be imported into your 'home' country. **However, it's rarely worthwhile buying duty-free alcohol when travelling to Portugal, as it's usually cheaper in Portuguese supermarkets and liquor stores.**

Visitors who are resident outside the EU can obtain a refund of value added tax *Imposto sobre o Valor Acrescentado (IVA)* on purchases of above around €60 made in one store. A special stamped form (Tax-Free Check) is provided and can be refunded at Tax-Free booths at international airports (Lisbon, Porto and Faro) and Lisbon harbour. A small administration fee is charged. Purchases must be carried by hand and not checked with your baggage. At the airport you present the goods, the cheque and your passport at the Tax-Free Shopping refund counter at customs (*alfândega*) for a cash, postal-note or credit card refund. Over 1,500 shops display the black and blue

Tax-Free sticker, called Europe Tax-Free Shopping Portugal. Items excluded from the tax-free scheme include food, books, prescription lenses, hotel costs and car rental.

PETS

If you plan to take a pet (*animal de estimação*) to Portugal, it's important to check the latest regulations with your nearest Portuguese embassy. Ensure that you have the correct papers, not only for Portugal but for all the countries you will pass through to reach Portugal. Particular consideration must be given before exporting a pet from a country with strict quarantine regulations, such as Britain. If you need to return prematurely, even after a few hours or days in Portugal, your pet may have to go into quarantine, e.g. for six months in Britain. Apart from the expense, this is distressing for both pets and owners. Norway and Sweden abolished quarantine on 1st May 1994 (but retain strict vaccination regulations) and Britain introduced a comprehensive review of its quarantine laws in 2000 (see below).

In order to import a dog or cat into Portugal you must present an animal health certificate issued in the country of origin by an official veterinary authority. The certificate must show that the animal has been examined within 48 hours prior to shipment and showed no sign of diseases (particularly rabies) and was in good health. In order for the certificate to be issued, you must provide proof that the animal has been vaccinated against rabies (*raiva*), either not less than six months and no more than a year prior to shipment if it's the first rabies vaccination, or not more than a year prior to shipment in the case of a booster vaccination. Note that the health certificate must be officially translated into Portuguese. Animals under the age of three months when imported into Portugal must be kept isolated in quarantine in your Portuguese home for a period after importation (usually six months or as determined by the Portuguese Animal Health Services). At the age of three months the animal must be vaccinated against rabies. Some animals require a special import permit from the Director General of Livestock (Ministerio da Agricultura, Largo da Academia Nacional de Belas Artes, 2, 1249 Lisbon, (☎ 213-239 500, 🖥 www.dgv.pt)) and pets from some countries are subject to customs duty and/or VAT.

Exporting & Importing Pets from the UK: Portugal is one of the countries that the UK includes in its Pet Travel Scheme (known as PETS), which allows cats and dogs from the UK to visit other countries and then return to the UK without having to go through a quarantine period. To qualify for this scheme your cat or dog must be fitted with a microchip, be vaccinated against rabies and have a blood test a month after vaccination. If the blood test is negative, your pet must be vaccinated and tested again.

You also need to provide the following documents as well as the International Vaccination Health Certificate and Export Certificate (see above):

● PETS re-entry certificate issued by a vet in the UK certifying that above conditions have been met;

● Certificate of Treatment against tapeworm and ticks. The treatment must be carried out by a vet between 24 and 48 hours after re-entering the UK;

● Declaration of Residence that certifies that your pet hasn't been outside any of the qualifying countries in the six months before entering the UK.

In order for your pet to qualify for the above scheme, all conditions must be met so it's important to plan well in advance and check with your vet before you make any firm travel arrangements. Further information is available from the Department for Environment, Food & Rural Affairs (DEFRA, 1A Page Street, London SE1P 4PQ, (☎ 020-7904 6000, 💻 www.defra.gov.uk).

British pet owners must complete an Application for a Ministry Export Certificate for Dogs, Cats and Rabies Susceptible Animals (form EXA1), available from the animal health section (International Trade) of DEFRA. A health inspection must be performed by a licensed veterinary officer before you receive an export health certificate (form EC2902), which must be issued no more than 48 hours before export (it's valid for ten days). If a dog travels via France it also requires a form EC2905 and if it travels via Spain it requires form EC2904. If you're transporting a pet to Portugal by ship or ferry, you should notify the ferry company. Some companies insist that pets are left in vehicles (if applicable), while others allow pets to be kept in cabins. If your pet is of nervous disposition or unused to travelling, it's best to tranquillise it on a long sea crossing.

If you intend to live permanently in Portugal, most veterinary surgeons (*veterinarios*) recommend that dogs be vaccinated against leptospirosis, parvovirus, hepatitis, distemper and kennel cough (in addition to rabies), and cats immunised against feline gastro-enteritis and typhus. It's recommended that cats also have an anti-rabies vaccination, although it isn't compulsory. Note that there are a number of diseases and dangers for pets in Portugal that aren't found in most other European countries. These include the fatal Leishmaniasis (also called Mediterranean or sandfly disease), processionary caterpillars, leeches, heartworm, ticks (a tick collar can prevent these), feline leukaemia virus and feline enteritis. Obtain advice from a vet on arrival in Portugal about the best way to protect your pets.

Dogs must be licensed after arrival in Portugal and the licence must be renewed annually at your local town hall (*câmara*). The licence fee costs from €2.50 to €3. You receive a dog licence and a numbered tag for your dog's collar, valid from 31st May until 31st May the following year. The annual licence also confirms a dog's annual rabies vaccination. A government veterinarian (*veterinário*) usually arrives in towns once a year (notice is given by the local municipality) to carry out a mass immunisation of dogs against rabies. A small charge is made (less than that charged by a veterinary clinic) and a certificate is provided.

Veterinary surgeons are well trained in Portugal, where it's a popular profession, and emergency veterinary care is also provided in animal clinics, some of which provide a 24-hour emergency service. Veterinary surgeons (including many English-speaking vets), animal clinics, and kennels and catteries advertise in English-language publications in Portugal. If you plan to leave your pet at a kennel or cattery, check whether it's a registered and bona fide establishment and book well in advance, particularly for school holiday periods. There are also foreign residents in resort areas who will look after your pet in their homes for a reasonable fee while you're away, which is preferable to leaving it at a kennel or cattery.

Bear in mind that there may be discrimination against pets when renting accommodation, particularly when it's furnished (the statutes of community properties can legally prohibit pets).

TELEVISION & RADIO

Portuguese television (TV) isn't renowned for its quality, although its generally no worse than the rubbish dished up in most European countries. In addition to terrestrial TV, satellite TV reception is excellent in most areas of Portugal and is particularly popular among the expatriate community (not that most of its output is any better than Portuguese TV). Cable TV isn't common in Portugal compared with northern European countries. Portuguese radio (including a number of 'foreign' stations) is generally good and the equal of most other European countries.

The Portuguese are avid TV viewers and according to recent surveys watch more TV than anyone else in Europe. Portuguese TV consists of a surfeit of moronic game shows (the staple diet of popular TV), soaps (*telenovelas*), chat shows, lots of football (Portuguese, Brazilian, Italian, British), bullfights and poorly dubbed films. Many programmes are imported from Brazil including the most popular soaps, watched by most of the population, and talk shows. There are excellent news, documentaries, and wildlife and history programmes. Like most countries, Portugal also imports many American and British shows, which are mostly subtitled rather than dubbed into Portuguese. Programmes are likely to change without notice and rarely start on time unless it's a live football match or other live event.

Portuguese terrestrial TV consists of two state TV channels managed by the RTP broadcasting company Televisão Portuguesa – RTP-1 and RTP-2 – plus two private networks, Sociedade Independente de Communicação (SIC) and TV Independente (TVI). All are available in most parts of the country. RTP broadcasts under RTP Azores in the Azores and RTP Madeira in Madeira. There are also around 15 cable TV companies. The most popular is TV Cabo who claim to have more than 4 million clients. TV Cabo offers a variety of products costing from around €16 a month. There's no TV or radio licence in Portugal. TV programmes are listed in all Portuguese newspapers and in special TV guides. Some Portuguese TV programmes are also listed in English-language newspapers and magazines, along with a selection of satellite TV programmes.

Standards: The standards for TV reception in Portugal **aren't the same as in some other countries**. Due to the differences in transmission standards, TVs and video recorders operating on the British (PAL-I), French (SECAM) or North American (NTSC) systems won't function in Portugal. Portugal (along with most other continental European countries) uses the PAL B/G standard. It's possible to buy a multi-standard European TV (and VCR) containing automatic circuitry that switches between different systems. Some multi-standard TVs also include the North American NTSC standard and have an NTSC-in jack plug connection allowing you to play back American videos. A standard British, French or US TV won't work in Portugal, although they can be modified. The same applies to 'foreign' video recorders, which won't operate with a Portuguese TV unless they're dual-standard. Some people opt for two TVs, one to receive Portuguese TV programmes and another (e.g. SECAM or NTSC) to playback their favourite videos.

If you decide to buy a TV in Portugal, you will find it advantageous to buy one with teletext, which, apart from allowing you to display programme schedules, also provides a wealth of useful and interesting information. It's possible to rent a TV, VCR or video camera in Portugal, particularly in resort areas. Most rentals are intended for long-term visitors and holidaymakers rather than for residents, and it's cheaper to buy a TV over a long term. You can buy a small colour portable TV for around €150 and can easily sell it for half this amount or more when it's no longer required.

Satellite Television

A number of geo-stationary satellites are positioned over Europe, carrying over 100 TV stations broadcasting in a variety of languages. There are millions of homes with satellite dishes in Europe, although Portugal has only a few hundred thousand, mostly owned by expatriates. The Portuguese generally prefer cable TV. TV addicts (easily recognised by their antennae and square eyes) are offered a huge choice of English and foreign-language stations which can be received throughout most of Portugal with an 80cm dish and receiver (costing from around €700). A bonus is the availability of foreign radio stations via satellite, including all the popular British Broadcasting Corporation (BBC) stations (see **Satellite Radio** on page 80).

Among the many English-language stations available on Astra are Sky One, Movimax, Sky Premier, Sky Cinema, Film Four, Sky News, Sky Sports (1, 2 and 3), UK Gold, Channel 5, Granada Plus, TNT, Eurosport, CNN, CNBC Europe, UK Style, UK Horizons, the Disney Channel and the Discovery Channel. Other stations broadcast in Dutch, German, Japanese, Swedish and various Indian languages. A few stations, such as Eurosport are multi-language and viewers can select the soundtrack language, e.g. English, Dutch, German or Portuguese. The signal from many stations is scrambled (the decoder is usually built into the receiver) and viewers must pay a monthly subscription fee to receive programmes. You can buy pirate decoders for some channels. Those best served by clear (unscrambled) stations are German-speakers (most German stations on Astra are clear).

BSkyB Television: You must buy a receiver with a Videocrypt decoder and pay a monthly subscription to receive all BskyB or Sky stations except Sky News (which isn't scrambled). Various packages are available costing from between £12 and £35 per month (for the premium package offering all movie channels plus Sky Sports). To receive scrambled channels such as Movimax and Sky Sports you need an address in Britain. Subscribers are sent a coded 'smart' card (similar to a credit card), which must be inserted in the decoder to switch it on (cards are frequently updated to thwart counterfeiters). Sky won't send smart cards to overseas viewers as they have the copyright for a British-based audience only and overseas homeowners need to obtain a card through a friend or relative in Britain. Satellite companies (most of whom advertise in the expatriate press) in Portugal can supply genuine BskyB cards, although you must pay a premium.

Digital Television: English-language digital satellite TV was launched on 1st October 1998 by BskyB in Britain. The benefits include a superior picture, better (CD) quality sound, wide-screen cinema format and access to many more stations (including around ten stations that show nothing but films). To watch digital TV you require a Digibox and a (digital) dish, which can be purchased at a subsidised price by customers in Britain. Customers have to sign up for a 12-month subscription and agree to have the connection via a phone line (to allow for future interactive services). In addition to the usual analogue channels (see above), BskyB digital provides BBC 1, BBC 2, ITV, Channel 4 and Channel 5, plus many digital channels (a total of 200 with up to 500 possible later). Digital satellite equipment is offered by a number of companies in Portugal (mainly based on the Algarve), although getting a Sky card isn't easy.

Eutelsat: Eutelsat was the first company to introduce satellite TV to Europe (in 1983) and it now runs a fleet of communications satellites carrying TV stations to over 50 million homes. Until 1995 Eutelsat broadcast primarily advertising-based, clear-access cable channels. However, following the launch in March 1995 of their Hot Bird 1 satellite (and others), Eutelsat has become a major competitor to Astra, although its channels are mostly non-English. The English-language stations on Eutelsat include Eurosport, BBC World and CNBC. Other channels are broadcast in Arabic, French, German, Italian, Polish, Portuguese and Turkish.

BBC World-wide Television: The BBC's commercial subsidiary, BBC World-wide Television, broadcasts two 24-hour channels: BBC World (24-hour news and information) and BBC Prime (general entertainment), transmitted via the Eutelsat Hotbird 5 satellite (13° east). BBC World is unencrypted (clear) while BBC Prime is encrypted and requires a D2-MAC decoder and a smart card available from BBC Prime, PO Box 5054, London W12 0ZY, UK (☎ 020-8433 2221, ✉ bbcprime@bbc.co.uk). For more information and a programme guide contact BBC World-wide Television, Woodlands, 80 Wood Lane, London W12 0TT, UK (☎ 020-8576 2555). A programme guide is also available on the Internet (🖳 www.bbc.co.uk/schedules) and both BBC World and BBC Prime have websites (🖳 www.bbcworld.com and www.bbcprime.com). When accessing them, you need to enter the name of your country of residence so that schedules are displayed in local time.

Equipment: A satellite receiver should have a built-in Videocrypt decoder (and others such as Eurocrypt, Syster or SECAM if required) and be capable of receiving satellite stereo radio. With a 1.2 or 1.5m motorised dish, you can receive hundreds of stations in a multitude of languages from around the world. If you wish to receive satellite TV on two or more TVs, you can buy a satellite system with two or more receptors. To receive stations from two or more satellites simultaneously, you need a motorised dish or a dish with a double feed antenna (dual LNBs). There are many satellite sales and installation companies in Portugal, most of which advertise in the expatriate press. Shop around and compare prices. Alternatively you can import your own satellite dish and receiver and install it yourself. **Before buying a system, ensure that it can receive programmes from all existing and planned satellites.**

Location: To receive programmes from any satellite, there must be no obstacles between the satellite and your dish, i.e. no trees, buildings or mountains must obstruct the signal, so check before renting or buying a home. Before buying or erecting a satellite dish, check whether you need permission from your landlord or the local authorities. Some towns and buildings (such as apartment blocks) have strict laws regarding the positioning of antennae, although generally owners can mount a dish almost anywhere without receiving any complaints. Dishes can usually be mounted in a variety of unobtrusive positions and can be painted or patterned to blend in with the background.

Communities: Note that when an apartment or townhouse is advertised as having satellite TV, it often means that it has a communal system and not its own satellite dish. Satellite stations are received via a communal satellite dish (or a number) and transmitted via cable to all properties in an urbanisation or complex. Only a limited number of programmes are usually available and no scrambled programmes may be included. Only a few English-language stations are currently unscrambled (free-to-air) on Astra including CNN, Sky News and Eurosport, although some communities pay to receive more.

TV Programme Guides: Many satellite stations provide teletext information and most broadcast in stereo. Sky satellite programme listings are provided in a number of British publications such as *What Satellite*, *Satellite Times* and *Satellite TV Europe* (the best), which are available on subscription and from international news stands in Portugal. Satellite TV programmes are also listed in expatriate newspapers and magazines in Portugal. The annual *World Radio and TV Handbook* edited by David G. Bobbett (Watson-Guptill Publications) contains over 600 pages of information and the frequencies of all radio and TV stations world-wide.

Radio

Radio was strictly controlled in Portugal during the Salazar dictatorship, although there has been a huge growth in the number of stations since democracy was restored. The Portuguese are a nation of radio listeners and spend a lot of time listening to the radio (even more than they do watching TV). There are many high-quality local, regional, national and foreign radio stations in Portugal, which has four national radio channels, three of which are state controlled: Antena 1 (MW and FM), Antena 2 (FM) and Antena 3 (FM). The other national station is the privately-operated Rádio Renascença (RR), although there are also literally hundreds of local private stations playing every type of music or a combination of music and chat. There are English-language 'expatriate' stations in the Algarve and Lisbon areas, where the emphasis is on music and chat with some news.

BBC: The BBC World Service is broadcast on short wave on several frequencies simultaneously and you can usually receive a good signal on one of them. A BBC wavelength guide is available in some English-language publications such as the Anglo-Portuguese News. The signal strength varies according to where you live in Portugal, the time of day and year, the power and positioning of your receiver, and atmospheric conditions. All BBC radio stations, including the World Service, are available on the Astra satellite. The BBC publishes a monthly magazine, *BBC On Air*, containing comprehensive information about BBC World Service radio and TV programmes. For a free copy and frequency information write to BBC, On Air Magazine, Room 207

NW, Bush House, Strand, London WC2B 4PH, UK (☎ 020-7240 4899, ✉ on.air.magazine@bbc.co.uk).

Satellite Radio: If you have satellite TV, you can also receive many radio stations via your satellite link. For example, BBC Radio 1, 2, 3, 4 and 5, BBC World Service, Sky Radio, Virgin 1215 and many foreign (i.e. non-English) stations are broadcast via the Astra satellites. Satellite radio stations are listed in British satellite TV magazines such as the *Satellite Times*. If you're interested in receiving radio stations from further afield you should obtain a copy of the *World Radio TV Handbook* edited by David G. Bobbett (Watson-Guptill Publications).

LEARNING PORTUGUESE

Apart from in the major cities and tourist areas, English isn't as widely spoken in Portugal as it is in many other countries (around 20 per cent of Portuguese speak English) and most Portuguese speak French as their second language rather than English. Also, don't be misled by its similarity to Spanish; although many words are identical or similar the pronunciation is often completely different. Portuguese speakers understand Spanish but don't always like to admit it and may even pretend not to understand it (there's little love lost between the Portuguese and Spanish). However, even Spaniards will be unlikely to understand the reply in Portuguese.

If you don't speak Portuguese, it's best to enrol in a course at a local language school, preferably before arriving in Portugal. If you're working in Portugal you will usually have little choice about learning Portuguese. However, it isn't always <u>essential</u> for retired residents and those who live and work among the expatriate community to learn Portuguese, but it certainly makes life easier and less frustrating. Unfortunately many residents (particularly British retirees) make little effort to learn Portuguese beyond the few words necessary to buy the weekly groceries, order a cup of coffee or a meal, and live as if they were on a brief holiday. **For anyone living in Portugal permanently, learning Portuguese shouldn't be seen as an option, but as a necessity.**

If you're a retiree, it's important to make an effort to learn at least the rudiments of Portuguese so that you can understand your bills, use the telephone, deal with servicemen, and communicate with your local town hall (plus performing myriad other 'daily' chores). If you don't learn Portuguese, you will be continually frustrated in your communications and will be constantly calling on friends and acquaintances to assist you, or even paying people (such as *despachantes*) to do jobs you could quite easily do yourself. **However, the most important reason to learn Portuguese is that in an emergency it could save your life or that of a loved one!** Learning Portuguese also helps you to appreciate the Portuguese way of life and make the most of your time in Portugal, and opens many doors that remain firmly closed to resident 'tourists'.

Portuguese is a difficult language to learn to speak, although it's easier to read, and is rich in phonetics with 13 vowel sounds associated with the letter 'a' alone! However, although it isn't easy, it's possible for most people to acquire at least a working knowledge of the language. 'All' that's required is a little hard work and some help and perseverance (particularly if you have only English-speaking colleagues and friends). You won't just 'pick it up' (apart from a few words), but must make a real effort to learn. Fortunately the Portuguese are tolerant of foreigners' tortured attempts to speak their language and any effort is appreciated.

Methods: Most people can teach themselves a great deal through the use of books, tapes, videos and even CD-ROM computer-based courses. However, even the best students require some help. Teaching Portuguese is a big business, with classes offered by language schools; colleges and universities; private and international schools; foreign and international organisations; local associations and clubs; chambers of commerce and town halls; and private teachers. Classes range from language courses for complete beginners, through specialised business or cultural courses, to university-level seminars leading to recognised diplomas. Most Portuguese universities offer language courses all year round, including special summer courses. These are generally cheaper than language schools, although classes may be much larger. If you already speak some Portuguese but need conversational practice, you may wish to enrol in an art or craft course at a local institute or club.

Language Schools: There are language schools in all Portuguese cities and large towns. Most offer a range of classes according to your current language ability, how many hours you wish to study a week, how much money you want to spend and how quickly you wish to learn. Courses are usually open to anyone over the age of 18 and some also accept students aged from 14. Courses are graded according to ability, e.g. beginner, intermediate or advanced, and usually last from 2 to 16 weeks. All schools offer free tests to help you find your correct level and a free introductory lesson.

Don't expect to become fluent in a short time unless you have a particular flair for learning languages or already have a good command of Portuguese. Unless you desperately need to learn quickly, it's usually better to arrange your lessons over a long period. However, don't commit yourself to a long course of study, particularly an expensive one, before ensuring that it's the right course for you. Courses generally fall into the following categories:

Category	Hours per Week
Extensive	4–10
Intensive	15–20
Total immersion	20–40+

Some schools offer combined courses where language study is linked with optional subjects including business Portuguese; Portuguese art and culture; reading and commentary of a daily newspaper; conversation; Portuguese history; and traditions and folklore. Some schools combine language courses with a range of social and sports activities such as tennis or golf.

The most common language courses in Portugal are intensive courses providing four hours tuition a day from Monday to Friday (20 hours a week). The cost of an intensive course is usually quite reasonable, e.g. a four-week intensive course costs around €400. The highest fees are charged in the summer months, particularly during July and August. Commercial courses are generally more intensive and expensive, e.g. €550 for two weeks and a total of 60 hours tuition. Courses that include accommodation are often excellent value and some schools arrange home stays with a Portuguese family (full or half board) or provide apartment or hotel accommodation. Accommodation with a host family typically costs €100 to €150 per week for half board. For those for whom money is no object (hopefully your employer!), there are total immersion courses where study is for eight hours a day, five days a week. Whichever course you choose, you should shop around as tuition fees vary considerably.

Private Lessons: You may prefer to have private lessons, which are a quicker although more expensive way to learn Portuguese. The main advantage of private lessons is that you learn at your own speed and aren't held back by slow learners or dragged along by the class genius. One way to get to know the Portuguese and improve your language proficiency is to find a Portuguese partner wishing to learn English (or your mother tongue), called a 'language exchange' (*intercâmbio*). Partners get together on a regular basis during which half the time is spent speaking English (or another language) and half speaking Portuguese. You can advertise for a private teacher or partner in local newspapers, on bulletin and notice boards (in shopping centres, supermarkets, universities, clubs, etc.), and through your and your spouse's employers. Don't forget to ask your friends, neighbours and colleagues if they can recommend a private teacher. Teachers often advertise in English-language publications in Portugal. Lessons cost from around €10 an hour at a school and from around €15 an hour from an experienced private tutor.

PUBLIC HOLIDAYS

The government has established 13 statutory national public holidays (*feriados obrigatórios* or *dias de festa*) a year plus one official local holiday. This is one of the highest numbers in the EU (only Spain has more). Note that foreign embassies and consulates in Portugal usually observe their own country's national holidays in addition to Portuguese public holidays. The following days are official national public holidays:

Date	Holiday
1st January	New Year's Day (*Ano Novo*)
Feb/March	Shrove Tuesday (*Entrudo*). Also called Carnival Day or Mardi Gras. It falls around six weeks before Easter.
March/April	Good Friday (*Sexta-feira Santa*)
25th April	Liberation Day (*Dia da Liberdade*). Celebrates the 1974 revolution.
1st May	Labour Day (*Dia do Trabalhador*)
June	Corpus Christi (*Corpus Christi*)
10th June	National Day or Day of Camões and the Community (*Dia de Portugal or Dia de Camões e das Communidades*). Celebrates the death of Portugal's most famous poet, Luís de Camões, on 10th June 1580 who wrote the epic poem *Os Lusíadas* in praise of the people of Portugal. The community part (*e das Communidades*) was added after the 1974 revolution.
15th August	Feast of the Assumption (Nossa Senhora da Asunção).
5th October	Republic Day (*Dia da República*). Commemorates the founding of the first republic in 1910.
1st November	All Saints Day (*Festa de Todos-os-Santos*).
1st December	Independence Day (*Dia de Restauração*). Commemorates the restoration of the Portuguese crown and independence from Spain in 1640.
8th December	Feast of the Immaculate Conception (*Imaculada Conceição*).
25th December	Christmas Day (*Dia de Natal*).

When a holiday falls on a Saturday or Sunday, another day isn't usually granted as a holiday unless the number of public holidays in a particular year falls below a minimum number. Holidays are occasionally moved to form long weekends and when a holiday falls on a Friday or Monday many businesses close for the entire holiday weekend (assuming they would normally work on a Saturday or Sunday). All public offices, banks and businesses are closed on public holidays, when only essential work is performed.

In addition to the national public holidays listed above, each province or town has its own feast days (*festas*), fairs (*feiras*) and pilgrimages (*romarias*). For example the 13th June (St. Anthony's Day) in Lisbon and 24th June (St. John the Baptist's Day) in Porto are official local public holidays. Although regional holidays aren't always official public holidays, most local businesses are closed, sometimes for a number of days. Public holidays are marked on most calendars, many of which also show saints' days (calendars are distributed free by local businesses such as banks in December/January).

TIME DIFFERENCE

Portugal (including Madeira) is on Greenwich Mean Time (GMT), which means that it's on the same time as Britain. The Azores are on GMT minus one hour in winter and GMT in summer. The country changes to summertime in the spring (on the last Sunday in March) when people put their clocks forward one hour. In autumn (on the last Sunday in October) clocks are put back one hour for wintertime.

Time changes are announced in local newspapers and on radio and TV. The time is given on the telephone 'speaking clock' service number (see your local phone book) and on a TV with a 'time' button. When making international telephone calls or travelling long-distance by air, check the local time difference with GMT, which is shown in phone books. The time difference between Portugal at noon and some major international cities is shown below:

LONDON	CAPE TOWN	BOMBAY	LOS ANGELES	TOKYO	NEW YORK
Noon	2pm	5.30pm	9pm	2am	7am

3.

FINANCE

One of the most important aspects of buying a home in Portugal and living there (even for relatively brief periods) is finance, which includes everything from transferring and changing money to mortgages and taxes. If you're planning to invest in a property or a business in Portugal financed with imported funds, it's important to consider both the present and possible future exchange rates. On the other hand, if you live and work in Portugal and are paid in euros this may affect your financial commitments abroad. **Bear in mind that if your income is received in a currency other than euros it can be exposed to risks beyond your control when you live in Portugal, particularly regarding inflation and exchange rate fluctuations.**

Although the Portuguese generally prefer to pay cash (*dinheiro de contado*), rather than use credit or charge cards, it's wise to have at least one credit card when visiting or living in Portugal (Visa and Mastercard are the most widely accepted). Even if you don't like credit cards and shun any form of credit, they do have their uses, for example no-deposit car rentals; no pre-paying hotel bills (plus guaranteed bookings); obtaining cash 24-hours a day; simple telephone and mail-order payments; greater safety and security than cash; and above all, convenience. Note, however, that not all Portuguese businesses accept credit cards, particularly not those in rural or remote areas.

Wealth Warning: If you plan to live in Portugal you must ensure that your income is (and will remain) sufficient to live on, bearing in mind devaluation (if your income isn't paid in euros), rises in the cost of living, and unforeseen expenses such as medical bills or anything else that may reduce your income (such as stock market crashes and recessions!). Foreigners, particularly retirees, shouldn't under-estimate the cost of living in Portugal, which has increased significantly in the last decade (although outside the major cities it's still among the lowest in western Europe). If you're planning to live permanently in Portugal, it's important to seek expert financial advice regarding Portuguese taxes. This will (hopefully) ensure that you take optimum advantage of your current tax status and don't make any mistakes that you will regret later.

This section includes information on Portuguese currency; importing and exporting money; banking; mortgages; taxes (property, income, capital gains, inheritance and gift); and the cost of living.

FISCAL NUMBER

All residents and non-resident foreigners with financial affairs in Portugal must obtain a tax card (*cartão de contribuinte*) and a fiscal number (*número de identificação fiscal/NIF*). The tax card is necessary before you can purchase a home in Portugal. You need to complete a form at the local tax office (*finanças*) in the area where you will be buying a home and provide a photocopy of the identification pages of your passport. You will usually be given a temporary fiscal number for the first few months and will receive a permanent number after the purchase of a property. Your fiscal number must be used in all dealings with the Portuguese tax authorities, when paying property taxes and in various other transactions, e.g. without a fiscal number you cannot register the title deed of a property or open a bank account in Portugal.

All non-residents who own a holiday or second home in Portugal must nominate a local resident (of any nationality) as their fiscal representative, who will receive all communications from the Portuguese tax authorities. You can also have your fiscal representative receive your bank statements, ensure that your bank is paying your standing orders (e.g. for utilities and property taxes) and that you have sufficient funds to pay them. If you let a home in Portugal through a Portuguese company, they may perform the above tasks as part of their services.

PORTUGUESE CURRENCY

As you're probably aware, the Portuguese unit of currency is now the euro, which became legal tender on 1st January 2002 in 12 European Union (EU) countries (Austria, Belgium, Finland, France, Germany, Greece, Ireland, Italy, Luxembourg, the Netherlands, Portugal and Spain). The escudo circulated alongside the euro for two months until 28th February 2002, when it was withdrawn from circulation. Escudos can still be exchanged for euros, but only at branches of the Bank of Portugal, located only in cities or large towns.

The euro, which is divided into 100 cents (*centavos*), is minted in coins (*moedas*) to the value of 1, 2, 5, 10, 20 and 50 cents, and 1 and 2 euros. Cent denomination coins are made of either brass or copper and the euro denomination coins have a brass middle and a silver (alloy) rim. Euro banknotes are printed in denominations of 5, 10, 20, 50, 100, 200 and 500 euros. The euro is usually written as € after the price (e.g. 5€), although in this book the euro sign is written before the price. When writing figures (for example on cheques), a full-stop (period) (.) is used to separate units of millions, thousands and hundreds, e.g. two thousand euros is written as 2.000€, and a comma is used to separate euros and cents, e.g. ten euros thirty cents is written as 10,30€. In this book, however, a comma is used to separate thousands and hundreds, and a full-stop to separate euros and cents.

It's best to obtain some euro coins and banknotes before arriving in Portugal and to familiarise yourself and your family with them. You should have some euros in cash (e.g. €100 in coins and small bills) when you arrive, although you should avoid carrying a lot of cash. This will save you having to queue to change money on arrival at a Portuguese airport (where exchange rates are usually poor). It's best to avoid €200 and €500 notes (unless you receive them as a gift!) which sometimes aren't accepted, particularly for small purchases or on public transport.

IMPORTING & EXPORTING MONEY

Exchange controls were abolished in Portugal on 1st January 1993 and there are no restrictions on the import or export of funds. A Portuguese resident is permitted to open a bank account in any country and to import (or export) unlimited funds in any currency. The import or export of gold in any form, currency and travellers' or other bearer cheques exceeding €12,470 in value must be declared to the customs' authorities. However, information relating to many types of transaction, even when they aren't subject to prior authorisation or checking, must be supplied to the Bank of Portugal for statistical purposes. In particular any transactions that aren't carried out through an authorised credit institution must be reported to the Bank of Portugal.

International Bank Transfers: When transferring or sending money to (or from) Portugal you should be aware of the alternatives and shop around for the best deal. A bank-to-bank transfer can be made by a normal transfer or by a SWIFT electronic transfer. A normal transfer is supposed to take three to seven days, but in reality it usually takes much longer (particularly when sent by mail), whereas a SWIFT telex transfer should be completed in as little as two hours (although SWIFT transfers aren't always reliable to and from Portugal). It's usually quicker and cheaper to transfer funds between branches of the same bank or affiliated banks, than between non-affiliated banks. **If you intend sending a large amount of money to Portugal or abroad for a business transaction such as buying a property, you should ensure you receive the commercial rate of exchange rather than the tourist rate.** Some banks levy high charges on the transfer of funds to Portugal to buy a home, which is the subject of numerous complaints. Check charges and rates in advance and agree them with your bank (you may be able to negotiate a lower charge or a better exchange rate). One specialist company that claims to offer the best deal when transferring cash from Britain is Currencies Direct, Hanover House, 73–74 High Holburn, London WC1V 6LR, UK (☎ 020-7813 0332, 🖥 www.currenciesdirect.com).

The cost of transfers varies considerably, not only in commission and exchange rates but also in transfer charges (such as the telex charge for a SWIFT transfer). Shop around a number of banks. It's usually better to convert money to euros before transferring it to Portugal, in which case you shouldn't incur any charges in Portugal, although some Portuguese banks deduct commission, whether a transfer is made in euros or a foreign currency. An EU directive limits banks in EU countries to being able to pass on to customers the costs incurred by sender banks only, and the money must be deposited in a customer's account within five working days.

Portuguese banks are among the slowest in Europe to process bank transfers and it isn't unusual for transfers to and from Portugal to get stuck in the pipeline (usually somewhere in Lisbon), which allows the bank to use your money for a period free of interest. For example, transfers between British and Portuguese banks sometimes take weeks and the money can 'disappear' for months or even completely! Except for the fastest (and most expensive) methods, cash transfers between international banks are a joke in this age of electronic banking, when powerful financiers can switch funds almost instantaneously.

Bank Drafts & Personal Cheques: Another way to transfer money is via a bank draft (*saque bancário*), which should be sent by registered mail. Note, however, that in the event that it's lost or stolen, it's impossible to stop payment and you must wait six months before a new draft can be issued. It's also possible to send a creditor a cheque drawn on a personal account, although they can take a long time to clear (usually a matter of weeks) and fees are high. Some people prefer to receive a cheque direct (by post) from their overseas banks, which they then pay into their Portuguese bank (although you must usually wait for it to clear). It's possible to pay cheques drawn on a foreign account into a Portuguese bank account. They can, however, take three or four weeks to clear, as they must be cleared with the paying bank, although some banks allow customers to draw against cheques in foreign currency issued on foreign banks from the day they're paid into an account.

Telegraphic Transfers: One of the quickest (it takes around ten minutes) and safest methods of transferring cash internationally is via a telegraphic transfer, but it's also one of the most expensive, e.g. commission of 7 to 10 per cent of the amount sent. Amex card holders can send money between American Express offices by using Amex's Moneygram service whereby money can be transferred to Portugal in just 15 minutes.

Charge, Credit & Debit Cards: One of the quickest methods of obtaining cash in Portugal is to draw cash on debit, credit or charge cards from *Multibanco* automatic teller machines (ATMs). You can usually withdraw up to €200 a day (note that you need a PIN number). Many foreigners living in Portugal (particularly retirees) keep the bulk of their money in a foreign account (perhaps in an offshore bank) and draw on it with a cash or credit card in Portugal. This is an ideal solution for holidaymakers and holiday-homeowners (although homeowners will still need a Portuguese bank to pay their bills).

Foreign Exchange: Most banks in major cities have foreign exchange (*câmbio*) windows (and there are banks with extended opening hours at international airports and main railway stations in major cities) where you can buy and sell foreign currencies, buy and cash travellers' cheques, cash euro-cheques, and obtain a cash advance on credit and charge cards. Banks charge around 1 per cent commission with a minimum charge (e.g. €3), so it's expensive to change small amounts, although some banks charge a flat fee irrespective of the amount changed. Banks at airports and railway stations usually offer the worst exchange rates and charge the highest fees. You can also change foreign banknotes (most major currencies) in automatic change machines, which are plentiful in main cities and tourist areas, although the exchange rate is usually poor.

There are numerous private *bureaux de change* in Portugal, many of which are open long hours. Most *bureaux de change* offer competitive exchange rates and charge no commission (but always check) and are also usually easier to deal with than banks. If you're changing a lot of money you may also be able to negotiate a better exchange rate. Note, however, that although commercial *bureaux de change* may charge less commission than banks, they don't usually offer the best exchange rates. The euro exchange rate for most European and major international currencies is listed in banks and daily newspapers, and announced on Portuguese and foreign radio and TV programmes. Shop around for the best exchange rate and the lowest commission, as they can vary considerably.

Travellers' Cheques: If you're visiting Portugal, it's safer to carry travellers' cheques (*cheques de viagem*) than cash, although they aren't as easy to cash as in some other countries. They aren't usually accepted as cash by businesses, except perhaps in some major hotels, restaurants and shops, which usually offer a poor exchange rate. You may wish to buy travellers' cheques in euros to take advantage of a favourable exchange rate. Fees charged by banks for cashing travellers' cheques make them an expensive option in Portugal. Banks charge up to 13 per cent of the amount on each travellers' cheque (even on small amounts) plus the government tax of 0.09 per cent of the amount. However, American Express travellers' cheques can be exchanged commission free at Top Tours, Portugal's American Express agent, which has offices in all major towns and cities (☎ 213-155 885). Savings banks (*caixas*) usually levy a lower fee than clearing banks and you may also get a better deal at some exchange bureaus or travel agencies than at a bank. Banks may offer a better exchange rate for travellers' cheques than for banknotes, but commission is also higher. You must show your passport when changing travellers' cheques.

Keep a separate record of travellers' cheque numbers and note where and when they were cashed. Most cheque issuers offer a replacement service for lost or stolen cheques, although the time taken to replace them varies significantly. American Express claim a free, three-hour replacement service at any of their offices world-wide, provided you know the serial numbers of the lost cheques (without the serial numbers, replacement can take three days or longer). Post-cheques are a useful alternative to travellers' cheques for Europeans travelling within Europe.

Footnote: There isn't a lot of difference in the cost between buying Portuguese currency using cash, buying travellers' cheques or using a credit card to obtain cash in Portugal. However, many people only carry cash when visiting Portugal, which is asking for trouble, particularly if you have no way of obtaining more cash locally, e.g. with a credit card or travellers' cheques. **One thing to bear in mind when travelling anywhere is never to rely on only one source of funds!**

BANKS

Banking in Portugal has changed out of all recognition in the last decade, during which the number of banks and branches has increased considerably, although during recent years there have been many take-overs and mergers. Banks in Portugal are generally highly profitable. There are two main types of banks in Portugal: clearing banks and savings banks (*caixas*). The major banking groups include Banco Commercial Portuguese (owns Banco Português do Atlântico), Champalimaud Group (includes Banco Totta e Açores and Banco Pinto e Sotto Mayor) and the Banco Espiríto Santo group (which includes Banco Espiríto Santo e Comercial de Lisboa). The main banks account for more than 80 per cent of the market share. Portugal's largest credit institution, measured by total assets, is the state-owned savings bank, Caixa Geral de Depósitos. All banks in Portugal are listed in the yellow pages under *Bancos*.

Since the revolution in 1974 and, more importantly, since joining the EU in 1986, Portugal's banks have (in general) emerged from the dark ages and are now more efficient. Banking has become highly automated in recent years, although Portuguese banks remain frustratingly slow and inefficient compared with banks in many other EU countries. Where human involvement is concerned Portuguese banks remain Neanderthal, although with regard to electronic banking they compare favourably with other European countries, and their ATMs (cash dispensers) are among the world's best. In recent years bank 'branches' have been established in supermarkets and Portugal has the most developed European supermarket banking network (e.g. Banco Portuguese do Atlantico teamed up with Jeronimo Martins' retail group to open branches called *Expresso Atlantico* in Pingo Doce and Feira Nova supermarkets, and in shopping centres). Supermarket outlets rely on telephone banking for personal banking services. There are no drive-in banks in Portugal.

There are also several foreign banks operating in Portugal, although there are fewer (with an overall smaller market share) than in most other European countries. Foreign banks are present in Lisbon and some also in Porto, but branches are rare in other towns, although in recent years branches have opened on the Algarve. Foreign banks include Barclays, Citibank, Deutsch Bank and Rheinhyp (a major German mortgage bank).

Most banks are open Monday to Friday from 8.30am to 3pm (or from 8.30am to 11.45am and from 1 to 3pm in smaller towns) and are closed at weekends and on public holidays. In Lisbon and some resorts on the Algarve, some bank branches open in the evening to change money.

Opening an Account

Although it's possible for non-resident homeowners to do most of their banking via a foreign account using debit and credit cards and euro-cheques, you will still need a Portuguese bank account (*conta bancária*) to pay your Portuguese utility and tax bills (which are best paid by direct debit). If you have a holiday home in Portugal, you can have all your correspondence (e.g. cheque books, statements, payment advices, etc.) sent to an address abroad. Since Portugal became a full member of the EU on 1st January 1993, banking regulations for both resident and non-resident EU citizens have been identical.

It's best to open a Portuguese bank account in person, rather than by correspondence from abroad. Ask your friends, neighbours or colleagues for their recommendations and just go along to the bank of your choice and introduce yourself. You must be aged at least 18 and provide proof of identity (e.g. a passport), your address in Portugal and your fiscal number (see page 88). If you wish to open an account with a Portuguese bank while you're abroad, you must first obtain an application form, available from foreign branches of Portuguese banks or direct from Portuguese banks in Portugal. You need to select a branch from the list provided, which should preferably be near to where you will be living in Portugal. If you open an account by correspondence, you will need to provide a reference from your current bank. There may be a minimum deposit to open an account, e.g. €250.

It isn't wise to close your bank accounts abroad, unless you're certain you won't need them in the future. Even when you're resident in Portugal, it's cheaper to keep money in local currency in an account in a country you visit regularly, rather than pay commission to convert euros. Many foreigners living in Portugal maintain at least two cheque (current) accounts, a foreign account for international and large transactions, and a local account with a Portuguese bank for day to day business and living expenses.

It's a criminal offence to bounce a cheque (i.e. write a cheque without sufficient funds in your account to cover it) in Portugal, for which you can be charged with fraud. You will also have to pay 20 per cent of the amount of the cheque in interest and fees, and can be blacklisted by the Banco de Portugal and refused a cheque account in future. In the past, the date on a cheque was irrelevant and post-dated cheques could be cashed or presented for payment at any time. However, under a new law banks now have to honour the date on a cheque and cannot cash (or attempt to cash) a post-dated cheque. If you pay a cheque drawn on a foreign bank into your Portuguese account, it may be credited immediately but can actually take up to three or four weeks to clear. In the meantime if you draw on an uncleared cheque you may incur high charges (*juros*) until it's cleared.

Offshore Banking

If you have a sum of money to invest or wish to protect your inheritance from the tax man, it may be worthwhile looking into the accounts and services (such as pensions and trusts) provided by offshore banking centres in tax havens such as the Channel Islands (Guernsey and Jersey), Gibraltar and the Isle of Man (around 50 locations world-wide are officially classified as tax havens). The big attraction of offshore banking is that money can be deposited in a wide range of currencies, customers are usually guaranteed complete anonymity, there are no double-taxation agreements, no withholding tax is payable, and interest is paid tax-free. Some offshore banks also offer telephone banking (usually seven days a week).

A large number of American, British and European banks, and miscellaneous other international financial institutions provide offshore banking facilities in one or more locations. Most institutions offer high-interest deposit accounts for long-term savings and investment portfolios, in which funds can be deposited in any major currency. Many people living abroad keep a local account for everyday business and maintain an offshore account for international transactions and investment purposes. **However, most financial experts advise investors never to rush into the expatriate life and invest their life savings in an offshore tax haven until they know their long-term plans.**

Accounts have minimum deposit levels, which usually range from the equivalent of around €800 to €16,000 (e.g. £500 to £10,000), with some as high as around €160,000 (£100,000). In addition to large minimum balances, accounts may also have stringent terms and conditions, such as restrictions on withdrawals or high early withdrawal penalties. You can deposit funds on call (instant access) or for a fixed period, e.g. from 90 days to one year (usually for larger sums). Interest is usually paid monthly or annually; monthly interest payments are slightly lower than annual payments, although they have the advantage of providing a regular income. There are usually no charges provided a specified minimum balance is maintained. Many accounts offer a cash card or a credit card (e.g. Mastercard or Visa) which can be used to obtain cash via ATMs throughout the world.

When selecting a financial institution and offshore banking centre, your first priority should be the safety of your money. In some offshore banking centres all bank deposits are guaranteed up to a maximum amount under a deposit protection scheme, whereby a maximum sum is guaranteed should a financial institution go to the wall (the Isle of Man, Guernsey and Jersey all have such schemes). Unless you're planning to bank with a major international bank (which isn't likely to fold until the day after the end of the world!), you should check the credit rating of a financial institution before depositing any money, particularly if it doesn't provide deposit insurance. All banks have a credit rating (the highest is 'AAA') and a bank with a high rating will be happy to tell you (but get it in writing). You can also check the rating of an international bank or financial organisation with Moody's Investor Service. You should be wary of institutions offering higher than average interest rates; if it looks too good to be true it probably will be – like the Bank of International Commerce and Credit (BICC) which went bust in 1992 costing investors £billions.

MORTGAGES

Mortgages or home loans (*hipotecas*) are available from most Portuguese banks (both for residents and non-residents), foreign banks in Portugal and offshore banks. In recent years, both Portuguese and foreign lenders have tightened their lending criteria due to the repayment problems experienced by many recession-hit borrowers. Some foreign lenders apply stricter rules than Portuguese lenders regarding income, employment and the type of property on which they will lend. Foreign lenders, e.g. offshore banks, may also have strict rules regarding the nationality and domicile of borrowers (some won't lend to Portuguese residents) and the percentage they will lend. Some lenders' terms (such as offshore lenders) don't permit long-term or regular letting (although how they would know is a mystery). If you raise a mortgage outside Portugal for a Portuguese property, you should be aware of any impact this may have on your foreign or Portuguese tax liabilities or allowances.

Although Portuguese banks are more keen to lend money on property nowadays, it's difficult for a foreign non-resident to obtain a Portuguese mortgage for a second home in Portugal. Portuguese mortgages are really only for someone living and working in the country, although if you're a non-resident you may be able to take out a mortgage with a Portuguese bank in your home country. Most banks are willing to finance the construction of a house, although you will usually need to buy and pay for the land out of your own resources. The bank will usually agree to advance the mortgage in stages in line with the agreed stage payments to the builder. Lenders usually require a life policy and building insurance for a property's full value.

In Portugal, it's customary for a property to be held as security for a home loan, i.e. the lender takes a first charge on the property, which is recorded at the property registry. If a loan is obtained using a Portuguese property as security, additional fees and registration costs are payable to the notary (*notário*) for registering the charge against the property. To obtain a mortgage from a Portuguese bank, you must usually provide proof of your monthly income and all outgoings such as mortgage payments, rent and other loans or commitments (although some lenders offer 'non-status' loans at higher interest rates). If you want a Portuguese mortgage to buy a property for commercial purposes, you must provide a detailed business plan in Portuguese. Note that a mortgage can be passed to the new owner when a property is sold.

Mortgages are granted on a percentage of the lender's valuation, which may be less than the purchase price. The maximum mortgage in Portugal is usually around 75 per cent of the purchase price, although loans of 50 to 60 per cent of the property valuation are more usual, particularly for non-residents. The normal term is 15 years, although mortgages can be repaid over 5 to 20 years (or up to the age of 65). The repayment period may be shorter for non-residents. Repayment mortgages are the most common type in Portugal, although endowment and pension-linked mortgages are also available. Payments can usually be made monthly or quarterly. As in most countries, mortgage interest rates in Portugal have fallen considerably in recent years and are now set by the European Central Bank. In mid-2002 mortgage interest rates were around 4 per cent. Note that a low interest rate (which usually increases after one year) may be more than offset by increased commission charges. Shop around for the best interest rate and ask the effective rate, including all commissions and fees.

When negotiating a mortgage, remember that you must add fees and expenses to the cost of a property. Fees can amount to 10 or 15 per cent of the purchase price (see **Fees** on page 144). For example, if you're buying a property for €100,000 and obtain a 75 per cent mortgage, you will have to pay €10,000 to €15,000 in fees. There are also various 'expenses' associated with mortgages, e.g. all lenders charge an 'arrangement' fee of 1 to 2 per cent, which is usually a minimum of €250 to €500. Although it's unusual to have a survey in Portugal, foreign lenders usually insist on a 'valuation survey' (usually costing from €325) for Portuguese properties before they will grant a loan. Note also that you must usually pay a deposit of 10 to 20/25?? per cent of the purchase price (see **Buying a New Completed Property or a Resale Property** on page 170).

Buying Through an Offshore Company: This is popular among foreign homebuyers in Portugal, as they can avoid paying Portuguese transfer tax (SISA), inheritance tax and possibly capital gains tax when they sell (see page 110). The shares of an offshore company can be used to secure a loan for the purchase of the property, with the shares being charged to the bank in return for a loan equal to a percentage of the value of the property.

Mortgages for Second Homes: If you have spare equity in an existing property, either in Portugal or abroad, then it may be more cost effective to re-mortgage (or take out a second mortgage) on that property, rather than take out a new mortgage for a second home. It involves less paperwork and therefore lower legal fees, and a plan can be tailored to meet your individual requirements. Depending on your equity in your existing property and the cost of a Portuguese property, this may enable you to pay cash for a second home. The disadvantage of re-mortgaging or taking out a second mortgage is that you reduce the amount of equity available in the property. When a mortgage is taken out on a Portuguese property, it's based on that property and not the individual, which could be important if you get into repayment difficulties.

Foreign Currency Loans: It's possible to obtain a foreign currency mortgage, other than in euros, e.g. pounds sterling, Swiss francs or US dollars. In previous years, relatively high Portuguese interest rates meant that a foreign currency mortgage was a good bet for many foreigners, although nowadays interest rates are set by the European Central Bank and are relatively low (3.25 per cent in mid-2002). However, you should be wary about taking out a foreign currency mortgage, as interest rate gains can be wiped out overnight by currency swings and devaluations. It's generally recognised that you should take out a mortgage in the currency in which you're paid or in the currency of the country where a property is situated. In this case if the foreign currency is devalued, you will have the consolation of knowing that the value of your Portuguese property will ('theoretically') have increased by the same percentage when converted back into the foreign currency.

When choosing between a euro loan and a loan in another currency, ensure that you take into account all costs, fees, interest rates and possible currency fluctuations. Irrespective of how you finance the purchase of a second home in Portugal, you should always obtain professional advice. Note that if you have a mortgage in a currency other than the currency in which you're paid, you must usually pay commission charges each time you transfer money into euros and remit money to Portugal. If you let a second home, you may be able to offset the interest (pro rata) on your mortgage against letting income.

VALUE ADDED TAX (IVA)

Value Added Tax (VAT or the 'Voracious Administration Tax'), called *Imposto sobre o Valor Acrescentado* (*IVA*) in Portugal, was introduced on 1st January 1986 when Portugal joined the European Community. Most prices in stores are quoted inclusive of *IVA*, although sometimes prices are quoted exclusive of tax (e.g. commercial goods). In June 2002 the standard rate of 17 per cent was raised to 19 per cent (one of the highest in the EU). Portugal levies *IVA* at the following rates:

Rate (%)	Applicability
5 – **reduced rate** (*taxa reduzida*)	essential foodstuffs such as cereals, meat, fish, milk, dairy products, olive oil, fruit and vegetables; table wines; books, newspapers and magazines; agricultural products and equipment; utilities such as water, gas and electricity; fuel oil and equipment for alternative energies; public transport; pharmaceuticals; sporting events; hotel accommodation; renting of camping areas; and civil works for municipalities and fire departments; farming equipment
12 – **intermediate rate** (*taxa intermédia*)	certain foodstuffs, restaurants, and miscellaneous items
19 – **standard rate** (*taxa normal*)	all goods and services (including new homes) which don't come under the reduced rate or aren't exempt

Note that the above rates are 4, 8 and 13 per cent respectively in the regions of the Azores and Madeira. Certain goods and services are exempt from *IVA*, including health care (e.g. medical and dental services); educational services; insurance, banking and certain financial services; social and welfare services; postal services; sale and lease of property (except new homes); agriculture; and acquisitions from other EU states. Exports are also exempt from *IVA*.

All businesses in Portugal must be registered for *IVA*. *IVA* returns are normally filed monthly and are due within two months of the end of the month to which they relate. Smaller enterprises with annual sales below €199,519 are permitted to file quarterly returns, which must be submitted before the 15th of the month following the quarter to which they apply. Any tax due must be paid when the return is filed. *IVA* fraud is rife in Portugal and payments are often made in cash to avoid *IVA*. Note that it's essential to have legitimate bills showing names and fiscal numbers to reclaim VAT.

IVA is payable on goods imported from outside the EU but not on goods purchased in an EU country where VAT has already been paid, although you may be asked to produce a VAT receipt. Enterprises located in other EU countries may obtain a refund of *IVA* paid on goods and services purchased in Portugal. *IVA* may also be refunded to enterprises from a non-EU country if Portugal and that country have a reciprocity agreement.

SOCIAL SECURITY TAXES

The social security (*segurança social* or *caixa*) system in Portugal is administered by the state and, in principle, applies to all individuals working in Portugal, either as employees or self-employed. It provides benefits for health care (see page 53), sickness, retirement, disability, death and old age, maternity, paternity and adoption. Both employers and employees must register and make contributions. Voluntary registration can also be made by those who aren't required to register. An employer must notify the Portuguese social security authorities of the commencement of work of an employee and deduct contributions from his gross salary and make payments to the authorities by the 15th of the following month. All compulsory social security contributions are tax deductible. Social security contributions are payable on the following:

- all remuneration, including payments in cash or kind, e.g. accommodation or food;
- regular bonus payments, commission or prizes;
- overtime payments;
- Christmas and holiday bonuses;
- unsociable hours payments (e.g. for shift work);
- regular payments for accommodation;
- danger money;
- remuneration resulting from suspension due to disciplinary action;
- compensation for unfair dismissal or termination of a contract;
- early retirement premiums.

The following kinds of income are exempt from social security contributions:

- travel expenses;
- subsistence allowances;
- payments in lieu of holidays;
- sick pay and pensions;
- payments made during military service;
- payments made towards the education of children (including university education);
- wedding gifts or irregular bonuses which are genuine ex-gratia payments;
- payments made towards medical bills;
- monthly expenses relating to board members or other professionals, the payment of which is required by contract;
- redundancy payments when made to all employees;

● canteen subsidies;

● profit-related pay.

Employees' contributions are based on their actual monthly income (i.e. there's no earnings cap), while contributions for the self-employed are calculated on an amount of between 1 and 12 times the minimum national wage, as chosen by the individual. For company directors, there's a monthly salary cap equal to 12 times the Portuguese minimum monthly wage (€348.01 in 2002), i.e. 12 x €348.01 = €4,176.12. However, those aged under 55 may choose to pay social security contributions based on their actual gross salary, if it exceeds the above limit. Social security contributions vary according to your profession and age, and whether you're an employee or self-employed, as shown below:

Activity	Percentage of Gross Income		
	Employee	Employer	Total
'normal' employees	11	23.75	34.75
agricultural workers	9.5	23	32.5
teachers	8	24.5	32.5
board members	10	22	32
domestic servants	9.3	20.7	30
professional soccer players	11	17.5	28.5
early retirement (under 55)	8	20.5	28.5
self-employed*	25.4/32	-	25.4/32
early retirement (over 55)	7	14.6	21.6
clergymen	4	8	12
fishermen	10	-	10

* Self-employed individuals may choose to pay contributions under the mandatory regime (25.4 per cent) or under an enlarged regime (32 per cent). The 25.4 per cent rate is for compulsory cover only (retirement, disability, death and old age, maternity, paternity and adoption) while the 32 per cent rate includes compulsory cover plus 'professional' sickness, illness subsidies and other family benefits (calculated on the adopted income basis). These rates apply on a monthly basis on an amount determined by the individual equal to between 1 and 12 times the Portuguese minimum monthly wage (€348.01 in 2002), i.e. 12 x €348.01= €4,176.12. The self-employed may reduce their contribution base without restriction; however, they may increase their contribution base only by one bracket, once a year, provided they're under 55 years of age. Contributions are limited to a maximum of six times the minimum monthly wage for those aged 55 or over.

Portugal has reciprocal social security agreements with all EU countries plus Andorra, Argentina, Australia, Brazil, Cabo Verde, Canada, Iceland, Norway, Switzerland, Turkey, Uruguay, the USA and Venezuela. These agreements allow for social security contributions paid in one country to be taken into account under the social security schemes of another country. Employees from the above countries who are transferred to Portugal for a limited period only and who continue to contribute to their home country's social security scheme, are exempt from paying contributions in Portugal for a period of one year. This exemption may be extended for a further year and in certain circumstances a five-year exemption may be granted. However, once the exemption period has elapsed, employees must pay social security contributions in Portugal. Employees of international organisations and diplomatic missions are usually exempt from paying social security contributions in Portugal.

The department of social security in Portugal has a free telephone hotline (*linha verde*) for information and enquiries operating Monday to Friday from 9am to 7pm (☎ 800-290 029) and a comprehensive website (in Portuguese only), which includes downloadable documents and forms (🖥 www.seg-social.pt).

INCOME TAX

Personal income tax (*Imposto sobre o Rendimento das Pessoas Singulares/IRS*) in Portugal is below the EU average, although it has increased considerably in recent years, and when social security taxes (see page 99) are included it's comparable with that in most other EU countries. Belgians, Dutch and Scandinavians will find Portuguese income tax low, while most other western Europeans will pay around the same or a little more. Paying Portuguese income tax can be advantageous, as there are more allowances for some people than there are in other countries. If you're able to choose the country where you're taxed, you should obtain advice from an international tax expert.

Portugal has a pay-as-you-earn (PAYE) system of income tax, whereby employees' tax is withheld at source by their employers, and they aren't responsible for paying their own income tax. Non-resident employees are subject to withholding tax on Portuguese income at a flat rate of 25 per cent. A husband and wife and their dependent children are taxed jointly as a family and a single tax return is submitted. For tax purposes, dependants include all children under 18 years of age; children aged from 18 to 24 who don't receive an income above the minimum wage, provided that in the year in question they've been registered in the 11th year of school; children unable to work; and minors under 18 years of age provided that they don't receive any income.

Moving to Portugal (or another country) often offers opportunities for legal 'favourable tax planning'. To make the most of your situation, it's best to obtain income tax advice before moving to Portugal, as there are usually a number of things you can do in advance to reduce your tax liability, both in Portugal and abroad. Be sure to consult a tax adviser who's familiar with both the Portuguese tax system and that of your present country of residence. For example, you may be able to avoid paying tax on a business abroad if you establish both residency and domicile in Portugal before you sell. On the other hand, if you sell a foreign home after establishing your principal residence in Portugal, it becomes a second home and you may then be liable to capital gains tax abroad (this is a complicated subject and you will need expert advice). You should inform the tax authorities in your former country of residence that you're going to live permanently in Portugal.

Tax evasion is illegal and a criminal offence in Portugal, for which offenders can be heavily fined or even receive a prison sentence. On the other hand, tax avoidance, i.e. legally paying as little tax as possible (if necessary by finding and exploiting loopholes in the tax laws) is a different matter altogether. Although Portuguese tax inspectors make a relatively small number of inspections, they target those among whom tax fraud is most prevalent, such as the self-employed. **Note that new legislation has been introduced to tackle fraud and it's now more difficult for 'fiscal nomads' to avoid Portuguese taxation in future. Offshore companies have been particularly targeted and it's now more difficult for them to avoid taxation.**

The Portuguese tax system was updated in 1989, prior to which taxes were relatively low and many people avoided paying taxes altogether. In the past, tax offices (*finanças*) tended to ignore foreigners in Portugal, although times have changed and in recent years they have become prime tax targets. The tax authorities may investigate foreign bank accounts held by EU residents in Portugal and abroad, and share tax information with other EU governments. Note that the Portuguese tax system is currently under reform and the information in this book was correct at the time of writing (mid-2002). It's therefore recommended to check updated information with an expert before taking any financial decisions regarding taxation.

Information about the Portuguese tax system is available from tax offices in main towns and cities, and from the Ministry of Finance website, which includes downloadable documents and tax returns (⌨ www.dgci.min-finanzas.pt). You can also file your tax return online. Note that information on the website in English is limited.

Liability

Your liability for income tax in Portugal depends on whether you're officially resident there. Under Portuguese law you become a **fiscal resident** in

Portugal if you spend 183 days there during a calendar year, either continuously or interrupted, or you have accommodation available in Portugal on 31st December and it can be assumed that you intend to use it as your habitual abode or residence. A family is considered to be resident if the person responsible for the family resides in Portugal. However, if another country has a double-taxation treaty with Portugal (see below), it will contain rules which determine in which country an individual is resident. Note that the 183 day rule also applies to other EU countries, and many countries (e.g. Britain) limit visits by non-residents to 182 days in any one year or an average of 90 days per tax year over a four-year period.

If you're a tax resident in two countries simultaneously, your 'tax home' may be resolved under the rules applied under international treaties. Under such treaties you're considered to be resident in the country where you have a permanent home; if you have a permanent home in both countries, you're deemed to be resident in the country where your personal and economic ties are closer. If your residence cannot be determined under this rule, you're deemed to be resident in the country where you have a habitual abode. If you have a habitual abode in both or in neither country, you're deemed to be resident in the country of which you're a citizen. Finally, if you're a citizen of both or neither country, the authorities of the countries concerned will decide your tax residence between them by mutual agreement.

If you intend to live permanently in Portugal, you should notify the tax authorities in your previous country of residence. You may be entitled to a tax refund if you depart during the tax year, which usually necessitates completing a tax return. The authorities may require evidence that you're leaving the country, e.g. evidence of a job in Portugal or of having purchased or rented a property there. If you move to Portugal to take up a job or start a business, you must register with the local tax authorities (*finanças*) soon after your arrival.

Double-taxation: Portuguese residents are taxed on their world-wide income, subject to certain treaty exceptions, while non-residents are taxed only on income arising in Portugal. Citizens of most countries are exempt from paying taxes in their home country when they spend a minimum period abroad, e.g. one year. Portugal has double-taxation treaties with many countries, designed to ensure that income that has already been taxed in one treaty country isn't taxed again in another treaty country. The treaty establishes a tax credit or exemption on certain kinds of income, either in the country of residence or the country where the income is earned. Portugal has double-taxation treaties with around 40 countries, including all EU countries plus Brazil, Bulgaria, Canada, China, Cuba, the Czech Republic, Hungary, India, Korea, Macao Mexico, Morocco, Mozambique, Norway, Pakistan, Poland, Romania, Russia, Singapore, Switzerland, Tunisia, Ukraine, the USA and Venezuela. Where applicable, a double-taxation treaty prevails over domestic law.

However, even if there's no double-taxation agreement between Portugal and another country, you can still obtain relief from double taxation. When there's no double-taxation agreement, tax relief is provided through direct deduction of any foreign tax paid or through a 'foreign compensation' formula. Note that if your tax liability in another country is lower than that in Portugal, you must pay the Portuguese tax authorities the difference. If you're in doubt about your tax liability in your home country, contact your nearest embassy or consulate in Portugal. The USA is the only country that taxes its non-resident citizens on income earned abroad (US citizens can obtain a copy of a brochure, *Tax Guide for Americans Abroad*, from American consulates).

Allowances, Deductions & Tax Credits

Before you're liable for income tax, you can deduct social security payments and certain costs from your gross income and from the sum due after establishing your tax base. The resultant figure is your taxable income. The term 'income' is broadly defined to include income from employment as well as business profits, rental income and capital gains. There are two types of allowable tax credits: those that are deducted in arriving at income under each of the categories of income shown below, and those deductible by reference to the personal expenditure or family circumstances of a taxpayer. It's essential to corroborate any deductions with receipts. Tax deductible expenses are subtracted from gross income to arrive at net income for each category, which are then totalled to give net income. A number of allowances laid down in the tax legislation are deducted from this value to give the net taxable income. IRS (2002) is calculated under the following nine categories of income:

A. Income from Employment: Includes salaries, wages, bonuses, fringe benefits in cash and kind, and other remuneration from employment. Deductions include 70 per cent of gross income up to a maximum of €2,484. When compulsory social security contributions exceed this amount they're deductible without limitation.

B. Income from Self-employment: Includes income earned by professionals, such as doctors and lawyers and royalties earned by authors or other original owners of intellectual property. A wide range of business expenses may be deducted in calculating the profits of a trade or business, including all expenses incurred by and related to a business activity except when they relate to vehicles (oil, insurance, depreciation, rents) or to entertainment expenses, which are 80 per cent deductible. For professionals, certain items such as entertainment and travelling expenses are deductible only to the extent that they don't exceed 10 per cent of gross income.

Depreciation of fixed assets and automobile operating expenses are 50 per cent deductible.

C. Commercial or Industrial Profits: Corporate Tax Code rules apply to this category with the possibility of carrying forward losses for five years where the trade was inherited on death. Tax may be levied by estimated assessment in certain cases.

D. Income from Farming/Agriculture: As for category C above.

E. Investment Income: No deduction is allowed from income earned from capital.

F. Income from Property: Income from property consists of rent from any assets owned in Portugal. Expenses for repairs and maintenance of buildings are deductible provided they're substantiated by documentation. Non-residents receiving income from a Portuguese source, e.g. from letting their Portuguese home, should instruct their fiscal representative to file an income tax declaration on their behalf (if they're unable to do it themselves). Letting income on property owned by non-residents or an offshore company is generally taxed at a flat rate of 25 per cent.

Rental income for property owned by offshore companies: from 2002, all offshore companies owning property in Portugal are subject to a rental tax on a fictional rental income irrespective of whether the property is let or not. This 'income' is assumed to be 6 per cent of the rateable (or 'patrimonial') value of the property and the tax is levied at 25 per cent of this 'income' value. For example, if the rateable value of your property is €150,000, the fictional rental income will be €9,000 and the rental tax will amount to €2,250. This tax is similar to a wealth tax such as the one levied on all non-resident property owners in Spain (see page 192).

Note that if the property has real rental income, the offshore company may be eligible for deductible expenses (see page 192). Note, however, that if a rental business is declared with all relevant costs and the rental income is lower than the above, the higher rate will apply!

G. Capital Gains: Exemptions include gains arising from corporate bonds or debentures acquired before 1st January 2001; units in investment funds; shares held for over one year; the disposal of a principal home provided that the proceeds are invested in a new home within two years of the sale or one year previous to the sale; plus a 50 per cent deduction on the gain from the sale of property used for residence purposes only, intellectual or industrial property, and a business or sub-lease. Capital losses can be offset against capital gains (see page 110).

H. Pensions: Annual income from pensions less than €7,058 may be excluded from taxable income. The capital element of a life annuity is excluded; when it isn't possible to distinguish between capital and interest, 65 per cent of the amount received is deductible.

I. Other Income: This category includes winnings from gambling and lotteries. There are no specific deductions.

As from 1st January 1999, most tax deductions were converted into tax allowances, although compulsory pension contributions and alimony may still be deducted without limit (provided such payments are evidenced in court decisions or agreements and proved by receipts or bank transfer slips). Note that all tax allowances must be suitably accredited by official receipts. In 2002 taxpayers could credit the following against their tax liability:

- €175.58 for each single taxpayer or €133.68 for each married taxpayer;

- €96.77 for each child;

- health expenses of the taxpayer and his dependants, up to the limit of €828 for unmarried taxpayers, up to €1,656 for married taxpayers and up to €174.58 for each dependent;

- 30 per cent of interest, amortisation of loan payments for the acquisition or improvement of a home in Portugal up to €1,536.30, or rental payments up to €1,536.30;

- 30 per cent of education expenses incurred by the taxpayer and his dependants, up to the limit of €828 for unmarried taxpayers, up to €1,656 for married taxpayers and up to €174.58 for each dependant;

- 25 per cent of life insurance and personal accident premiums, limited to €359.13 for married taxpayers and to €179.57 for single taxpayers. 25 per cent of health insurance, limited to €179.57 for single taxpayers, €359.13 for married taxpayers;

- 25 per cent of contributions to individual pension plans, limited to the lower of 5 per cent of gross income. These limits may be increased for taxpayers under 35;

- 25 per cent of donations to the state or municipalities, increased by 20, 30 or 40 per cent according to the type of beneficiary;

- 25 per cent of donations to religious institutions, public utility collective persons (i.e. non-profit entities with a public purpose officially recognised by the government), schools, museums, libraries, cultural associations, philanthropic and charitable institutions;

- advance personal income tax payments and taxes previously deducted at source.

Any personal income taxes paid in another country will also be deducted from your tax base. Note, however, that if you pay higher tax abroad than would have been paid in Portugal, you won't receive a rebate from the Portuguese tax authorities!

Withholding Tax: Income from certain sources is subject to final withholding tax applied at the following rates:

- 35 per cent: winnings from lotteries, draws and competitions;

- 25 per cent: income from shares; non-resident income earned in Portugal; pensions received by a non-resident in Portugal.

- 20 per cent: interest on demand and fixed-term deposits; income from securities; income corresponding to the difference between the amounts paid as a redemption, advance payment or maturity of a life insurance policy.

Tax Rates

Portuguese income tax is progressive and levied at rates of between 12 and 40 per cent (2002), as shown in the table below:

Taxable Income (€)	Tax Rate (%)	Cumulative Tax (€)
up to 4,100.12	12	492.01
from 4,100.12 to 6,201.42	14	786.19
from 6,201.42 to 15,375.45	24	2,987.96
from 15,375.45 to 35,363.52	34	9,783.90
from 35,363.52 to 51,251.48	38	15,821.32
above 51,251.48	40	

For example, if your taxable income is €15,000, you pay 12 per cent on the first €4,100.12 (€492), 14 per cent on the next €2,101.30 (€294.18) and 24 per cent on the next €8,798.58 (€2,111.66), making a tax bill of €2,897.84.

A system of income splitting is applied, whereby the income of a married couple is divided by two for the purpose of applying the tax tables and the resulting tax liability is doubled. However, when one partner earns over 95 per cent of the total income, the splitting factor is reduced to 1.95, effectively increasing the tax liability to compensate for the fact that two sets of rate bands are available (see **Tax Calculation** below).

Tax Calculation

The following tax calculation is for a married employee with two children, employment income only, a non-working spouse, social security paid in Portugal, and no expenses.

	Sum (€)
Gross Annual Income	25,000.00
Deductions & Tax Credits:	
– social security (11%)	-3,300.00
– various	-1,000.00
– taxpayer/spouse	-267.36
– children (2)	-193.54
Net Income	20,239.10
Splitting (x 1.95)	10,379.03
Net Taxable Income (x 2)	20,758.06
Income Tax Payable	4,818.05

Tax Returns & Bills

The tax year in Portugal is the same as the calendar year and residents are sent a tax return to complete at the beginning of the year. The standard tax form (*modelo IRS1*) is supplemented by a number of special forms for declaring different types of income (called *annexes*). Residents with employment (category A) and pensions (category H) income only are required to make an annual tax return between 1st February and 15th March. All other residents must file a tax return between 16th March and 30th April. If a non-resident has rental income or capital gains from property, he must also file a tax return by 30th April. If you have tax to pay you will receive a tax bill four to eight weeks after filing, which must be paid within 30 days. Any balance of tax due is usually payable by the 31st May and overpayments are refunded by 31st August. If a refund is due it will automatically be paid into the bank account specified on your return. Foreign residents may need to provide a copy of their IRS tax declarations when renewing their residence card (*residência*).

PROPERTY TAX

Property tax or rates (*contribuição autárquica/CA*) are levied annually on land or buildings by the local authority (*câmara municipal*). The tax is payable by property owners and not by tenants. Property tax is based on the fiscal or rateable value (*valor tributavel*) of a property as shown in the fiscal register (*matriz predial*). Previously the fiscal value of a property was well below its actual value, although there have been a number of re-valuations in the last decade and fiscal values are now closer to actual values. A property's fiscal value is based on its market value, location and the standard of local services.

Property is valued under three classifications: urban property (*prédios urbano*), rural property (*prédios rustica*) and a mixture of these two (*prédios misto*). For urban property the tax rate is between 0.7 and 1.3 per cent of a property's fiscal or rateable value (*valor tributavel*). Therefore, if you own a property with a fiscal value of €100,000 situated in a town, your property tax will be between €700 and €1,300. For rural property (i.e. non-building land outside an urban site and houses and buildings used strictly for agriculture and rural activities) the tax rate is a flat 0.8 per cent of the fiscal value (€800 for a property worth €100,000).

Note that under a new law introduced in 2002 property in Portugal owned by entities resident in a jurisdiction with a more favourable tax regime than Portugal, e.g. offshore companies, is subject to property tax at a fixed rate of 2 per cent. Therefore a property with a fiscal value of €100,000 situated in a town will be liable for €2,000 property tax annually.

You should receive a notification of the amount payable between January and April from the *Direcção das Contribuições e Impostos* of the Ministry of Finance in Lisbon. If you don't receive a notification you should contact your local tax office, as it may not have been sent or been lost in the post. Property tax is usually invoiced in arrears and payable in two instalments, the first in April and the second in September. Therefore in September 2002 you would be invoiced for the second instalment of property tax for 2001. Payment can be made at your local tax office (*finanças*), a main post office and at designated banks. Always ensure that you receive a receipt.

If you've purchased a property and paid SISA (see page 144), you may be exempt from paying property tax for up to ten years, depending on the property's fiscal value. To qualify the property must be occupied within six months of signing the deeds, the owner must be a permanent resident and the property owned in the name of a private individual (not a company). An application for exemption must be made to the local tax office within 90 days of the completion of the sale. If you make a late application or pay property tax when it isn't due, you cannot claim a refund or extend the exemption period, which runs from the date of completion. If you sell within the exemption period, a subsequent owner can also claim an exemption from property tax.

CAPITAL GAINS TAX

Capital gains tax (*imposto de mais valias*) is payable on the profit from the sale of certain assets in Portugal. Gains that are not specifically exempt are taxed as normal income using the applicable income tax rate. The sale of shares acquired prior to 1st January 2001 are taxed at 10 per cent. Capital losses can be offset against capital gains, but not against ordinary income.

Capital losses in excess of gains can be carried forward and offset against future gains for a five-year period.

Capital gains tax applies to property; securities; private companies' share capital; the sale of industrial or intellectual property such as trade marks and registered designs if the seller isn't the original owner; rental rights; and the transfer of a taxpayer's property to a taxpayer's business. Exemptions from capital gains include profits from the sale of corporate bonds and debentures acquired before 1st January 2001; investment fund participation; shares held before 1st January 1989 or held for more than one year prior to 1st January 2001; securities acquired on or after 1st January 2001 if the positive difference between capital gains and losses is €997.60 or less; property (except land for construction) owned prior to 1st January 1989; and the disposal of a principal home provided that the proceeds are invested in a new home (or in a building or extending a building, or in land for this purpose) within two years of the sale or one year prior to the sale.

Property: A capital gain on property is based on the fiscal value (*valor tributável*) of your home and not its market value. To calculate the capital gain on the sale of property, the fiscal value when it was purchased is indexed by an official government coefficient to take into account inflation. Allowances are made for the costs associated with buying and selling a property, as are costs for improvements and maintenance. Only 50 per cent of a gain made on the sale of property acquired since 1989 (plus intellectual or industrial property and a business or sub-lease) is taxable. Note that draft legislation in 2002 proposed changing the regulations regarding capital gains tax paid by offshore companies who were previously exempt from this tax. The new legislation (introduced to prevent entities resident in offshore jurisdictions from avoiding tax) rules that if property represents more than 50 per cent of the company's total assets then capital gains tax is payable at the usual rates. At the time of writing, this law was still at draft stage.

STAMP DUTY

Stamp duty is levied on numerous transactions in Portugal, and is payable either in the form of a previously purchased stamp which you affix to the document or is included in the price. The most frequent transactions involving stamp duty are as follows:

- loans or credit (5 per cent on the total amount);
- insurance premiums (generally 9 per cent) except for life insurance which is exempt;
- sale of property by auction (7.5 per cent);
- rental of rural property on yearly rental income (6 per cent);

- rental of urban property on monthly rental income (6 per cent up to €50, 10.5 per cent on any exceeding amount);
- leasing (8 per cent of value).

INHERITANCE & GIFT TAX

As in most countries, dying doesn't free you (or more correctly, your beneficiaries) entirely from the clutches of the tax man. Portugal imposes an inheritance and gift tax (*imposto sobre as sucessões e doações*), called estate tax or death duty in some countries, on assets or monies received as an inheritance or gift. The estates of both residents and non-residents are subject to Portuguese inheritance tax if they own property or have other assets in Portugal. In Portugal, inheritance tax is paid by the beneficiaries, e.g. a surviving spouse, and not by the deceased's estate (as in some other countries). The country where beneficiaries pay inheritance and gift tax is usually decided by their domicile.

The tax office of the area where the deceased's assets are located must be notified (and a copy of the death certificate filed) within 30 days of the death of a local resident, or within 60 days if the deceased resided in another area of Portugal. If the deceased was a non-resident, the tax office must be notified within 180 days. A list of the deceased's assets must be filed at the tax office within 60 days of the notification of the death. If the liquidation is immediate, the amount payable may be reduced, although beneficiaries are permitted to pay any tax due in instalments (when interest is levied).

Inheritance tax is progressive and levied at rates from 0 to 52 per cent, according to the value of the estate or gift and the relationship between the donor and the beneficiary. Transfers below €3,491.59 made to spouses or children are exempt, while the maximum 52 per cent rate is payable on estates valued above €341,676.56 passing to an unrelated person. The amount of inheritance tax payable for first degree (children, spouses) and second degree (siblings and ascendants) relatives is shown in the table below:

Value of Taxable Assets (€)	Tax Payable (%)	
	First Degree	Second Degree
Up to 3,491.59	0	7
3,491.60 to 13,716.94	6	10
13,716.95 to 34,915.85	9	13
34,915.86 to 68,584.71	12	16
68,584.72 to 172,085.27	16	21
172,085.28 to 341,676.56	20	26
Over 341,676.56	25	32

Inheritance and gift tax is due only on assets held in Portugal, irrespective of whether the beneficiaries are foreign residents or non-residents. Loans are considered to be located in the lender's country, while shares and bonds issued by Portuguese resident companies are deemed to be located in Portugal, irrespective of where the holder is resident. Assets are divided into 'active' (e.g. bank accounts, property, shares, cars, moveables and personal items) and 'passive' (i.e. debts such as mortgages, loans, bills, etc.). The value of a home is based on its fiscal value, listed in the property's registration document (*caderneta predial*).

It's important for both residents and non-residents owning property in Portugal to decide in advance how they wish to dispose of their Portuguese property. Ideally this should be decided even <u>before</u> buying property in Portugal. Property can be registered in a single name; both names of a couple or joint buyers' names; the names of children, giving the parents sole use during their lifetime (*usufruto* or *interesse vitalício*); or in the name of a Portuguese or foreign company or trust. You should obtain professional advice regarding the registration of a Portuguese property. It's wise for a couple not only to register joint ownership of a property, but to share their other assets and have separate bank accounts, which will help reduce their dependants' liability for inheritance tax. Portuguese law doesn't recognise the rights to inheritance of a non-married partner, although there are a number of solutions to this problem, e.g. a life insurance policy.

One way of reducing your liability to inheritance tax is to transfer legal ownership of property to a relative as a gift during your lifetime. However, this is treated as a sale (at the current market price) and incurs fees of around 10 to 15 per cent plus capital gains tax, which need to be compared with your inheritance tax liability. Whether you should make a will or 'sell' a property to someone depends on the value of the property and your relationship (it may be cheaper for a beneficiary to be taxed under the inheritance laws). If you're elderly, it may pay you to make the title deed (*escritura*) of your Portuguese home directly in the names of your children. Inheritance and gift tax isn't payable in Portugal when a property is owned by an offshore company (see page 172).

Portuguese inheritance law is a complicated subject and professional advice should be sought from an experienced lawyer who understands both Portuguese inheritance law and the law of any other countries involved. Your will (see below) is also a vital component in reducing Portuguese inheritance and gift tax to the minimum or deferring its payment.

WILLS

It's an unfortunate fact of life (and death) that you're unable to take your hard-earned money with you when you make your final exit, even if you plan to return in a later life. All adults should make a will (*testamento*) irrespective of how large or small their assets (each spouse should make a separate will). If a foreigner dies intestate in Portugal, i.e. without a will, his estate may be automatically disposed of under Portuguese law and the law regarding compulsory heirs applied. As in many European countries, a surviving spouse and children have certain inheritance rights under Portuguese law and cannot be disinherited. However, foreigners aren't generally bound by Portuguese inheritance rules and are free to leave their property to whom they wish according to the law of their home country, provided a will is valid under the law of that country. If you've lived in Portugal for a long time, it may be necessary to create a legal domicile in your home country for the purpose of making a will.

Although it isn't <u>necessary</u> to have a Portuguese will for Portuguese property, it's wise to have a separate will for <u>any</u> country where you own property. When a person dies, assets can be dealt with immediately under local law without having to wait for the granting of probate in another country, which can take months. Having a Portuguese will for your Portuguese assets speeds up the will's execution and simplifies the administration of the estate, and can save substantial costs such as the translating and legalising (proving) of wills made abroad. If you have two or more wills, you <u>must</u> ensure that they don't contradict or invalidate one another. You should periodically review your will to ensure that it reflects your current financial and personal circumstances.

There are two kinds of Portuguese will: a public will and a private (or closed) will. A **public will** is the normal and most suitable kind of will for most people. It's written in Portuguese at a notary's office and entered into notarial books as if it were a deed. A public will must be signed in front of a notary by the testator and two witnesses, who can be any nationality. The original remains at the notary's office and the notary provides the testator with notarised (legalised) copies. It's unnecessary to employ a lawyer to prepare a public will, although it's usually recommended. It must, however, be prepared by a notary who's responsible for ensuring that it's legal and properly drafted. If you don't understand Portuguese, you will need an official translation in a language that you speak fluently and a translator must be present at the signing if the testator or the witnesses cannot speak Portuguese.

A **closed or private will** can be written in English (or another foreign language) and be in English form, although a Portuguese translation is necessary. It must be written in your own hand writing as clearly as possible (it can be copied from a draft made by a lawyer) and must be signed before a notary and two witnesses. The notary will validate the will by endorsing it as a 'minute of approval' (*minuta de aprovacão*) and will seal the will and return it to you. It should be kept in a safe place or can be filed by the notary. Portuguese wills can be drawn up by Portuguese lawyers and notaries abroad, although it's cheaper to do it in Portugal. Note that the rules relating to witnesses are strict and if they aren't followed precisely can render a will null and void.

Executors aren't required under Portuguese law. However, if you appoint an executor you should inform your heirs so that they will know who to notify in the event of your death. It isn't wise to name a Portuguese bank or a lawyer who doesn't speak Portuguese as the executor, because they must instruct a Portuguese lawyer (*advogado*) whose fees may be impossible to control. It's best to appoint a Portuguese resident (such as a lawyer) as the executor, which will ease the problems of administering the estate. However, it's important to agree the fee in advance.

Your beneficiaries must provide the Portuguese authorities with an original death certificate or an authorised copy. If you die abroad, a foreign death certificate must be legally translated and legalised for it to be valid in Portugal. Inheritance tax must be paid in advance of the release of the assets to be inherited in Portugal and beneficiaries may therefore need to borrow funds to pay the tax before they receive their inheritance. Bear in mind that the winding-up of an estate can take a long time in Portugal.

Keep a copy of your will(s) in a safe place and another copy with your lawyer or the executor of your estate. Don't leave them in a bank safe deposit box, which in the event of your death is sealed for a period under Portuguese law. You should keep information regarding bank accounts and insurance policies with your will(s), but don't forget to tell someone where they are!

Note that Portuguese inheritance law is a complicated subject and it's important to obtain professional legal advice when writing or altering your will(s). See also **Inheritance & Gift Tax** on page 112.

COST OF LIVING

No doubt you would like to try to estimate how far your euros will stretch and how much money (if any) you will have left after paying your bills. The cost of living in Portugal has risen considerably in the last decade or so and in the major cities is now around the EU average, although it's still relatively low in rural areas. The country has a low standard of living compared with most other EU countries. In the UBS *Prices & Earnings Around the Globe* report (2000 edition), Lisbon ranked 47th out of the 58 most expensive cities in the world. Inflation is low at less than 3 per cent, although unemployment is relatively high, particularly in resort areas.

In the last few decades, increased costs (particularly salaries) have brought the price of many goods and services in Portugal in line with most other European countries and imported goods can be particularly expensive. Among the more expensive items in Portugal are quality clothes (although fewer are needed in resort areas), cars and many consumer goods. Shopping for expensive consumer and household goods in other European countries or North America can yield considerable savings. However, many things in Portugal remain cheaper than in northern European countries, including property and rents outside the major cities and top resort areas (where they can be astronomical), fresh food, alcohol, dining out and general entertainment.

It's difficult to calculate an average cost of living in Portugal, as it depends very much on each individual's particular circumstances and lifestyle. The actual difference in your food bill will depend on what you eat and where you lived before moving to Portugal. Food in Portugal costs around the same as in the USA, but is cheaper than in most northern European countries. €200 to €300 should feed two adults for a month, including (inexpensive) wine but excluding fillet steak, caviar and expensive imported foods. A couple owning their home can 'survive' on a net income of as little as €1,000 per month (many pensioners actually live on less) and most can live quite comfortably on an income of around €2,000 per month (excluding rent or mortgage payments). In fact most northern Europeans who live modestly in Portugal without over-doing the luxuries will find that their cost of living is up to 50 per cent lower than in their home country.

ALL MANOR OF PROPERTY

manor-park.com

manor-park.info

algarve-resorts.com

algarvemanor.com

homes-unique.com

algarve-property.info

WHETHER YOU ARE LOOKING FOR A COUNTRY
ESTATE OR AN EXCLUSIVE RESORT PROPERTY,
OR INDEED AN INVESTMENT OPPORTUNITY,
LET US LOCATE IT ON YOUR BEHALF THROUGH
OUR EXTENSIVE SEARCH NETWORK.

AT MANOR PARK WE ALSO PRIDE OURSELVES ON
PROVIDING A SPECIAL SERVICE FOR PROPERTY
OWNERS WISHING TO SELL.

MANOR PARK IS A LICENSED REAL ESTATE AGENT SPECIALISING
IN THE LUXURY PORTUGUESE PROPERTY MARKET OF QUINTA DO
LAGO, VALE DO LOBO, VILAMOURA AND ALMANCIL. WE ALSO
SUPPORT AN EXTENSIVE NETWORK THROUGHOUT PORTUGAL
WITH SPECIAL EMPHASIS ON THE ALGARVE.

MANORPARK
PROPERTIES

Rua Cristóvão Pires Norte - R/C - D
Apartado 3207 - 8135-903 Almancil
Algarve - Portugal
info@manor-park.com
Tel **(351) 289 391303**
Fax (351) 289 391304

AMI NUMBER 2198

4.

FINDING YOUR DREAM HOME

A fter deciding to buy a home in Portugal, your first tasks will be to choose the region and what sort of home to buy. **If you're unsure where and what to buy, the best decision is usually to rent for a period.** The secret of successfully buying a home in Portugal (or anywhere else for that matter) is research, research and more research, preferably before you even set foot there. You may be fortunate and buy the first property you see without doing any homework and live happily ever after. However, a successful purchase is much more likely if you thoroughly investigate the towns and communities in your chosen area; compare the range and prices of properties available and their relative values; and study the procedure for buying property. It's a wise or lucky person who gets his choice absolutely right first time, but there's a much better chance if you do your homework thoroughly.

One of the things which attracts many buyers to Portugal is the generally high quality of property compared with some other European countries, which usually provides good value for money. However, although more Portuguese own their own homes than people in some other European Union (EU) countries, the Portuguese don't normally buy property as an investment and you shouldn't expect to make a quick profit when buying property in Portugal. Property values usually increase at an average of around 5 per cent (if you're lucky) a year or in line with inflation, meaning that you must own a house for around three years simply to recover the fees associated with buying. Property prices rise faster than average in some fashionable areas, although this is generally reflected in higher purchase prices. The stable property market in Portugal acts as a discouragement to speculators wishing to make a quick profit, and capital gains tax (see page 110) can also take a large slice out of any profit made on the sale of a second home.

Like many other countries, the Portuguese property market was hard hit by the recession in the early 1990s during which it experienced a severe slump, particularly on the Algarve. By the mid-1990s the market started to recover and now (2002) there's a strong property market throughout the country, particularly in properties on luxury developments (offering a wide range of leisure and sports facilities) and luxury villas. In the 1970s and 1980s, over-development (when a rash of ugly high-rise buildings were constructed) spoilt some areas of the Algarve and there are now strict planning controls (among the strictest in Europe). A new planning law, **(Plano Regional de Ordenamento do Território Algarve/PROTAL)** introduced in 1993 to curb uncontrolled development, has stabilised and increased prices and most new developments are now low-density buildings in harmony with their surroundings.

There are many foreign property owners in Portugal, which is one of Europe's favourite countries for second homes, particularly among buyers from Britain, Germany, Ireland and Scandinavia. Most foreigners are concentrated on the Algarve coast, although buyers are now venturing further afield and investigating other regions, including both coastal and rural areas. Many foreign property owners in Portugal are residents (some 50,000 Britons live there), the majority of whom are retired. A slice of the good life needn't cost the earth, with 'old' apartments and village homes available from as little as €50,000, modern apartments from around €75,000 and detached villas from €125,000. However, if you're seeking a substantial home with a sizeable plot of land and a swimming pool, you will usually need to spend at least €250,000 (depending on the area –considerably more in the Algarve). For those with the financial resources the sky's the limit, with luxury villas costing well over a million euros.

This chapter is designed to help you decide what sort of home to buy and, most importantly, its location. It will also help you avoid problems and contains information about regions, research, location, renting, the cost, fees, buying new and resale, community properties, timesharing (and other part-ownership schemes), estate agents, inspections and surveys, conveyancing, purchase contracts, completion, renovation and restoration, moving house, security, utilities, heating and air-conditioning, property income and selling a home.

REGIONS

For the purposes of this section, Portugal has been divided into the six tourist regions defined by the Portuguese National Tourist Office: Algarve, Costa de Lisboa, Costa Verde, Costa de Prata, Montanhas and Planícies (as shown on the map on page 244).

Algarve: The Algarve region (the name is derived from the Arabic *Al Gharb*, meaning 'the west' or 'the land beyond') in the south of the country is also an official province and has a totally different character from other Portuguese regions. It was occupied by the Moors between the 8th and 13th centuries and was the last region to be re-conquered from them in 1292. Even today there's evidence of the Moors' former presence, particularly in the local architecture, e.g. low white houses with distinctive fretwork chimneys. The Algarve stretches 160km/100mi from Cape St Vincent (Cabo de Sao Vicente) to Vila Real de Santo António on the Spanish border and boasts one of Europe's most beautiful coastlines. It's renowned for its long sandy beaches, idyllic coves, distinctive red cliffs and picturesque fishing villages. However, the Algarve is more than a strip of coastline and includes a 30km/20mi stretch of unspoilt countryside noted for its pine forests, rolling hills and almond, fig, olive and orange trees.

Although many of its bustling resorts are worlds away from the quintessential Portugal, the region still possesses an abundance of unspoilt charm, historic beauty and Moorish character. Despite some towns having been ravaged by over-development, half the coast is totally unspoilt and there are still a number of traditional fishing villages (e.g. Ferragudo, Sagres and Tavira) where the 20th century has barely intruded. Sagres is Europe's most south-westerly town and in recent years has become popular with foreign buyers, attracted by the several golfing complexes built in the area, including Parque da Floresta. Attractive inland towns include Loulé, Monchique, São Bartolomeu de Messines and Silves (once the capital of the Moors). Monchique is the capital of the beautiful mountainous area of Serra de Monchique, which marks the boundary between the Algarve and the Alentejo. Nearby are the hot springs of Caldas de Monchique, where thermal baths were built by the Romans.

The Algarve coastline is generally divided into three areas: western, central and eastern. The western Algarve stretches from Cape St. Vincent (Cabo de Sao Vicente) to Albufeira and includes the towns of Lagos (from where many of Portugal's voyages of discovery set sail), Portimão and Lagoa (a wine-producing area). Albufeira is a large commercial and market town and a bustling tourist resort in summer (the largest on the Algarve), but it still manages to retain a certain amount of charm. The central Algarve extends from Albufeira to Faro and takes in Vilamoura and the exclusive resorts of Dunas Douradas, Quinta do Lago and Vale do Lobo (the so-called 'golden triangle'). Vilamoura, situated to the west of Quarteira (an unattractive mass of high-rise apartment blocks), is one of Europe's largest residential developments with a large marina. Other marinas on the Algarve are at Albufeira, Lagos, Portimão and Vila Real de San Antonio. The marina at Faro, currently under construction, is expected to be completed in 2003.

The eastern Algarve, from Faro to Vila Real de Santo António (on the Spanish border), is the quietest and least developed (i.e. unspoilt) stretch of the Algarve. It's noted for its sleepy fishing villages and farming communities (e.g. Estói, Olhão and Tavira) which are a world away from the manicured tourist complexes and bustling resort towns further west. Faro (pop. 30,000) is the historic capital of the Algarve and its economic and administrative centre. It's a port and a university town, with an attractive old centre boasting some of the best architecture in the region. The eastern Algarve is noted for its lagoon and offshore islands (*ilhas*), with superb deserted beaches which comprise the Parque Natural da Ria Formosa.

The Algarve accounts for some 90 per cent of all property sales to foreign buyers in Portugal, thanks largely to its excellent year-round climate which includes over 3,000 hours of sunshine. Although some towns have been spoilt by unsightly tower blocks, recent development has been more in tune with the environment and today the watchword is quality rather than quantity. The Algarve is noted for its many luxury developments and self-contained estates ('hermetically' sealed from the outside world). It's also a sportsman's paradise with extensive facilities for golf, tennis, horse-riding and water sports. Popular towns among foreign homebuyers include Prai da Rocha, Carvoeiro,

Luz, Armacao de Pera and Praia da Gale. The region has good road connections with the rest of the country and with neighbouring Spain (via the IP1 highway). The coastal motorway is now complete and most resorts are within one hour's drive of Faro airport. There are also excellent bus and rail connections (along the coast and with Lisbon and Porto), and an international airport at Faro which opened in 1963 and whose second terminal was recently finished.

Costa de Lisboa (Lisbon Coast): The Costa de Lisboa region encompasses the area from around Ericeira in the north to just below Sines in the south, taking in the southern portions of Estremadura and Ribatejo provinces, and the capital Lisbon built on seven hills alongside the River Tagus (Tejo). Lisbon (pop. 1.3m) is one of Europe's great historic cities (although destroyed by an earthquake in 1755) and despite being one of western Europe's shabbiest, slowest and most decaying capital cities, is an elegant, cosmopolitan and vibrant city, steeped in history and tradition. It's a city of stark contrasts, slowly being dragged into the 21st century (much of the city has recently been undergoing a facelift) and noted for its cobbled streets, ancient trams and funiculars; a wealth of museums, monuments and diverse architecture; and, above all, the friendliness of its people. If you're bored of sterile, modern resorts and yearn for some good old-fashioned charm, then Lisbon (a city with a soul) may be just what you're seeking.

The coastal area to the west of Lisbon is known variously as the Costa do Sol (sunshine coast), Estoril Coast and Portuguese Riviera. It has a number of elegant and sophisticated resorts, famous for their luxury hotels, extravagant villas, casinos and fine beaches. Estoril has long been a traditional refuge for Europe's deposed royalty (hence the nickname 'the coast of kings') and is a favoured resort of the rich and famous. Sintra is a charming town that was the summer home of the Portuguese Royal family and before them the Moorish Lords of Lisbon. Cascais is the centre of the Portuguese Riviera (a new marina has recently been built) and is a stylish and colourful resort. Among the region's many architectural gems are the superb Manueline monastery at Belèm (from where Vasco da Gama set sail on his two-year voyage to India in 1497) which has been declared a UNESCO World Heritage site; the monumental palace-convent at Mafra (Portugal's equivalent of Spain's El Escorial); and the wedding-cake Palácio de Queluz.

The Costa de Lisboa has many fine beaches, including those at Caparica, Estoril, Guincho, Praia Adraga and Tróia. Ericeira is an attractive fishing village with a cliff-top town (one of the liveliest night spots on the coast) and Sesimbra (west of Setúbal) is another picturesque fishing village with a medieval castle. Setúbal (pop. 80,000) on the Costa Azul (blue coast) is one of Portugal's most ancient cities and its third largest port, noted for its impressive suspension bridge spanning the Tagus (one of the longest in Europe). Nearby Palmela is a pretty town with a magnificent castle.

The Estoril Coast is home to a small group of (wealthy) expatriates and the area has been enhanced in recent years by a number of new golf developments. Not surprisingly, the Costa de Lisboa boasts some of the most expensive property in Portugal. The region has excellent air, rail and road connections with the rest of the country and internationally.

Costa de Prata (Silver Coast): The Costa de Prata (so named because of the silver reflection of the sun on the sea) is the name given to a region encompassing most of the provinces of Estremadura, Ribatejo (meaning 'beside the Tejo') and the Beira Litoral, stretching from just north of Lisbon almost to Porto. It's one of the most economically developed regions of the country and an area of infinite diversity, from vast expanses of fine, sandy beaches to rolling hills and wooded mountain ranges in the interior. The Costa de Prata boasts a wealth of natural beauty and history and includes many of the country's most stunning architectural masterpieces: the splendid monasteries of Alcobaça and Batalha (both UNESCO World Heritage sites); Òbidos castle; Tomar's Convento de Cristo (former headquarters of the Knights Templar); and Queen Leonor's Thermal Spa City of Caldas da Rainha.

The region's largest town is Coimbra (pop. 85,000), situated on the banks of the Mondego river. It was the capital of Portugal in the 12th and 13th centuries and is one of Portugal's most historic and colourful cities, home of the Portuguese traditional song *fado*. Coimbra is Portugal's third largest city and one of Europe's oldest university towns (Velha University was founded in 1290 in Lisbon and established in Coimbra in 1537). Òbidos is a medieval walled city where time seems to have stood still – it's considered the most romantic town in Portugal and among its prettiest with its narrow cobbled streets and blue and white houses. Dubbed the 'wedding city', Òbidos was a traditional bridal gift of the kings of Portugal to their queens. The Òbidos lagoon is popular among holiday homeowners and is an area of outstanding natural beauty and tranquil, clean beaches. West of Òbidos is the fishing village of Peniche which has Portugal's second largest fishing fleet, from where ferries leave for the Ilhas Berlengas (Berlenga Islands) 12km/7mi offshore.

The Costa de Prata is acclaimed for its excellent beaches and is a top European destination for surfers. The coastline is dotted with traditional unspoilt fishing villages and, not surprisingly, is noted for its excellent seafood. Popular beach resorts include Figueira da Foz, Nazare, São Martinho do Porto and Vila do Conde (famous for its lace). Newer resorts include the Praia d'El Rey resort, which boasts one of Europe's best golf clubs, and Costa Nova. Other places of note include Aveiro (the Venice of Portugal, famous for its lagoon and canals); Santarém (capital of the province of Ribatejo), an attractive country town which was one of the Moors' strongholds in Portugal;

and the Sanctuary of Fátima, which is visited annually by millions of Roman Catholic pilgrims and is second only to Lourdes in popularity.

The Costa de Prata is popular with Portuguese and Spanish holidaymakers, and in recent years has become increasingly popular with foreign visitors and property buyers. The area forms a popular alternative to the Algarve since property prices are lower. The region has good rail and road connections with the rest of the country, which have been improved by the opening of the new A1 motorway in recent years, and is served by both Lisbon and Porto international airports.

Costa Verde (Green Coast): The Costa Verde is Portugal's northernmost region bordering Galicia in Spain and includes the province of Minho and the coastal region of the Douro (Portugal's smallest province). Minho is Portugal's most unspoilt province where many villages remain lost in time and are virtually untouched by modern developments. The people even have their own dialect which has more in common with the Galician language spoken over the border in Spain than it does with Portuguese. Minho (which produces *vinho verde* or green wine) clings to its conservative rural traditions and many farmers still rely on ox-drawn carts and ploughs (the countryside is among the poorest in western Europe). It's Portugal's most beautiful province, noted for its verdant, densely wooded hills and lush river valleys fed by the Cavado, Douro, Lima and Minho rivers. Minho is also Portugal's most colourful and lively province, famous for its local festivities and picturesque old towns full of quiet charm and interest. The region is a haven for hikers and nature lovers, particularly the 70,000 hectare Parc National de Peneda-Gerês, and is home to many rare plants and animals.

The region takes in Porto (Oporto in English), Portugal's second largest city and its commercial centre, with a population of around 500,000. Magnificently situated on the banks of the Douro River (river of gold), it's famous for its port wine lodges (*fábricas*) at Vila Nora de Gaia, where visitors can sample Portugal's most famous wine. Porto (the birthplace of Prince Henry the Navigator, Portugal's most famous seafarer) is Portugal's most sophisticated, modern and best-developed city, and is acclaimed for its monuments, picturesque streets and spectacular graceful bridges. The grapes for port wine are grown on the land either side of the River Douro, which has one of the most beautiful valleys in Europe; a spectacular railway (opened in 1887) runs from Porto to Pinhão (150km/93mi), following the river for around half its journey.

Braga is the capital of Minho and the country's ecclesiastical capital; it was once the seat of the Primate of Portugal and is dubbed the Rome of Portugal on account of its many churches, cathedral and archbishop's palace. Guimarães was the first capital of Portugal in the 12th century and is known as the cradle of Portuguese independence. It's the birthplace of King Alfonso Henríques, Portugal's first king, who set out from here to re-conquer the south of the country from the Moors. The region has many picturesque fishing villages (including Caminha, Esposende and Ofir) and popular resorts which include Espinho (with one of the largest markets in Portugal), the once sleepy fishing village of Póvoa do Varzim (now a fashionable resort with a vibrant nightlife), Viana do Castelo (a major cultural centre noted for its pottery) and Vila do Conde (a handicrafts centre famous for its lace). The area is also famous for its fascinating market towns which include Barcelos (noted for its Thursday market) and the romantic town of Ponte de Lima, plus its many fortified towns, among the best of which are Monção, Melgaço and Valença (do Minho).

Porto has good rail and road connections (it's linked to Lisbon by the A1 motorway) with the rest of the country and an international airport. Apart from Porto, which has a sizeable foreign community (particularly British expatriates working in the port wine industry), the Costa Verde isn't well known among visitors from other countries and attracts few foreign homebuyers.

Madeira: The Madeira archipelago (situated in the North Atlantic around 545km/338mi off the coast of north-west Africa, 978km/607mi from Lisbon) includes the islands of Madeira, Porto Santo, and the uninhabited Desertas and Selvagens. All the islands were uninhabited at the time of their discovery by the Portuguese in the 15th century (1419). Madeira (pop. 250,000, half of whom live in Funchal) is 57km/35mi long and 22km/14mi wide and covers an area of 741km^2/286mi^2. It has been an autonomous region since 1976 with its own locally elected government and parliament, but it remains legally and politically part of Portugal and is therefore a full member of the EU.

Madeira (the name means wood in English) is the mountain peak of a volcanic mass created at the same time as the Canary Islands and was originally covered in trees. Nowadays every available strip of land has been cultivated and the mountain slopes are terraced and irrigated by a complex network of water channels (*levadas*) extending to over 2,000km/1,250mi (which are used as hiking paths by visitors). The coastline mainly consists of dramatic peaks and cliffs (Cape Girão is the second highest cliff in the world) and the island has no beaches. The nearest beach is on the island of Porto Santo, 43km/27mi north-east of Madeira. Porto Santo is much flatter and drier (almost barren) than Madeira, but its saving grace is its glorious sandy beaches. It has its own airport with flights to Madeira and Lisbon and is also served by a ferry service from Madeira (1.5 hours).

Madeira is one of the oldest tourist destinations in Europe and a popular port of call for cruise ships. It's noted for its stunning scenery and is one of the world's most beautiful islands (it's known as the 'Pearl of the Atlantic'). Lapped by the warm waters of the Gulf Stream, it has an excellent year-round mild climate ('eternal spring') and is a popular destination for northern Europeans seeking a winter refuge. Madeira is a lush green island with a mass of exuberant vegetation and is often referred to as the flower garden of the Atlantic. The capital, Funchal, tumbles down the mountainside towards the sea and offers a unique combination of hustle and bustle, and charm and elegance. Funchal has a wonderful market, which is a riot of colour and exotic smells. The island boasts two spectacular golf courses and a wealth of other sports facilities. Madeira has been famous for its hearty Madeira wines since the 18th century.

Madeira doesn't have a very active property market, although it's possible to buy your own slice of paradise and several new developments are currently underway. Property isn't cheap, although it's less expensive than in many parts of the Algarve, particularly on the island's more remote north coast away from the capital Funchal. Old country properties are particularly attractive. Communications are good and the island is served by regular international flights from Portugal and many other European countries. The airport was recently expanded to allow larger planes to land.

Montanhas (mountains): The Montanhas region includes the province of Trás-os-Montes (literally 'beyond the hills'), the inland Beiras (Alta and Baixa) and part of the Douro (the region is crossed by the River Douro). Trás-os-Montes is Portugal's lost land, trapped in a medieval time warp, where ploughing with oxen and wooden-wheeled ox carts are still commonplace (as in Minho). The locals are a proud, independent people who have maintained their centuries-old traditions of costume, dancing and song (with a strong Celtic influence). It's the poorest and most backward part of the country, but has a charm, beauty and tranquillity that's rare elsewhere in Portugal. The region has a harsh climate, which is described locally as 'nine months of winter and three months of hell'.

The Montanhas region contains the wildest (still home to wolves and wildcats) and most dramatic landscapes in Portugal, including Montezinho National Park, the Serra do Gerês (part of the 170,000 acre Peneda-Gerês National Park, which straddles the border with Spain) and the Serra de Estrêla. The Serra de Estrêla contains Portugal's only winter sports venue (at Torre) and is home to the country's highest peak at 1,992m/6,500ft. The region is popular with outdoor sports lovers and is a popular canoeing, climbing, fishing, hiking and hunting destination. Palaeolithic prehistoric rock art was discovered in 1994 at Foz Côa (the Côa Valley, near the town of Vilanova de Foz Côa) during work on a hydroelectric dam, which was due to flood the valley. The site was saved and is now designated the Parque Arqueológico do Vale de Côa.

The region's main towns include Bragança, Castelo Branco (13th century castle), Chaves (a beautiful, historic spa city), Guarda (described as cold, rich, strong and ugly, commanding spectacular views over Spain), Lamego (Sanctuary of Nossa Senhora dos Remédios), Vila Real (noted for its splendid religious architecture) and Viseu (once the heart of Roman Lusitania).

Bragança, in the extreme north-east of the country, is dominated by its imposing medieval 13th century castle and was the seat of the Bragança family who ruled Portugal from 1640 to 1910. The Montanhas region also contains many unspoilt historic villages, including Almeida, Idhana-a-Velha, Monsanto, Piódão and Sortelha.

Although crossed from the west to east by the IP3, IP4 and IP5 highways, the region doesn't have particularly good road communications and public transport is relatively poor (many areas are accessible only by private car). The region is of little interest to foreign homebuyers, although it's an excellent choice for those wishing to escape the 20th century with a love of the outdoor life.

Planícies (plains): The Planícies region includes the inland provinces of the Alentejo (the provinces of Alto Alentejo and Baixo Alentejo) and most of the province of Ribatejo. It's Portugal's largest and least populated region covering around a third of the country from the River Tagus (or River Tejo – Alentejo simply means 'beyond the Tejo') in the north to the Algarve in the south, and from the Atlantic Ocean to the Spanish border. South of the River Tagus (which divides Portugal in two) the huge Alentejo plain of rolling grasslands and wheat fields stretches all the way to the Algarve. It's a majestic, timeless land of vast plains and rolling hills, with an austere beauty that's a constant delight to nature lovers. The land is divided into vast agricultural estates, which are still based on the original country estates (*latifúndio*) established by the Romans two thousand years ago. Virtually the only industry in the region is agriculture augmented by forestry and tourism. The fertile coastal areas are the granary of Portugal and produce most of the country's food (the region is famous for its traditional cooking, virtually unchanged for centuries), while further inland are huge cork-oak forests (Portugal is the world's largest producer of cork) and numerous olive groves. The region is also noted for its horse (Arabian) and bull breeding.

Planícies is famous for its wealth of striking fortified villages, many perched on hilltops surrounded by medieval walls, including Alter do Chão, Castelo de Vide, Evora-Monte, Marvão, Nisa, Monsaraz and Portalegre (famous for its old tapestry factory). Évora, the capital of Alto Alentejo, was once the political centre of Roman Iberia and is one of the most beautiful and historic towns in Portugal (it has UNESCO World Heritage status). Borba, Estremoz and Vila Viçosa (which was often given to Portugal's queens as a wedding present) are known as 'marble towns' after their marble streets, mansions and marble-adorned churches. Other historic towns include Arraiolos (famous for its tapestries and rugs), Beja (the capital of Baixa Alentejo founded by Julius Caesar), Elvas (a fortress town with Roman-Arab castle), Mèrtola, Santarém and Serpa. There are a number of low-key resorts on the Atlantic coast with good beaches, including Odeceixe, Vila Nova de Milfontes and Zambujeira do Mar.

Although the region has reasonable road communications, it doesn't have any motorways and public transport is poor (many areas are accessible only by private car). The region has traditionally been of little interest to foreign homebuyers, although it will appeal to those seeking peace and solitude.

RESEARCH

There's a huge choice of property for sale in Portugal, which is a buyers' market in most areas (the exceptions are Lisbon, Porto and luxury developments on the Algarve) and is likely to remain that way for many years. As when buying property anywhere, it's never wise to be in too much of a hurry. It's a wise or lucky person who gets his choice absolutely right first time, which is why most experts recommend that you rent before buying unless you're absolutely sure what you want, how much you wish to pay and where you want to live. Have a good look around in your chosen region(s) and obtain an accurate picture of the types of properties available, their relative prices and what you can expect to get for your money. However, before doing this, you should make a comprehensive list of what you want (and don't want) from a home, so that you can narrow the field and save time on wild goose chases. In most areas, properties for sale include derelict farmhouses, unmodernised village homes, modern townhouses and apartments with all modern conveniences, and a wide choice of detached villas. You can also buy a plot of land and have an individual, architect-designed house built to your own specifications. If, however, after discussing it at length with your partner one of you insists on a new luxury apartment on the Algarve and the other an 18th century farmhouse in Trás-os-Montes, the easiest solution may be to get a divorce!

To reduce the chances of making an expensive error when buying in an unfamiliar region, it's often prudent to rent a house for a period (see **Renting** on page 139), taking in the worst part of the year (weather-wise). This allows you to become familiar with the region and the weather, and gives you plenty of time to look around for a home at your leisure. There's no shortage of properties for sale in Portugal (indeed, in many resort areas there's a glut) and whatever kind of property you're looking for, you will have an abundance from which to choose. Wait until you find something you fall head over heels in love with and then think about it for another week or two before rushing headlong to the altar! One of the advantages of buying property in Portugal is that there's usually another 'dream' home around the next corner – and the second or third dream home is often even better than the first. Better to miss the 'opportunity of a lifetime' than end up with an expensive pile of stones around your neck! **However, don't dally too long, as good properties at the right price don't remain on the market forever.**

If you're looking for a holiday home (*segunda casa/residência*), you may wish to investigate mobile homes or a scheme that restricts your occupancy of a property to a number of weeks each year. These include shared ownership, leaseback and timesharing (see page 158). However, don't rush into any of these schemes without fully researching the market and before you're absolutely clear about what you want and what you can realistically expect to get for your money. The more research you do before buying a property in Portugal the better, which should (if possible) include advice from those who already own a home there, from whom you can usually obtain invaluable information (often based on their own mistakes). Many people set themselves impossible deadlines in which to buy a property or business (e.g. a few days or a week) and often end up bitterly regretting their impulsive decision. Although it's a common practice, mixing a holiday with property purchase isn't wise, as most people are inclined to make poor decisions when their mind is fixed on play, rather than business.

Publications & Exhibitions: Outbound Publishing produces *World of Property* (see **Appendix A**), a bimonthly magazine containing many properties for sale in Portugal (and other countries) and organise regular property exhibitions in the UK. Other international property exhibitions that include Portugal are organised by *International Property* magazine (see **Appendix A**). Property is also advertised for sale in many newspapers and magazines in Portugal and abroad (see **Appendix A**), and on the Internet.

Independent Advice and Information: A useful source of information for prospective homebuyers in Portugal is the Association of Foreign Property Owners in Portugal (AFPOP), Rua Infante D. Henrique 22-2º, 8500 Portimão (☎ 282-458 509, ✉ afpop@ip.pt). AFPOP publishes a newsletter; provides accountancy, building, investment and legal consultancies; maintains a list of recommended professionals; and offers advice on anything to do with buying, letting and maintaining a home in Portugal.

AVOIDING PROBLEMS

The problems associated with buying property abroad have been highlighted in the last decade or so, during which the property market in many countries has gone from boom to bust and (almost) back again. From a legal viewpoint, Portugal isn't always one of the safest places in which to buy a home, although buyers have a high degree of protection under Portuguese law. However, although the pitfalls must never be ignored, buying property in Portugal is usually safe. There are tens of thousands of foreign property owners in Portugal and several million Portuguese owners, the vast majority of whom are happy with their purchases and who encountered few or no problems when buying their homes. This should be borne in mind when you hear or read horror stories concerning foreign buyers in Portugal.

The possible dangers haven't been emphasised to discourage you, but simply to ensure that you go into a purchase with your eyes open and to help you avoid problems (forewarned is forearmed). It cannot be emphasised too strongly that anyone planning to buy property in Portugal must take expert, independent legal advice. Never sign anything, or pay any money, until you've sought legal advice in a language in which you're fluent, from an independent lawyer who's experienced in Portuguese property law. If you aren't prepared to do this, you shouldn't even think about buying property in Portugal!

Legal Advice: The vast majority of buyers in Portugal (and most other countries) don't obtain independent legal advice. Most people who experience problems take no precautions whatsoever when purchasing property and of those that do take legal advice, many do so only after having already paid a deposit and signed a contract (or when they hit problems). You will find that the relatively small price (in comparison to the cost of a home) of obtaining legal advice to be excellent value for money, if only for the peace of mind it affords. Trying to cut corners to save on legal costs is foolhardy in the extreme when tens of thousands (or hundreds of thousands) of euros are at stake. **However, be careful whom you engage, as some lawyers are part of the problem rather than the solution (overcharging is also common)!** Don't pick a lawyer at random, but engage one who has been recommended by someone you can trust.

Employing Professionals: There are professionals speaking English and other foreign languages in many areas of Portugal, and a number of expatriate professionals (e.g. architects, builders and surveyors) also practise there. However, don't assume that because you're dealing with a fellow countryman that he will offer you a better deal or do a better job than a Portuguese (the contrary is often true). It's wise to check the credentials of all professionals you employ, whatever their nationality. It's never wise to rely solely on advice proffered by those with a financial interest in selling you a property, such as a developer or estate agent, although their advice may be excellent and totally unbiased. **You should also avoid 'cowboy' agents and anyone who does property deals on the side (such as someone you meet in a bar or restaurant), as dealing with them often leads to heartache.**

Problems: Among the problems that can be experienced by buyers in Portugal are properties purchased without a legal title; properties built or enlarged illegally without planning permission; properties with missing infrastructure; builders or developers going bust or absconding with their clients' money; undischarged mortgages from the previous owner; properties sold with outstanding bills for utilities or rates; intermediaries disappearing with the seller's proceeds (possibly after having been given power of attorney); overcharging by vendors (particularly when selling to foreigners); and properties sold to more than one buyer. Note that in the not too distant past, many properties in Portugal were built without planning permission, weren't constructed according to the approved plans or were built on land that wasn't zoned for building in the first place.

Mistakes: Among the mistakes made by buyers in Portugal are buying in the wrong area (**rent first!**); buying a home that's unsaleable; buying a property for renovation and grossly underestimating the restoration costs; not having a survey done on an old property; not taking legal advice; not including the necessary conditional clauses in the contract; buying a property for business, e.g. to convert to self-catering accommodation, and being too optimistic about the income; and taking on too large a mortgage. It's possible when buying a property directly from the vendor that he may suggest you pay part of the price with an 'under the table' cash payment, thus lowering the price declared to the tax authorities and reducing the vendor's capital gains tax liability. You will also save money on taxes and fees, but will have a higher capital gains tax bill when you sell. Bear in mind that if you're selling a property and the buyer refuses to make the 'illicit' payment after the contract has been signed, you will have no legal redress! **You should steer well clear of this practice, which is naturally strictly illegal.** Checks must be carried out both before signing a promissory contract (*contrato de promessa de compra e venda*) and before signing the deed of sale (*escritura*). If you get into a dispute over a property deal it can take years to have it resolved in the Portuguese courts and even then there's no guarantee that you will receive satisfaction.

Subrogation: One of the Portuguese laws that property buyers should be aware of is the law of subrogation, whereby property debts, including mortgages, local taxes and community charges, remain with a property and are inherited by the buyer. This is an open invitation to dishonest sellers to 'cut and run'. It is, of course, possible to check whether there are any outstanding debts on a property and this should be done by your legal advisor on the day of completion (see page 173), although the system isn't failsafe. When buying property in Portugal you should deal only with a government-registered estate agent (*mediador autorizado*) and employ an English-speaking lawyer to protect your interests and carry out the necessary searches. It's necessary to ensure that a property is free of debts and liens via a certificate (*certidão de registro*) from the local land registry. The deeds (*escritura*) must be registered as soon as possible after completion.

Buying Off-plan: Many problems can arise when buying off-plan, i.e. unbuilt properties, or a property on an unfinished development (urbanisation). Because of the problems associated with buying off-plan, such as the difficulty in ensuring that you actually get what is stated in the contract and that the developer doesn't go broke, some people advise against buying an unfinished property. A 'finished' property is a property where the building is complete in every detail (as confirmed by your own architect), all communal services have been completed, and all infrastructure is in place such as roads, parking areas, external lighting, landscaping, water, sewerage, electricity and telephone services. A builder is supposed to provide buyers who purchase off-plan with an insurance policy or banker's 'termination' guarantee, which protects buyers against the builder going broke before construction is completed.

Take Your Time: Many people have had their fingers burnt by rushing into property deals without taking proper care and consideration. It's all too easy to fall in love with the attractions of a home in the sun and to sign a contract without giving it sufficient thought. If you aren't absolutely certain, don't allow yourself to be rushed into making a hasty decision, e.g. by fears of an imminent price or exchange rate rise or of losing the property to another buyer who has 'made an offer'. Although many people dream of buying a holiday or retirement home in Portugal, it's vital to do your homework thoroughly and avoid the 'dream sellers' (often fellow countrymen) who will happily prey on your ignorance and tell you anything in order to sell you a home.

CHOOSING THE LOCATION

The most important consideration when buying a home in Portugal is usually its location – or as the old adage goes, the three most important points are location, location and location! A property in a reasonable condition in a popular area is likely to be a better investment than an exceptional property in a less attractive location. There's usually no point in buying a dream property in a terrible location. Portugal offers almost anything that anyone could want, but you must choose the right property in the right spot. **The wrong decision regarding location is one of the main causes of disenchantment among foreigners who have purchased property in Portugal.**

Where you buy a property in Portugal will depend on a range of factors, including your personal preferences, your financial resources and, not least, whether you plan to work or not. If you have a job in Portugal, the location of your home will probably be determined by the proximity to your place of employment. However, if you intend to look for employment or start a business, you must live in an area that allows you the maximum scope. Unless you have good reason to believe otherwise, it would be foolish to rely on finding employment in a particular area. If, on the other hand, you're looking for a holiday or retirement home, the whole of Portugal is your oyster. The most popular areas are the Algarve and the Costa do Sol in the Lisbon Coast region. When seeking a permanent home, don't be too influenced by where you've spent an enjoyable holiday or two. A town or area that was adequate for a few weeks' holiday may be totally unsuitable for a permanent home, particularly regarding the proximity to shops, medical services, and sports and leisure facilities. Bear in mind when buying an investment property that you're planning to let, that you must choose the location and local amenities with this in mind (the property may not be what you would choose for yourself or for your retirement).

If you have little idea about where you wish to live, read as much as you can about the different regions of Portugal (see **Regions** on page 121) and spend some time looking around your areas of interest. Bear in mind that the climate, lifestyle and cost of living can vary considerably from region to region (and even within a particular region). Before looking at properties it's important to have a good idea of the type of property you want and the price you wish to pay, and to draw up a shortlist of your areas or towns of interest. Most importantly, make a list of what you want and don't want in a property, as if you don't do this, you're likely to be overwhelmed by the number of properties to be viewed.

The 'best' area in which to live depends on a range of considerations, including the proximity to your place of work, schools, bars, shops, businesses, public transport, bars, entertainment and sports facilities (and bars), etc. Also whether you wish to be located in the country or a town, on the coast or inland. There are beautiful areas to choose from throughout Portugal, most within easy travelling distance of a town or city (and a bar). Don't, however, always believe the travelling times and distances stated in adverts and quoted by estate agents. According to some developers and agents, everywhere in the Algarve is handy for Faro airport and anywhere on the Costa de Prata is a stone's throw from Lisbon or Porto airport. When looking for a home, bear in mind travelling times and costs to your place of work, shops and schools (and the local bar/restaurant). If you buy a remote country property, the distance to local amenities and services could become a problem, particularly if you plan to retire to Portugal. Although Portugal is a small country, if you live in the country you will need to use the car for everything (which will increase your cost of living) and will also generally need to be much more self-sufficient than if you live in a town.

If possible you should visit an area a number of times over a period of a few weeks, both on weekdays and at weekends, in order to get a feel for a neighbourhood (it's better to walk rather than drive around). A property seen on a balmy summer's day after a delicious lunch and a few glasses of *vinho branco* may not be nearly so attractive on a subsequent visit *sem* sunshine and the warm inner glow. If possible, you should also visit an area at different times of the year, e.g. in both summer and winter, as somewhere that's wonderful in summer can be forbidding and inhospitable in winter (or vice versa if you don't like extreme heat). In any case, you should view a property a number of times before deciding to buy it. If you're unfamiliar with an area, most experts recommend that you rent for a period before deciding to buy (see **Renting** on page 139). This is particularly important if you're planning to buy a permanent or retirement home in an unfamiliar area. Many people change their minds after a period and it isn't unusual for buyers to move once or twice before settling down permanently.

If you will be working in Portugal, obtain a map of the area and decide the maximum distance you will consider travelling to work, e.g. by drawing a circle with your workplace in the middle. Obtain a large-scale map of the area and mark the places that you've seen, at the same time making a list of the plus and minus points of each property. If you use an estate agent, he will usually drive you around and you can then return later to the properties that you like best at your leisure (provided that you've marked them on your map!). However, agents may be reluctant to give you the keys to visit a property on your own.

There are many other points to consider regarding the location of a home, which can roughly be divided into the local vicinity, i.e. the immediate surroundings and neighbourhood, and the general area or region. You will also need to take into account the present and future needs of all the members of your family, including the following:

- Do you want or need winter and summer sunshine? If you want it to be relatively warm all year-round, then the only real choice is Madeira. Although the Algarve is mild and pleasant in winter with daytime temperatures often a maximum of around 15 to 20°C. (60 to 68°F.), this can seem quite cool if you're accustomed to the heat of high summer (when air-conditioning is a blessed relief). Consider both the winter and summer climate, position of the sun, average daily sunshine, plus the rainfall and wind conditions (see **Climate** on page 50). The orientation or aspect of a building is vital and if you want morning or afternoon sun (or both) you must ensure that balconies, terraces and gardens are facing in the right direction.

- Check whether an area is particularly susceptible to natural disasters such as floods, storms or forest fires. If a property is located near a waterway, it may be expensive to insure against floods (or flash floods) which are a threat in some areas. In areas with little rainfall (such as the Algarve) there can be droughts resulting in water restrictions and high water bills.

- Noise can be a problem in Portugal. Although you cannot choose your neighbours, you can at least ensure that a property isn't located next to a busy road, industrial plant, commercial area, building site, discotheque, night club, bar or restaurant (where revelries may continue into the early hours). Look out for 'objectionable' neighbouring properties which may be too close to the one you're considering and check whether nearby vacant land has been zoned for commercial activities. In community developments (e.g. apartment blocks) many properties are second homes and are let short-term, which means you may need to tolerate boisterous holidaymakers as neighbours throughout the year (or at least during the summer months). In towns, traffic noise, particularly from motorcycles, may continue all night!

- Bear in mind that if you live in a popular tourist area, e.g. on the Algarve coast, you may be inundated with tourists in the summer. They will not only jam the roads and pack the beaches and shops, but also occupy your favourite table at your local bar or restaurant (heaven forbid!). Although a 'front-line' property on the beach sounds attractive and may be ideal for short holidays, it isn't always the best solution for permanent residents. Many beaches are hopelessly crowded in the peak season, streets may be smelly from restaurants and fast food joints, parking may be impossible, services stretched to breaking point, and the incessant noise may drive you crazy. You may also have to put up with water shortages, power cuts and sewage problems. Some people prefer to move inland to higher ground, where it's less humid, you're isolated from the noise and can also enjoy excellent views. On the other hand, getting to and from hillside properties can be precarious and roads are sometimes poorly maintained, narrow and lacking crash barriers (and are for sober, confident drivers only).

- Do you wish to live in an area with many other expatriates from your home country or as far away from them as possible (practically impossible in most areas of the Algarve)? If you wish to integrate with the local community, avoid the foreign 'ghettos' and choose a Portuguese village or an area or development with mainly local inhabitants. However, unless you speak fluent Portuguese or intend to learn it, you should think twice before buying a property in a village, although residents in rural areas who take the time and trouble to integrate into the local community are warmly welcomed. If you're buying a permanent home, it's important to check on your prospective neighbours, particularly when buying an apartment. For example, are they noisy, sociable or absent for long periods? Do you think you will get on with them? **Good neighbours are invaluable, particularly when buying a holiday home in a village.**

- On the other hand, if you wish to mix only with your compatriots and don't plan to learn Portuguese, then living in a predominantly foreign community may be ideal. Note that many developments and towns are inhabited largely by second homeowners and are like ghost towns for most of the year. In these areas many facilities, businesses and shops are closed outside the main tourist season, when even local services such as public transport and postal collections may be curtailed.

- Do you wish to be in a town or do you prefer the country? Inland or by the sea? How about living on an island? If you buy a property in the country you will need to tolerate poor public transport, relatively long travelling distances to a town of any size, solitude and remoteness, and possibly the high cost and amount of work involved in the upkeep of a country house and garden. You won't be able to pop along to the local shop for fresh bread, drop into the local bar for a glass of your favourite tipple with the locals, or have a choice of restaurants on your doorstep. In a town or large village, the weekly market will be just around the corner, the doctor and pharmacy close at hand, and if you need help or run into any problems, your neighbours will be nearby. If you live in a remote rural area, drainage is likely to be a septic tank, you will need to have your own well, take your garbage to a collection point and may even need to generate your own electricity.

On the other hand, in the country you will be closer to nature, will have more freedom (e.g. to make as much noise as you wish) and possibly complete privacy, e.g. to sunbathe or swim *au naturel*. Living in a remote area in the country will suit those looking for peace and quiet who don't want to involve themselves in the 'hustle and bustle' of town life (not that there's a lot of this in Portuguese rural towns). If you're after peace and quiet, make sure that there isn't a busy road or railway line nearby or a local church within 'donging' distance. Bear in mind that many people who buy a remote country home find that the peace of the countryside palls after a time and they yearn for the more exciting city or coastal nightlife. If you have never lived in the country, it's best to rent before buying. Note also that while it's cheaper to buy in a remote or unpopular location, it's usually much more difficult to find a buyer when you want to sell.

- If you're planning to buy a country property with a large garden or plot of land, bear in mind the high cost and amount of work involved in its upkeep. If it's to be a holiday home, who will look after the house and garden when you're away? Do you want to spend your holidays mowing the lawn and cutting back the undergrowth? Do you want a home with a lot of outbuildings? What are you going to do with them? Can you afford to convert them into extra rooms or guest accommodation?

- If you plan to work in Portugal, how secure is your job or business likely to be and are you liable to move to another area in the near future? Can you find other work in the same area, if necessary? If there's a possibility that you may need to move within a few years, you should rent or at least buy a property that will be relatively easy to sell and recoup the cost.

- What about your partner's and children's jobs, or your children's present and future schooling? What is the quality of local schools? Even if your family has no need or plans to use local schools, the value of a home is often enhanced by the quality and proximity of schools, and will be easier to sell.

- What local health and social services are provided? How far is the nearest hospital with an emergency department? Are there English-speaking doctors and dentists and 'foreign' clinics or hospitals in the area?

- What shopping facilities are provided in the neighbourhood? How far is it to the nearest sizeable town with good shopping facilities, e.g. a super/hypermarket? How would you get there if your car was out of order? Many rural villages are dying and have few shops or facilities, and aren't necessarily a good choice for a retirement home.

- What's the range and quality of local leisure, sports, community and cultural facilities? What is the proximity to sports facilities such as a beach, golf course, tennis courts, ski resort or waterway? Properties in or close to coastal resorts are considerably more expensive, although they also have the best letting potential.

- Is the proximity to public transport, e.g. an international airport, port or railway station, or access to a motorway important? Don't believe all you're told about the distance or travelling times to the nearest airport, railway station, motorway junction, beach or town, but check it yourself.

- If you're planning to buy in a town or city, is there adequate private or free on-street parking for your family and visitors? Is it safe to park in the street? It's important to have secure off-street parking in Portuguese cities if you value your car. Parking is a problem in cities and most large towns, where private garages or parking spaces are unobtainable or expensive. Traffic congestion is also a problem in many towns and tourist resorts, particularly during the high season. Note also that an apartment or townhouse in a town or community development may be some distance from the nearest road or car park. How do you feel about carrying heavy shopping hundreds of metres to your home and possibly up several flights of stairs? If you're planning to buy an apartment above the ground floor, you may wish to ensure that the building has a lift.

- What is the local crime rate? In many resort areas the incidence of housebreaking and burglary is high, which also results in more expensive home insurance. On the other hand, many modern developments in resort areas are noted for their high security. Check the crime rate in the local area, e.g. burglaries, housebreaking, stolen cars and crimes of violence. Is crime increasing or decreasing? Professional thieves like isolated houses, particularly those full of expensive furniture and other belongings, that they can strip bare at their leisure. You're much less likely to be the victim of thieves if you live in a village, where crime is usually low (strangers stand out like sore thumbs in villages, where their every move is monitored by the local populace).

● Is the local council well run? What are the views of other residents? If the municipality is efficiently run you can usually rely on good local services and facilities. In areas where there are many foreign residents, the town hall (*câmara*) may have a foreign residents' department (*departamento de estrangeiros*).

RENTING

If you're uncertain about exactly what sort of home you want and where you wish to live, it's best to rent for a period in order to reduce the chances of making a costly error. **Renting long-term before buying is particularly prudent for anyone planning to live in Portugal permanently.** If possible you should rent a similar property to that which you're planning to buy, during the time of year when you plan to occupy it. Renting allows you to become familiar with the weather, the amenities and the local people; to meet other foreigners who have made their homes in Portugal and share their experiences; and, not least, to discover the cost of living at first hand. Provided you still find Portugal appealing, renting 'buys' you time to find your dream home at your leisure. You may even wish to consider renting a home long-term (or even 'permanently') as an alternative to buying, as it saves tying up your capital and can be surprisingly inexpensive in many regions. Some people let out their family homes abroad and rent one in Portugal, when it's even possible to make a profit.

If you're looking for a rental property for a few months, e.g. three to six months, it's best not to rent unseen, but to rent a holiday apartment for a week or two to allow yourself time to look around for a longer term rental. Properties for rent are advertised in local newspapers and magazines (where you can also place a 'wanted' ad.), particularly in English-language publications. They can also be found through property publications in many other countries (see **Appendix A** for a list). Estate agents in Portugal often offer both short and long-term rentals, and developers may also rent properties to potential buyers. A rental contract (*contrato de arrendamento*) is necessary when renting a property in Portugal, whether long or short-term.

Long-term Rentals: Portugal doesn't have a flourishing long-term (i.e. six months or longer) rental market in resort areas, where it's more common for people to buy, although there's an adequate choice of long-term rentals in most regions, including everything from studio apartments to luxurious villas with private swimming pools. Most properties in resort areas are let furnished (*mobiliado*), whether long or short-term, and long-term unfurnished (*desmobiliado, sem mobília*) properties are difficult to find. On the other hand, in major cities long-term rentals are usually let unfurnished and furnished properties are difficult to find. Rental costs vary considerably according to the size (number of bedrooms) and quality of a property, its age and the facilities provided. However, the most significant factor affecting rents is the region, the city or town, and the particular neighbourhood.

Long-term rentals are good value in resort areas outside the main summer season (when they're rare), where it's possible to rent a property for the entire winter season. Rentals of one year or longer are difficult to find in the Algarve and are generally very expensive. In major cities, rents are high (in relation to salaries) and contracts are commonly for one year and renewable by mutual agreement between the landlord and tenant. Portuguese law is heavily weighted in favour of tenants and this acts as a deterrent to landlords who fear being unable to get rid of a tenant when a contract terminates. Long-term rentals don't usually include utilities such as gas and electricity (or heating).

Short-term Rentals: Short-term rentals are always furnished and are usually for holiday lets of a few weeks or months. A short-term or temporary contract is necessary, which provides tenants with less rights than a long-term contract. There's an abundance of self-catering properties for rent in Portugal, including apartments, cottages, farmhouses, townhouses and villas. Rents for short-term rentals are much higher than for longer lets, particularly in popular holiday areas where many properties are let as self-catering holiday accommodation. However, many agents let self-catering properties in resort areas at a considerable reduction during the 'low' season, which may extend from October to April.

The rent for an average one or two bedroom furnished apartment or townhouse during the low season is usually from €600 to €900 per month for a minimum one or two month let. Rent is usually paid one month in advance with one month's rent as a deposit. Lets of less than a month are more expensive, e.g. €300 to €450 per week for a two-bedroom apartment in the low season, which is some 50 per cent of the rent levied in the high season. Many hotels and hostels also offer special low rates for long stays during the low season (see below). Note, however, that when the rental period includes the peak letting months of July and August, the rent can be prohibitively high (the Algarve is one of Europe's most expensive regions in which to rent a summer holiday home). Standards vary considerably, from dilapidated ill-equipped apartments to luxury villas with every modern convenience. Check whether a property is fully equipped (which should mean whatever you want it to mean) and whether it has heating if you're planning to rent in winter. Rentals can be found by contacting owners advertising in the publications listed in **Appendix A** and through estate agents in most areas of Portugal, many of whom also handle short-term lets.

Hotels: Hotel rates in Portugal vary with the time of year, the exact location and the individual establishment, although you may be able to haggle over rates outside the high season and for long stays. Hotels located in large towns and cities, coastal resorts and spa towns are the most expensive, and rates in Lisbon and Porto are similar to other major European cities. However, inexpensive hotels and other accommodation can be found in most towns, where a single room (*quarto individual*) can usually be found for €20 to €30 and a double (*quarto duplo*) for €30 to €40 (usually with a private bath or shower). Hotel rates are fairly consistent throughout Portugal.

Minimum and maximum rates are fixed according to the facilities and the season, although there's no season in the major cities or in Madeira. Rates are considerably higher in tourist areas during the high season of July and August, when rooms at any price are hard to find. On the other hand, outside the main season (particularly in winter) some hotels offer low half or full board rates, when a double room with a bath, including dinner (buffet) and breakfast can be found for €40 for two (there are even better rates for stays of a week or longer). Some hotels and apart-hotels ('hotels' consisting of self-contained apartments) also offer special low rates for long-stay winter guests. However, hotels aren't usually a cost-effective, long-term solution for home hunters, although there may be little choice if you need accommodation for a short period only. Inexpensive bed and breakfast (e.g. a *pensão, residéncia* or *quarto*) accommodation is also available in Portugal.

Home Exchange: An alternative to renting is to exchange your home abroad with one in Portugal. This way you can experience home-living abroad for a relatively small cost and may save you the expense of a long-term rental (if you decide you don't want to buy a home there). Although there's an element of risk involved in exchanging your home with another family – depending on whether your swap is made in heaven or hell! – most agencies thoroughly vet clients and have a track record of successful swaps. There are home exchange agencies in most countries, many of which are members of the International Home Exchange Association (IHEA).

The best place to find or contact home exchange organisations is via the Internet where you will find 🖳 www.digsville.com (American-oriented with a retro-hippy feel), 🖳 www.intervac.com (large membership, long-established), www.homebase-hols.com, 🖳 www.homeexchange.com (boasts 250,000 requests per month from over 70 countries, with most properties in North America), 🖳 www.homelink.org.uk (over 12,000 members – one of the largest and best-known companies), 🖳 www. landfair.com (provides a custom-matching service for US$250) and 🖳 www. webhomeexchange.com (American oriented). There are also many specialist agencies for particular groups such as teachers (🖳 www.teacherstravelweb. com), Christians (🖳 www.christianhomeexchange.com) and gays (🖳 www.well.com/user/ homeswap). See also **Property Income** on page 192.

COST

Property prices soared throughout Portugal in the 1980s, particularly in the major cities, where prices rose dramatically. In resort areas such as the

Algarve, rising prices were fuelled by the high demand for holiday homes from foreigners. However, as the recession hit Portugal in the late 1980s and early 1990s, the stream of buyers dried up leaving developers and agents with a glut of unsold properties. During this period there were bargains around when some owners and developers were forced to sell, although prices held up remarkably well during the recession (although sales plummeted). In contrast, prices in the major cities have continued rising due to a constant and largely unfulfilled demand for homes from Portuguese flocking to the cities from rural areas. There's a chronic housing shortage in Lisbon and Porto, where housing costs are very high compared with the relatively low standard of living. The Algarve property market has made a spectacular recovery from the recession in the 1990s and sales are currently booming, particularly at the top end of the market where villas cost well over €1m. In some parts of the Algarve prices have risen by as much as 40 per cent since 1999, although the average price rise is around 15 per cent a year. Experts predict that this trend will continue for the next few years and at present in most resort areas in Portugal it's very much a seller's market. Demand for new and resale villas is exceptionally high and good quality properties are now in short supply.

Property prices in Portugal generally rise slowly and steadily (with the exception of the Algarve where the price rise has been spectacular since 1999), and are fairly stable, particularly in rural areas where there's little local demand and few non-resident owners. Apart from obvious factors such as size, quality and land area, the most important consideration influencing the price of a house is its location. The closer a property is to a major city or beach, the more expensive it will be. An average two-bedroom apartment on the Algarve coast costs at least two or three times as much in central Lisbon or Porto. Property is cheapest in rural areas, where a farmhouse with outbuildings and a large plot of land can cost the same as a studio apartment in a luxury Algarve development.

Properties for restoration and modernisation are widely available in rural areas, although you usually need to spend two to three times the purchase cost on restoration. The quality of properties varies considerably in respect to materials, fixtures and fittings, and workmanship. Value for money also varies considerably and you should compare at least five to ten properties to get a good idea of their relative values. You usually pay a premium for a beachside 'front-line' property or a property situated on or near a golf course. Property on the Algarve coast is generally of a high standard and good value for money (although not cheap), particularly for foreigners paying in currencies (such as the GB£) that have made large gains against the euro in recent years.

When property is advertised in Portugal, the total living area in square metres (*metros quadrados*), written as m^2, and the number of bedrooms (*quartos*) are usually stated. When comparing prices, compare the cost per square metre of the habitable or built area (*área de contrução*), excluding patios, terraces and balconies, which should be compared separately. If you're in any doubt about the size of rooms you should measure them yourself, rather than rely on the measurements provided by the vendor or agent. A garage (*garajem*) is rarely provided with apartments or townhouses in Portugal, although there may be a private parking space or a communal off-road parking area. Some apartment blocks have underground garages, and lock-up garages can sometimes be purchased separately for apartments and townhouses in resort areas. Villas usually have their own car port or garage. Without a garage, parking can be a nightmare, particularly in cities or busy resort towns and developments in summer.

Approximate prices for average properties on the Algarve coast (in an average resort or development) are listed below. Prices in other regions of Portugal (apart from Lisbon and Porto and a few fashionable areas such as the Lisbon coastal resorts of Cascais and Estoril) are lower than on the Algarve, while prices in Madeira are similar.

Property	Price (€)
Studio apartment	from 90,000
1 bedroom apartment	from 120,000
2 bedroom apartment	from 150,000
3 bedroom apartment	from 180,000
1 bedroom townhouse	from 150,000
2 bedroom townhouse	from 200,000
3 bedroom townhouse	from 250,000
2 bedroom-modernised cottage or village house	from 200,000
2 bedroom detached villa	from 400,000
3 bedroom detached villa	from 600,000
4 bedroom detached villa	from 900,000

It's possible to buy cheaper properties than those quoted above in unfashionable areas of towns and in rural areas, particularly older properties. On the other hand, properties in luxury developments offering a wide range of leisure and sports facilities are much more expensive (golf properties can be particularly expensive). For example, €200,000 for a tiny studio or one bedroom apartment, from €350,000 for a two bedroom apartment and €500,000 or more for a three bedroom apartment or townhouse. Bear in mind that the more expensive your home, the more you will have to pay in property taxes, which are based on a property's fiscal value (*valor tributável*).

Community fees for a community property (see page 153) also rise in direct relation to the size (and value) of a property. Luxury developments generally have high annual maintenance fees, e.g. from around €2,000 for a studio apartment to over €4,500 for a three-bedroom villa.

FEES

A variety of fees are payable when you buy a property in Portugal, which usually add between 10 and 15 per cent to the purchase price, which is higher than in many other EU countries. Most fees are based on the 'declared' or fiscal value (*valor tributável*) of the property, which was traditionally much lower than the actual price paid. However, the fiscal value of most properties has been reassessed in recent years and may now be close to actual market values. **Buyers should beware of declaring a price that's well below the actual value, for which there are stiff penalties.** The fees payable when buying a property in Portugal may include the following:

- transfer tax (resale properties only);
- value added tax (new properties only);
- notary's fees;
- legal fees;
- deed registration fee;
- surveyor's fee (optional);
- selling agent's fees;
- mortgage fees;
- utility fees (new properties only).

Most taxes are paid by the buyer or are included in the price. Always ensure that you know exactly what the total fees will be before signing a contract. **Note that transfer tax (SISA), notary and deed registration fees aren't applicable when buying a property owned by an offshore company (see page 172).**

Transfer Tax (SISA): SISA is one of Portugal's most controversial taxes and over recent years successive governments have made plans for legislation to either abolish the tax altogether or to substantially reduce its rates. However, in spite of much publicity and many hours of parliamentary time, SISA rates are much as they ever were and look like remaining so for the immediate future. This does not mean to say, however, that SISA won't be abolished in the future. At present SISA is payable on all resale properties (i.e. any property that isn't being sold for the first time) and is adjusted annually for inflation. In 2002 SISA rates were as shown in the table below:

Price (€)	SISA (%)	Deduction (€)
Up to 60,015	0	3,000
60,015 to 82,207	5	3,000
82,207 to 109,678	11	7,933
109,678 to 137,098	18	15,610
137,098 to 166,055	26	26,578
Over 166,055	10	none

Note that SISA isn't based on a sliding scale and the rate shown applies to the whole of the value of the property. The appropriate deduction is made after multiplying the property value by the relevant percentage. For example, if the declared value of a property is €150,000, SISA is 26 per cent (€39,000) minus €26,578, which equals a SISA bill for €12,422 (around 8 per cent). For a property declared as costing €200,000, SISA would be €20,000 (10 per cent).

SISA is charged at a fixed rate of 8 per cent on rustic (rural) property where no construction exists. Rural land with ruins and uninhabitable buildings registered as 'urban property' attract SISA at the rate of 8 per cent on the land and at the usual rates on the construction. Note, however, that it's unusual for a ruin to be valued at more than 8 per cent and many ruins are valued at a lower rate or are SISA exempt. SISA is payable at usual rates on building plots and land for construction. SISA must be paid before the signing of the final deed of sale (*escritura*) and is usually paid a few days earlier. The receipt must be presented to the notary at the completion and is retained by him (so obtain a copy for your records).

If the sale isn't made in euros, a statement must be obtained from a local bank stating the rate of exchange for the SISA calculation. If you're buying a new apartment or townhouse and are the first purchaser, a proportion of the original SISA paid on the land should be deducted from the SISA payable (but you must apply for this concession). If you pay SISA on a property you may not be required to pay property tax for a period, depending on the property's rateable value (see **Property Tax** on page 109).

Value Added Tax: Value added tax (*IVA*) of 19 per cent is levied on new properties purchased from a developer or builder and being sold for the first time. VAT should be included in an advertised or agreed price and not added afterwards, but you should check this carefully.

Notary's Fees: The fees for the notary who officiates at a sale are fixed by law and used to depend on the sale price. However, new legislation has introduced a fixed system under which notaries charge around €153 per transaction plus additional charges of €1.25 per amendment or clause in the document. There may also be other additional costs (usually small amounts).

Legal Fees: Legal fees for the conveyancing (see page 166) involved in a property sale are usually 1 to 2 per cent of the purchase price for an average property. The actual amount depends on the work involved, although there's usually a minimum charge, e.g. €1,000. Fees, which should be agreed in writing beforehand, are much lower if a lawyer is engaged only to vet the sales contract. **Engaging a lawyer and paying legal fees is optional, although it's highly recommended.**

Deed Registration Fee: The registration fees for registering a deed of sale at the land registry (*conservatória do registo predial*) are approximately 0.75 to 1 per cent of the property's value. The deed registration fee is paid to the notary with his fee for completing the sale.

Surveyor's Fee: If you employ a surveyor (see page 164) to inspect a building or plot of land, the fee will depend on the type of survey, any special requirements and the value of the property. A homebuyer's survey and valuation for a property valued at up to €200,000 is usually from around €550 and a full structural survey on the same property is around €800.

Selling Agent's Fees: The selling agent's fees are usually between 5 and 10 per cent of the selling price, depending on the cost of the property and the type of contract, and are paid by the vendor. However, they're usually allowed for in the asking price, so in effect are paid by the buyer.

Utility Fees: If you buy a new property you may need to pay for electricity, gas and water connections, and the installation of meters. If they aren't included in the price, you should ask the builder or developer to provide the cost of connection to all services in writing.

Mortgage Fees: Mortgage fees may include a commitment fee, an arrangement fee (usually 1 per cent of the loan amount), an administration fee (e.g. 1 per cent), and an appraisal or valuation fee.

Running Costs: In addition to the fees associated with buying a property, you should also take into account the running costs. These include local property taxes (rates); community fees for a community property (see page 153); garden and pool maintenance (for a private villa); building and contents insurance (see page 61); standing charges for utilities (electricity, gas, telephone, water); plus a caretaker's fees or management charges if you leave a home empty or let it. Annual running costs usually average around 2 to 3 per cent of the cost of a property.

BUYING A NEW HOME

New properties are widely available in Portugal and include coastal and city apartments and townhouses, luxury developments (e.g. golf or marina) and a wide range of individually designed villas. Most new properties (particularly in the Algarve) are part of purpose-built developments, many of which are planned as holiday homes and may not be attractive as permanent homes. If you're buying an apartment or house that's part of a community development, check whether your neighbours will be mainly Portuguese or foreigners. Some foreigners don't wish to live in a community consisting mainly of their fellow countrymen (or other foreigners) and this may also deter buyers when you wish to sell. On the other hand, some foreigners don't want to live in a Portuguese community, particularly if they don't speak Portuguese.

Prices of new properties vary considerably with their location and quality, from around €100,000 for a studio or one-bedroom apartment in a resort; from €130,000 for a two-bedroom apartment or from €150,000 in the case of a townhouse; from €150,000 for a three-bedroom apartment or townhouse; and from around €700,000 for a four-bedroom detached villa. It's often cheaper to buy a new home than an old property requiring modernisation or renovation, as the price is fixed, unlike the cost of renovation which can soar way beyond original estimates (as many people have discovered to their cost). If required, a new property can usually be let immediately and modern homes have good resale potential and are considered a good investment by Portuguese buyers. On the other hand, new homes may be smaller than older properties, have smaller gardens and rarely come with a large plot of land. New properties are covered by a warranty against structural defects.

Most new properties are sold by property developers (*promotor/ promovedor*) or builders (*construtor*), although they're also marketed by estate agents. New developments usually have a sales office and a show house or apartment (*casa modelo*). When a building is purchased off-plan, payment is made in stages as building work progresses. **Note that it's important to ensure that each stage is completed satisfactorily before making payments.** If you aren't able to do this yourself, you should engage an independent representative (e.g. an architect or structural engineer) to do it on your behalf. It has been calculated that around half of all new properties have construction defects or deficiencies and in around a third of cases the contract conditions aren't fulfilled, particularly regarding the completion date and the quality of materials used. If you're buying a property off-plan, you can usually choose your bathroom suite, kitchen, fireplace, wallpaper and paint, wall and floor tiles, and carpet in bedrooms, all of which may be included in the price. You may also be able to alter the interior room layout, although this will increase the price. It's best to make any changes or additions to a property during the design stage, such as including a more luxurious kitchen, a chimney or an additional shower room, as they will cost much more to install later.

The quality of new property in Portugal has improved considerably in recent years and generally ranges from good to excellent. The best (and most expensive) properties are often built by foreign builders, possibly using quality imported materials and fittings such as doors, windows, and bathroom and kitchen suites, in order to ensure a high standard. The quality of a building and the materials used will be reflected in the price, so when comparing prices ensure that you're comparing similar quality. Cheaper properties aren't usually the best built, although there are exceptions. If you want a permanent, rather than a holiday home, you're better off opting for quality rather than quantity. The average price for new properties on the Algarve is between €500 to €1,750 per square metre, depending on the quality, plus the cost of land.

The word luxury is often used loosely by builders and developers in Portugal and should be taken with a pinch of salt (it should mean what you want it to mean). A luxury apartment or townhouse should include some or most of the following: a full-size, fully fitted kitchen (possibly with a microwave, hob/oven with extractor hood, dishwasher, fridge/freezer and washing machine); a utility room; large bathrooms (often en suite to all bedrooms) with bidets and dressing areas; a separate shower room; air-conditioning and central heating (possibly under-floor) in the lounge and bedrooms; double glazing and shutters (possibly electric) on all windows; cavity walls (for sound deadening and cooling); one or more fireplaces; a wall safe; ceramic tiled floors in the kitchen and bathrooms, and marble-tiled floors in other rooms; fitted carpets in all bedrooms and dressing rooms; built-in mirror-fronted wardrobes in bedrooms; communal satellite TV; telephone outlets; 24-hour security and resident concierge; panic call buttons and intercom to a concierge; automatic lifts; basement car parking; and a lockable basement storage room.

Luxury properties that are part of a community (see page 153) also have a wide range of quality community facilities such as indoor (heated) and outdoor swimming pools, tennis courts and beautiful landscaped gardens. Some properties have an associated golf or country club with a golf course, tennis and squash courts, health spa, gymnasium, swimming pools, sauna, Jacuzzi, snooker and indoor bowling, plus a restaurant and bar. Most new developments have their own sales offices, usually offering a full management and rental service for non-resident owners. If you wish to furnish a property solely for letting, furniture packages are available and are usually good value for money. The complete furnishing of a holiday home costs from around €3,000 for one bedroom, €3,500 for two bedrooms and €4,000 for three bedrooms, although if you require good quality or luxury fittings prices are considerably higher.

Resale 'New' Homes: Buying 'new' doesn't necessarily mean buying a brand new home where you're the first occupant. There are many advantages in buying a modern resale home which may include better value for money; an established development with a range of local services and facilities in operation; more individual design and style; the eradication of 'teething troubles'; furniture and other extras included in the price; a mature garden and trees; and a larger plot of land. With a resale property you can see exactly what you will get for your money (unlike when buying off-plan), most problems will have been resolved, and the previous owners may have made improvements or added extras (such as a swimming pool) which may not be fully reflected in the asking price. See also **Buying a Resale Home** on page 152.

Building Your Own Home

If you want to be far from the madd(en)ing crowd, you can buy a plot of land (*lote*) and have an individual architect-designed house built to your own design and specifications or to a standard design provided by a builder (some properties are specifically designed so that you can start with one or two bedrooms and add more later if desired or as your finances allow). Note, however, that building a home in Portugal isn't for the faint-hearted. Portuguese red tape and the often eccentric ways of doing business can make building your own home a nightmare and it's fraught with problems. However, there are many excellent builders in Portugal (both Portuguese and foreign) who will build an individually designed house on your plot of land or will sell you a plot and build a house chosen from a range of standard designs.

The Cost: The cost of land with planning approval in Portugal varies considerably depending on the area, e.g. from around €25 to €40 per m² for a rural location, from €125 to €140 per m² for a rural location in easy reach of the coast and from €400 to €900 per m² for a prime coastal plot in the Algarve (or even more for the very best locations) where there's currently a shortage of plots. However, further inland the price may be just a tenth of that on the coast and in rural areas agricultural land can be exceedingly cheap, costing as little as a few euros per m². Land usually represents as much as half the cost of building a home in a prime area, although it's still possible in many areas to buy a plot of land and build a bigger and better home for less than the cost of a resale property. Building your own home allows you to not only design your own home, but to ensure that the quality of materials and workmanship are first class. Building costs range from around €500 to €1,500 per square metre in resort areas, depending on the quality and the location. SISA at 10 per cent is payable on building land (see page 144).

Buying a Building Plot: You must take the same care when buying land as you would when buying a home. The most important point is to ensure that it has been approved for building and that the plot is large enough and suitable for the house you plan to build. It may also be possible to build on agricultural land, but there are strict limits on plot and building sizes. You can obtain this information from the local town hall in a usage licence (*licença de utilização*). Some plots are unsuitable for building, as they're too steep or require prohibitively expensive foundations. Also check that there aren't any restrictions such as high-tension electricity lines, water pipes or rights of way which may restrict building.

Bear in mind that the cost of providing services to a property in a remote rural area may be prohibitively expensive and it must have a reliable water supply. When buying land for building, you should ensure that the purchase contract is dependent on obtaining the necessary building licence (*licença de obras*). Obtain a receipt showing that the plot is correctly presented in the local property register and check for yourself that the correct planning permission has been obtained (don't simply leave it to the builder). If planning permission is flawed or a building is built illegally, you can be heavily fined and a building may even need to be demolished! Note that it can take a long time to obtain planning permission in Portugal.

Most builders offer package deals, which include the land and the cost of building your home. However, it isn't always wise to buy the building plot from the builder who's going to build your home, and you should shop around and compare separate land and building costs. **If you do decide to buy a package deal from a builder, you must insist on separate contracts for the land and the building, and obtain the title deed for the land before signing a building contract.** If you're having a home built on an existing urbanisation, you must ensure that the urbanisation has been approved.

Finding an Architect & Builder: When looking for an architect (*arquitecto*) and builder (*construtor*) it's best to obtain recommendations from local people you can trust, e.g. an estate agent (*notário*) neighbours and friends. Note, however, that estate agents and other professionals aren't always the best people to ask, as they may receive a commission. You can also obtain valuable information from local residents and from owners of properties in an area that you particularly like. Many Portuguese architects speak English and there are also architects from other EU countries working in the main resort areas. Architects' fees are usually calculated as a percentage of the total costs of the work, usually around 10 per cent, which doesn't encourage them to cut costs.

The most important consideration when building a new home is the reputation (and financial standing) of the builder. An architect should be able to recommend a number of reliable builders, who must be registered and have a permit (*alvará*), but you should also do your own research. However, you should be wary of an architect with his 'own' builder (or a builder with his own architect), as it's the architect's job to ensure that the builder does his work according to the plans and specifications (so you don't want their relationship to be too cosy). Inspect other homes a builder has built and check with the owners what problems they have had and whether they're satisfied. Building standards in Portugal vary considerably and you should never assume that the lowest offer is the best value for money.

It's imperative that the builder has an insurance policy (or 'termination' guarantee) to cover you in the event that he goes bust before completing the property and its infrastructure, which must be specified in the contract. An agreed court of arbitration should be included in the contract in the event of a dispute. If you want a house built in Portugal exactly to your specifications, you will need to personally supervise it every step of the way or employ an architect or structural engineer as a project manager. This will add around 5 per cent to the total building cost. Without close supervision it's highly likely that your instructions won't be followed.

Contracts: You should obtain written quotations (*citaçãos*) from a number of builders before signing a contract. One of the most important features of a home in Portugal is good insulation (against both heat and cold) and protection against humidity. The contract must include a detailed building description (down to the last detail such as light switches and power points) and a list of the materials to be used (with references to the architect's plans); the exact location and orientation of the building on the plot; the building and payment schedule, which must be in stages according to building progress (see page 169); a penalty clause for late completion; the retention of a percentage (e.g. 5 to 10 per cent) of the building costs as a guarantee against defects; and how disputes will be settled.

Ensure that the contract includes all costs, including the architect's fees (unless contracted separately). Note that architects' fees are set by the Architects' Association with whom all architects must be registered. Landscaping (if applicable); all permits and licences (including the costs of land segregation, the declaration of new building, and the horizontal division for a community property); and the connection of utilities (water, electricity, gas, etc.) to the house, not just to the building site, should be included in the contract. Before accepting a quotation, it's wise to have it checked by a building consultant to confirm that it's a fair deal. You should check whether the quotation (which must include *IVA* at 19 per cent) is an estimate or a fixed price, as sometimes the cost can escalate wildly due to contract clauses and changes made during building work. **It's vital to have a contract checked by a lawyer, as building contracts are often heavily biased in the builder's favour and give clients few rights in law.**

Warranties: Under Portuguese law, builders are responsible for minor defects for one year after completion and for structural defects for five years (less than in many other countries). It isn't uncommon to have problems during construction, particularly regarding material defects. If you do have problems, you must usually be extremely patient and persistent to obtain satisfaction. You should have a completed building checked by a structural surveyor for defects and a report drawn up, and if there are any defects, he should determine exactly who was responsible for them. Architects and builders in Portugal are required by law to have indemnity insurance, although many still try to avoid claims.

Habitation Licence & Registration: When a property has been completed the builder must arrange for an inspection (*visitoria*) by the local council to ensure that it has been constructed according to the plans and building regulations. After a satisfactory inspection, the local council issues a habitation licence (*licença de habitação*) and the final payment is due only after this has been issued. When this has been completed a property must be registered with the local authority (the plot must be registered before building work commences), the local tax office (*finanças*) and at the local land registry (*conservatória de registo predial*).

BUYING A RESALE HOME

Resale properties often represent good value for money in Portugal, particularly in resort areas, where the majority of apartments and townhouses are sold fully furnished, although the quality varies considerably (from beautiful to junk) and may not be to your taste. Luxury properties and villas are generally marketed as unfurnished, although it's common practice for the buyer to make an offer for all or part of the furniture. Another advantage of buying a resale property is that you can see exactly what you will get for your money and will save on the cost of installing water and electricity meters and telephone lines, or extending these services to a property. When buying a resale property in a development, it's best to ask the neighbours about any problems, community fees, planned developments and anything else that may affect your enjoyment of the property. Most residents are usually happy to tell you, unless of course they're trying to sell you their own property!

If you want a property with abundant charm and character, a building for renovation or conversion, outbuildings, or a large plot of land, then you must usually buy an old property. Note, however, that there's a relatively small market for old country homes such as farmhouses in Portugal, particularly inexpensive properties requiring renovation. Most old homes purchased by foreigners are in the hinterland of the Algarve, although houses for renovation for a reasonable asking price are becoming more difficult to find and you may need to look further afield. In many rural areas (including villages close to the coast), it's possible to buy old properties from around €50,000 (although the asking prices are sometimes ridiculous), but you will need to carry out major renovation and modernisation which may well double or treble the price.

Many old homes lack basic services such as electricity, a reliable water supply and sanitation. Because the purchase price is often low, many foreign buyers are lulled into a false sense of security and believe they're getting a wonderful bargain, without fully investigating the renovation costs. If you aren't into do-it-yourself in a big way, you may be better off buying a new or recently built property, as the cost of restoration can be prohibitively expensive. If you're planning to buy a property that needs restoration or renovation and you won't be doing the work yourself, obtain an accurate estimate of the costs before signing a contract. You should consider having a survey (see page 164) done on a resale property, as major problems can be found even in relatively new homes.

Bear in mind that if you buy and restore a property with the intention of selling it for a profit, you must take into account not only the initial price and the restoration costs, but also the fees and taxes included in the purchase, plus capital gains tax if it's a second home. It's often difficult to sell an old renovated property at a higher than average market price, irrespective of its added value. The Portuguese have little interest in old restored properties, which is an important point if you need to sell an old home quickly in an area that isn't popular with foreign buyers. If you're buying for investment, you're usually better off buying a new home.

Owners often advertise their property directly in the Portuguese and expatriate press in Portugal (see **Appendix A**) or by simply putting a for-sale (*vende-se*) sign in the window. Although you can save money by buying direct from an owner, particularly when he's forced to sell, you should employ a lawyer to carry out the necessary checks (see **Conveyancing** on page 166). If you're unsure of the value of a property, you should obtain a professional valuation.

COMMUNITY PROPERTIES

In Portugal, properties with common elements (whether a building, amenities or land) shared with other properties are owned outright through a system of co-ownership, similar to owning a condominium (*condomínio*) in the USA. Community properties include apartments, townhouses, and detached (single-family) homes on a private estate with communal areas and facilities. Almost all properties that are part of a development (*urbanização*) are community properties. In general, the only properties that don't belong to a community are detached houses built on individual plots in public streets or on rural land. Owners of community properties not only own their homes, but also own a share of the common elements of a building or development, including foyers, hallways, passages, lifts, patios, gardens, roads, and leisure and sports facilities (such as swimming pools and tennis courts). When you buy a community property, you automatically become a member of the community of owners (*comunidade de proprietários*), which includes over two-thirds of all foreign property owners in Portugal.

Many community developments are located in or near coastal resorts and offer a range of communal facilities such as a golf course, swimming pools, tennis courts, a gymnasium or fitness club, and a bar and restaurant. Golf homes are popular, as no one can build in front of you and spoil your view, and you can consider the golf course as your lawn and garden. They also usually include discounts on green fees or even 'free' golf membership. Most developments have landscaped gardens and some also offer high security and a full-time porter (*porteiro*). At the other extreme, cheaper, older developments may consist of numerous cramped, tiny apartments with few, if any, amenities. Bear in mind that many community developments are planned as holiday homes and may not be attractive as permanent homes.

Advantages: The advantages of owning a community property include increased security; lower property taxes than detached homes; a range of community sports and leisure facilities; community living with lots of social contacts and the companionship of close neighbours; no garden, lawn or pool maintenance; fewer of the responsibilities of home ownership; ease of maintenance; and the opportunity to live in an area where owning a single-family home would be prohibitively expensive or impossible, e.g. a beach front or town centre.

Disadvantages: The disadvantages of community properties may include excessively high community fees (owners may have no control over increases); restrictive rules and regulations; a confining living and social environment and possible lack of privacy; noisy neighbours (particularly if neighbouring properties are rented to holidaymakers); limited living and storage space; expensive covered or secure parking (or insufficient off-road parking); and acrimonious owners' meetings, where management and factions may try to push through unpopular proposals (sometimes using proxy votes). Bear in mind that unless it's prohibited in the community rules, anyone can buy up community properties and turn them into timeshares.

Research: Before buying a community property it's wise to ask current owners about the community. For example, do they like living there; what are the fees and restrictions; how noisy are other residents; are the recreational facilities easy to access; would they buy there again (why or why not?); and, most importantly, is the community well managed. You may also wish to check on your prospective neighbours and if you're planning to buy an apartment above the ground floor you may want to ensure that the building has a lift. Note that upper floor apartments are both colder in winter and warmer in summer and may incur extra charges for the use of lifts (they do, however, offer more security than ground floor apartments). An apartment that has other apartments above and below it will generally be more noisy than a ground or top floor apartment.

Community of Owners: In an apartment block or community development the developer divides the costs of the communal areas between the owners, who must form a community of owners (*comunidade de proprietários*). You should never buy a property in an urbanisation where there isn't a legal community of owners. Some communal areas (such as roads) may be cared for by the local municipality, provided it has approved the urbanisation plan and has included it in its general plan for the municipality. An approved urbanisation has the same right to public support as any other part of a municipality. Before buying a community property, it's essential to obtain a copy of both the law of horizontal division (*lei de propiedade horizontal*) and the community rules, and have them explained to you. Portuguese law requires that all communities have their own set of statutes (*estatutos/regras*) which identify property that's owned privately and property owned communally.

Cost: Community properties vary enormously in price and quality, for example from around €80,000 for a studio or one bedroom apartment in an average location to several hundred thousand euros for a luxury apartment, townhouse or villa in a prime location. Garages and parking spaces must usually be purchased separately in developments, although it's unusual for developments to have lock-up garages or spaces in an underground car park. If you're buying a resale property, check the price paid for similar properties in the same area or development in recent months, but bear in mind that the price you pay may have more to do with the seller's circumstances than the price fetched by other properties. Find out how many properties are for sale in a particular development; if there are many on offer you should investigate why, as there could be management or structural problems. If you're still keen to buy, you can use any negative points to drive a hard bargain.

Management: A community of owners has an elected president (*presidente*) and a paid administrator (*administrador*), who may be a professional administrator from outside the community. The general running of a community is carried out by the administrator, a position that's automatically assumed by the president if an administrator isn't elected. The community of owners must be registered and all community books and documentation must be in Portuguese, although they can be translated into other languages for owners. All owners are required to attend an annual general meeting during the first two weeks of January, although they can name someone to represent and vote for them by proxy. The meeting is to discuss and approve the accounts for the previous year, approve expenses for the current year, and elect the president and committee members.

Community Fees: Owners of community properties must pay community fees (*gastos de comunidade*) for the upkeep of communal areas and for communal services. Charges are calculated according to each owner's share (*quota/acção de proprietário*) of the development or apartment building and not whether they're temporary or permanent residents. Shares are calculated according to the actual size of properties, e.g. ten properties of equal size would each pay 10 per cent of community fees. The percentage to be paid is detailed in the property deed (*escritura*). Shares not only determine the share of fees to be paid, but also voting rights at general meetings.

Fees go towards road cleaning; green zone maintenance (including communal and possibly private gardens); cleaning, decoration and maintenance of buildings; porterage or concierge; communal lighting in buildings and grounds; water supply (e.g. swimming pools, gardens); insurance; administration fees; urbanisation rates; maintenance of radio and TV aerials; and satellite TV charges. Fees may also include the external painting of individual villas; rubbish collection; telephone message and mail forwarding services; reading utility meters; police registration; paying utility bills; reception service (possibly 24-hour); airing of properties when not in use; and security. A float (deposit) may be required to cover ongoing expenses such as electricity, gas, water, insurance and maintenance.

Always check the level of general and any special charges before buying a community property. Fees are usually billed monthly or bi-annually and adjusted at the end of the year when the actual expenditure is known and the annual accounts have been approved by the committee. If you're buying an apartment from a previous owner, ask to see a copy of the service charges for previous years and the minutes of the last annual general meeting, as owners may be 'economical with the truth' when stating service charges, particularly if they're high. You should obtain receipts for the previous five years (if applicable).

Community fees vary considerably according to the communal facilities provided. For example, fees for a small apartment in a small, older block may be as little as €300 per year, whereas fees for a large luxury penthouse in a modern prestigious development can be well over €1,000 per year. Fees for a typical two-bedroom apartment costing around €150,000 are around €300 per year. In luxury developments with extensive sports and leisure facilities fees may range from €2,000 for a studio to over €4,500 for a three-bedroom villa. High fees aren't necessarily a negative point (assuming you can afford them), provided you receive value for money and the community is well managed and maintained. The value of a community property depends to a large extent on how well the development is maintained and managed. **Note, however, that many communities in Portugal aren't well run.**

Non-payment of Fees: Some communities have severe debt problems because of the non-payment of fees, which in turn leads to management failing to maintain facilities such as lifts, lighting and security systems when they break down. Check how many defaulters there are in a development and avoid those with a large number. Try to find out why people have defaulted, as it may be that an urbanisation has problems. **Ensure that fees have been paid up to date before buying a community property, otherwise you could be liable for any unpaid fees.** Owners with unpaid community fees may have their voting rights at general meetings cancelled, although a community may not cut off services such as water to an owner who fails to pay his community fees. If an owner doesn't pay his community fees, his property can be embargoed by the community of owners and if he continues to refuse to pay it can eventually be forcibly sold at auction. A community of owners may also be able to recover debts in Portugal from owners or previous owners by suing them in another country.

Maintenance & Repairs: If necessary, owners can be assessed an additional amount to make up any shortfall of funds for maintenance or repairs. You should check the condition of the common areas (including all amenities) in a development and whether any major maintenance or capital expense is planned for which you could be assessed. Old run-down apartment blocks can have their community fees increased substantially to pay for new installations and repairs (such as a new water supply or sewage installations). Enquire about any planned work and obtain a copy of the minutes of the last annual meeting where important matters are bound to have been raised. Owners' meetings can become rather heated when finances are discussed, particularly when assessments are being made to finance capital expenditure.

Restrictions: Community rules allow owners to run a community in accordance with the wishes of the majority, while at the same time safeguarding the rights of the minority. Rules usually include such things as noise levels; the keeping of pets (usually permitted, although some communities prohibit all pets); renting; exterior decoration and plants (e.g. the placement of shrubs); garbage disposal; the use of swimming pools and other recreational facilities; the activities of children (e.g. no ball games or cycling on community grounds); parking; business or professional use; use of a communal laundry room; the installation and positioning of satellite dishes; and the hanging of laundry. Check the rules and discuss any restrictions with residents.

Holiday Homes: If you're buying a holiday home that will be vacant for long periods (particularly in winter), don't buy in an apartment block where heating and/or hot water charges are shared, otherwise you will be paying towards your co-owners' bills. This is unusual in resort areas in Portugal, although water and garbage collection may be charged communally. You should also check whether there are any rules regarding short or long-term rentals or leaving a property unoccupied for any length of time. Bear in mind that when buying in a large development, communal facilities may be inundated during peak periods, e.g. a large swimming pool won't look so big when 100 people are using it and getting a game of tennis can be difficult during peak periods.

Retirement Homes

Purpose-built retirement communities (or sheltered housing) are becoming increasingly common in Portugal, particularly on the Algarve. Most urbanisations are developed by foreign companies for foreigners, as the Portuguese prefer to live among their family and friends in their 'twilight' years. Some sheltered housing developments attract elderly people, e.g. aged 70 plus, with limited mobility.

Developments may consist of one and two-bedroom apartments or a combination of apartments, townhouses and villas, which can be purchased freehold or leasehold, i.e. a lifetime residency. Note that if you buy leasehold, you don't have to pay Transfer Tax (SISA). Typical prices (leasehold) for one bedroom properties are from €140,000 and from €270,000 for a three bedroom property. Properties usually have central heating, air-conditioning, fully-fitted kitchens and satellite TV. A wide range of communal facilities and services are usually provided which may include a medical centre (possibly with a resident doctor), nursing facilities, lounges, laundry, housekeeping, sauna, jacuzzi, restaurant, bar, meal delivery, handyman, mini-supermarket, post and banking, guest apartments, free local transport, 24-hour security with closed-circuit TV, intercom service, personal emergency alarm system and a 24-hour multi-lingual reception. Sports and leisure services may include swimming pools, tennis courts, lawn bowling, gymnasium, video room, library and a social club. Most sheltered housing developments levy monthly service charges, e.g. between €225 and €500, which may include a number of weeks' 'free' nursing care each year in a residents' nursing home. Charges usually include heating and air-conditioning, hot water, satellite TV and all the other services listed above.

TIMESHARE & PART-OWNERSHIP SCHEMES

If you're looking for a holiday home abroad, you may wish to investigate a scheme that provides sole occupancy of a property for a number of weeks each year. These include co-ownership, leaseback and timesharing. **Don't rush into any of these schemes without fully researching the market and before you're absolutely clear what you want and what you can realistically expect to receive for your money.**

Co-ownership: Co-ownership (*compropriedade*) includes schemes such as a consortium of buyers owning shares in a property-owning company and co-ownership between family, friends or even strangers. Some developers offer a turn-key deal whereby a home is sold fully furnished and equipped. Co-ownership allows you to recoup your investment in savings on holiday costs and still retain your equity in a property. A common deal is a 'four-owner' scheme (which many consider to be the optimum number of co-owners), where you buy a quarter of a property and can occupy it for up to three months a year. However, there's no reason why there cannot be as many as 12 co-owners, with a month's occupancy each per year (usually divided between high, medium and low seasons).

Co-ownership offers access to a size and quality of property that would otherwise be impossible, and it's even possible to have a share in a substantial *castelo*, where a number of families could live together simultaneously and hardly ever see each other if they didn't want to. Co-ownership can be a good choice for a family seeking a holiday home for a few weeks or months a year and has the added advantage that (because of the lower cost) a mortgage may be unnecessary. It's usually cheaper to buy a property privately with friends than through a developer, when you may pay well above the market price for a share of a property (check the market value of a property to establish whether it's good value). **Co-ownership is much better value than a timeshare and needn't cost much more.** However, a water-tight contract must be drawn up by an experienced lawyer to protect the co-owners' interests.

One of the best ways to get into co-ownership, if you can afford it, is to buy a property yourself and offer shares to others. This overcomes the problem of getting together a consortium of would-be owners and trying to agree on a purchase in advance, which is difficult unless it's just a few friends or family members. Many people form a Portuguese or offshore company to buy and manage the property, which can in turn be owned by a company in the co-owners' home country, thus allowing any disputes to be dealt with under local law. Each co-owner receives a number of shares according to how much he has paid, entitling him to so many weeks' occupancy a year. Owners don't need to have equal shares and can all be made direct titleholders. If a co-owner wishes to sell his shares he must usually give first refusal to the other co-owners, although if they don't wish to buy them and a new co-owner cannot be found, the property will need to be sold.

Leaseback: Leaseback or sale-and-leaseback schemes are designed for those seeking a holiday home for a limited number of weeks each year. Properties sold under a leaseback scheme are always located in popular resort areas where self-catering accommodation is in high demand. Buying a property through a leaseback scheme allows a purchaser to buy a new property at less than its true cost, e.g. 30 per cent less than the list price. In return for the discount the property must be leased back to the developer, e.g. for 9 to 11 years, so that he can let it as self-catering holiday accommodation. The buyer owns the freehold of the property and the full price is shown in the title deed. The purchaser is also given the right to occupy the property for a period each year, usually six or eight weeks, spread over high, medium and low seasons. These weeks can usually be let to provide income or possibly be exchanged with accommodation in another resort (as with a timeshare scheme). The developer furnishes and manages the property and pays all the maintenance and bills (e.g. for utilities) during the term of the lease, even when the owner occupies the property. It's important to have a contract checked by your lawyer to ensure that you receive vacant possession at the end of the leaseback period, without having to pay an indemnity charge, otherwise you could end up paying more than a property is worth.

Timesharing: Also called various other names, including 'holiday ownership', 'vacation ownership', 'co-ownership' or 'holidays for life', timesharing is easily the most popular form of part-ownership in Portugal, where there are many timeshare resorts. Timesharing is more tightly controlled in Portugal than in some other countries and the contract must be in a language you understand and must be signed in the presence of a notary. Timeshare owners in Portugal either have a real right of ownership (which they can sell), which is known as Actual Timesharing Rights and can be in perpetuity or for a minimum of 30 years, or they own club type accommodation (known as Touristic Habitation Right), where the buyer buys the right to occupy a property for a specified period for a specific number of years (from 2 to 15) and has no real right of ownership.

Timesharing doesn't have a good reputation in Europe, largely due to the dubious hard-sell methods employed by many timeshare companies. However, there are many reputable timeshare companies operating in Portugal, where the best timeshare developments are on a par with luxury hotels and offer a wide range of facilities, including bars, restaurants, entertainment, shops, swimming pools, tennis courts, health clubs, and other leisure and sports facilities. If you don't wish to holiday in the same place each year, choose a timeshare development that's a member of an international organisation such as Resort Condominium International (RCI) or Interval International (II), which allow you (usually for an additional fee) to exchange your timeshare with one in another area or country.

If you're thinking about buying a timeshare in Portugal, you should be extremely wary of who you deal with. Timeshare 'muggers' or touts (variously termed 'outside personal contacts', 'outside people catchers', 'off-project contracts' or OPCs) are rife in the Algarve throughout the main tourist season, despite the fact that touting in streets is prohibited. Touts compete vigorously to induce tourists (they usually target couples only) to attend a 'presentation' (sales pitch) by pretending to be conducting surveys, using scratch cards and other competitions (everyone's a winner – provided that you attend a sales pitch), and offering free drinks, free golf, free one day membership with lunch, a free pass to local attractions, meals, wine, cash (e.g. €60), excursions and other baubles. If you're tempted to attend a sales pitch (lasting at least two or three hours), you should be aware that you will invariably be subjected to some of the most aggressive, high-pressure sales methods employed anywhere on earth and many people are simply unable to resist (the sales staff are experts).

If you decide to go to a presentation, which under Portuguese law can only take place at the timeshare itself, don't take your cheque book, credit cards or a lot of cash with you, so that you won't be pressured into paying a deposit without thinking it over. You will often be offered inducements to sign on-the-spot such as a 'discount', e.g. €300 or even a 50 per cent discount (the fanciful list price is a joke), a bonus week and no legal fees. However, if you're 'persuaded' to buy, all isn't lost, as you have a 14-day cooling-off period, during which you can cancel and receive a full refund (although it may take some time and you will need to persevere!). Note that you must cancel by registered letter. Avoid the hard-sell merchants like the plague, as reputable companies don't need to resort to hard-sell tactics and <u>never</u> tout for business on street corners. There are so many scams associated with timeshares that it would take a dedicated book to recount them all (and it would need to be updated every few months). **Suffice to say that many people bitterly regret the day they signed up for a timeshare!**

If you do make the decision to buy under a timeshare scheme, before you sign a contract you should make sure the seller gives you the following documentation: Authorisation from the Tourist Board (*Direcção Geral do Turismo*), the public deeds of the Actual Timesharing Rights and the Title of Constitution from the Land Registry (*Registo Predial*). Be very suspicious of a company that refuses to give you any documentation. Before signing a contract you should have these documents checked by a legal expert.

It isn't difficult to understand why there are so many timeshare companies and why salespersons often employ such intimidating hard-sell methods. A week's timeshare in an apartment worth around €100,000 can be sold for €13,000, making a total income of some €650,000 for the timeshare company if they sell 50 weeks (over six times the market value of the property!), plus management and other fees. **Most experts believe that there's little or no advantage in a timeshare over a normal holiday rental and that it's simply an expensive way to pay for your holidays in advance.** It doesn't make any sense to tie up your money for what amounts to a long-term reservation on an annual holiday. Timeshares cost from €13,000 for one week in a one or two-bedroom apartment in a top-rated resort, to which must be added annual management or maintenance fees, e.g. €300 or more for each week and other miscellaneous fees (note that fees can rise dramatically unless limited in the contract). Most financial advisers believe you're better off putting your money into a long-term investment, where you retain your capital and may even earn sufficient interest to pay for a few weeks' holiday each year. For example, €13,000 invested at just 5 per cent yields €650 per year, which when added to the saving on management fees, say €300 for a week, makes a total of €950. **Sufficient to pay for a week's holiday in a self-catering apartment almost anywhere.**

Often timeshares are difficult or impossible to sell at any price and 'pledges' from timeshare companies to sell them for you or buy them back at the market price are just a sales ploy, as timeshare companies aren't interested once they have made a sale. In fact some companies even persuade those wanting to sell to buy another timeshare, while offering to buy or sell their existing timeshare for well above its market value (which naturally they never do). **Note that there's no real resale market for timeshares and if you need to sell you're highly unlikely to get your money back.** If you're selling, avoid pirate resale agencies, as they're interested only in raking in sellers' registration fees.

If you want to buy a timeshare, it's best to buy a resale privately from an existing owner or a timeshare resale broker, when they sell for a fraction of their original cost. A realistic resale price is 20 to 50 per cent of the developer's current sale price. When buying a timeshare privately you can usually drive a hard bargain and may even get one 'free' simply by assuming the current owner's maintenance contract. Further information about timesharing can be obtained from the Timeshare Council in Spain (☎ 952-663 966, 💻 www.timesharecouncil.net) and the Timeshare Helpline in the UK (☎ 020-8296 0900, 💻 www.timeshare.freeserve.co.uk).

ESTATE AGENTS

The vast majority of property sales in Portugal are handled by estate agents (*imobiliárias*), particularly those where overseas foreign buyers are involved. It's common for foreigners in many countries, particularly Britain, to use an agent in their own country who works in co-operation with Portuguese agents and developers. Many Portuguese agents also advertise abroad, particularly in the publications listed in **Appendix A**, and in expatriate magazines and newspapers in Portugal. Most Portuguese agents in resort areas such as the Algarve have staff who speak English and other foreign languages. If you want to find an agent in a particular town or area, you can look under *imobiliárias* in the local Portuguese yellow pages (available at main libraries in many countries).

Qualifications: Portuguese estate agents are regulated by law and must be professionally qualified and licensed (*mediador autorizado*). You should choose an agent who's a member of a professional association such as the *Associação de Mediadores Imobiliários (AMI)*, *Sociedade de Mediação Imobiliária* or the *Associação dos Mediadores do Algarve (AMA)*. Ask to see an agent's licence, which should be displayed. You may also be afforded extra protection if the agent is a member of an international organisation, such as the European Federation of Estate Agents. However, although they're licensed, agents in Portugal aren't regulated, don't require professional indemnity insurance and aren't bound by consumer protection legislation. The rules for estate agents also apply to foreigners, who cannot sell property in Portugal without a full Portuguese licence (although some Portuguese agents are little more than sleeping partners in foreign-owned companies). However, there are a number of unlicensed, amateur 'cowboy' agents operating in Portugal (particularly in resort areas), who should be avoided. **If you pay a deposit to an agent, you must ensure that it's deposited in a separate (preferably bonded) account.** Note that not all Portuguese agents have indemnity insurance and even when they do it's limited to a relatively small sum.

Fees: There are no government controls on agents' fees in Portugal, where an agent's commission is usually between 5 and 10 per cent and allowed for in the sale price (so is effectively paid by the vendor). Foreign agents located abroad often work with Portuguese agents and share the standard commission, so buyers usually pay no more by using them (check, however, that this is the case). **Also check whether you need to pay any extra fees in addition to the sale price (apart from the normal fees and taxes associated with buying a property in Portugal).**

Viewing: If possible, you should decide where you want to live, what sort of property you want and your budget before visiting Portugal. Obtain details of as many properties as possible in your chosen area and price range, and make a shortlist of those you wish to view. Usually the details provided by Portuguese estate agents are sparse and few agents provide detailed descriptions of properties. Photographs may not do a property justice. It's also possible to view properties via the Internet.

There are no national property listings in Portugal, where agents jealously guard their list of properties, although many work with overseas agents in areas that are popular with foreign buyers. Portuguese agents who advertise in foreign journals or who work closely with overseas agents usually provide coloured photographs and a full description, particularly for the more expensive properties. The best agents provide an abundance of information. Agents vary enormously in their efficiency, enthusiasm and professionalism. If an agent shows little interest in finding out exactly what you want, you should look elsewhere. If you're using a foreign agent, confirm (and reconfirm) that a particular property is still for sale and the price, before travelling to Portugal to view it.

A Portuguese agent may ask you to sign a document before showing you any properties, which is simply to protect his commission should you obtain details from another source or try to do a deal with the owner behind his back. In Portugal you're usually shown properties personally by agents and won't be given the keys (especially to furnished properties) or be expected to deal with tenants or vendors directly. You should make an appointment to see properties as agents don't usually like people just turning up. **If you cannot make an appointment, you should call and cancel it.** If you happen to be on holiday it's okay to drop in unannounced to have a look at what's on offer, but don't expect an agent to show you properties without an appointment. If you view properties during a holiday, it's best to do so at the beginning so that you can return later to inspect any you particularly like a second or third time. Portuguese agents don't usually work during lunch hours and most close on Saturdays and Sundays.

You should try to view as many properties as possible during the time available, but allow enough time to view each property thoroughly, to travel between properties and for breaks for sustenance (it's mandatory to have a good lunch in Portugal). Although it's important to see sufficient properties to form an accurate opinion of price and quality, don't see too many in one day (around six is usually a manageable number), as it's easy to become confused over the merits of each property. If you're shown properties that don't meet your specifications, tell the agent immediately. You can also help an agent narrow the field by telling him exactly what's wrong with the properties you reject. It's wise to make notes of both the good and bad features and take lots of photographs of the properties you like, so that you're able to compare them later at your leisure (but keep a record of which photos are of which house!). It's also wise to mark each property on a map so that should you wish to return later on your own, you can find them without getting lost (too often). The more a property appeals to you, the more you should look for faults and negative points; if you still like it after stressing all the negative points, it must have special appeal.

Viewing Trips: Most agents and developers arrange viewing trips with inexpensive accommodation for prospective buyers, and usually refund the cost if you buy a property. By all means take advantage of inspection flight offers, but don't allow yourself to be pressurised into buying on a viewing trip. Allow sufficient time to view and compare properties from a number of agents and developers. A long weekend isn't long enough to have a good look around, unless you know exactly what you want to buy and where, or are planning to view one or two specific properties only.

Most agents offer after-sales services and will help you arrange legal advice, insurance, utilities, interior decorators and builders, and offer a full management and rental service on behalf of non-resident owners. Note, however, that agents often receive commissions for referrals and therefore you may not receive independent advice (you can always ask). Many agents will also handle the legal side of a sale (conveyancing), although this may be risky and it's best to employ an independent lawyer. You should never allow an agent to do the conveyancing if he's acting for both the seller and buyer.

INSPECTIONS & SURVEYS

When you've found a property that you like, you should make a close inspection of its condition. Obviously this will depend on whether it's an old house in need of complete restoration, a property that has been partly or totally modernised, or a modern home. One of the problems with a property that has been restored is that you don't know how well the job has been done, particularly if the owner did it himself. If work has been carried out by local builders, you should ask to see the bills.

Some simple checks you can do yourself include testing the electrical system, plumbing, mains water, hot water boiler and central heating. Don't take someone else's word that these are functional, but check them for yourself. If a property doesn't have electricity or mains water, check the nearest connection point and the cost of extending the service to the property, as it can be very expensive in remote rural areas. If a property has a well or septic tank, you should also have them tested. An old property may show visible signs of damage and decay, such as bulging or cracked walls, rising damp, missing roof slates (you can check with binoculars) and rotten woodwork. Some areas are prone to flooding, storms and subsidence, and it's wise to check an old property after a heavy rainfall, when any leaks should come to light. If you find or suspect problems, you should have the property checked by a builder or have a full structural survey carried out by a surveyor. You may also wish to have a property checked for termites, which are found in many areas of Portugal.

A Portuguese buyer wouldn't make an offer on an old property before at least having it checked by a builder, who will also be able to tell you whether the price is too high, given any work that needs to be done. However, it's unusual to have a survey (*inspeção*) on a property in Portugal, particularly a property built in the last 10 or 20 years. Nevertheless, some homes built in the 1970s and 1980s are sub-standard and were built with inferior materials, and even relatively new buildings can have serious faults. It's important to check who the developer or builder was, as a major company with a good reputation is unlikely to have cut corners. A property over five years old won't usually be covered by a builder's warranty, although warranties are transferable if a property is sold during the warranty period.

If you're buying a detached villa, farmhouse or village house, especially one built on the side of a hill, it's always recommended to have a survey carried out. Common problems include rusting water pipes and leaky plumbing; inadequate sewage disposal; poor wiring; humidity and rising damp (no damp course); uneven flooring or no concrete base; collapsing façades; subsidence; and cracked internal and external walls. Some of these problems are even evident in developments less than five years old. A good yardstick to use is that if you would have a survey done if you were buying a similar property in your home country, then you should have one done in Portugal.

You could ask the vendor to have a survey done at his expense, which, provided it gives the property a clean bill of health, will help him sell it even if you decide not to buy. You can make a satisfactory survey a condition of a contract, although this isn't usual in Portugal and a vendor may refuse or insist that you carry out a survey before signing the contract. **If a vendor refuses to allow you to do a survey before signing a contract, you should look elsewhere.** Some foreign lenders require a survey before approving a loan, although this usually consists of a perfunctory valuation to ensure that a property is worth the purchase price. You can employ a foreign (e.g. British) surveyor practising in Portugal, who will write a report in

English. However, a Portuguese surveyor (*agrimensor*) may have a more intimate knowledge of local properties and building methods. If you employ a foreign surveyor, you must ensure that he's experienced in the idiosyncrasies of Portuguese properties and that he has professional indemnity insurance covering Portugal (which means you can happily sue him if he does a bad job!).

Discuss with the surveyor exactly what will be included, and most importantly, what will be excluded from the survey (you may need to pay extra to include certain checks and tests). A full structural survey should include the condition of all buildings, particularly the foundations, roofs, walls and woodwork; plumbing, electricity and heating systems; and anything else you want inspected such as a swimming pool and its equipment, e.g. filter system or heating. A survey can be limited to a few items or even a single system only, such as the wiring or plumbing in an old house. You should receive a written report on the structural condition of a property, including anything that could become a problem in the future. Some surveyors will allow you to accompany them and provide a video film of their findings in addition to a written report. For a property costing up to €150,000 a valuation costs around €325, a homebuyer's survey and valuation €550 and a full structural survey some €800, which is a relatively small price to pay for the peace of mind it affords.

Buying Land: Before buying a home on its own plot of land you should walk the boundaries and look for fences, driveways, roads, and the overhanging eaves of buildings that might be encroaching upon the property. If you're uncertain about the boundaries you should have the land surveyed, which is wise in any case when buying a property with a large plot of land. When buying a rural property in Portugal, you may be able to negotiate the amount of land you want included in the purchase. If a property is part of a larger plot of land owned by the vendor or the boundaries must be redrawn, you will need to hire a surveyor to measure the land and draw up a new plan. You should also have your lawyer check the local municipal plans to find out what the land can be used for and whether there are any existing rights of way. The town hall will provide a certificate (*parecer camarário*) specifying what can be built on a plot of land.

CONVEYANCING

Conveyancing is the legal term for processing the paperwork involved in buying and selling property and transferring the deeds of ownership. In Portugal, some aspects of conveyancing, such as drawing up the deeds and witnessing the signatures, can be performed only by a public notary (*notário*). A *notário* represents the Portuguese government and one of his main tasks is to ensure that all state taxes are paid on the completion of a sale. **He doesn't**

verify or guarantee the accuracy of statements made in a contract or protect you against fraud! Many Portuguese estate agents will also undertake the conveyancing, although this can be risky and it's essential to engage your own lawyer (*advogado*). You should <u>never</u> allow an agent to do the conveyancing if he's acting for both the seller (*vendedor*) and buyer (*comprador*). Conveyancing should include the following checks:

- Verifying that a property belongs to the vendor, as shown in the deed (*escritura*) and listed at the land registry (*conservatória do registro predial*) or that he has the legal authority to sell it. The owner should produce a certified notarial copy of the *escritura* and a land registry certificate (*certidão de registro*). The description of the property at the land registry and the tax office (see below) should be identical.

- Checking that the owner has an official tax document (*caderneta predial*) issued by the local tax office and showing the fiscal value (*valor trubutável*) of the property, and that the property description agrees with the land registry certificate.

- Checking that there are no pre-emption rights over a property and that there are no plans to construct anything which would adversely affect the value, enjoyment or use of the property, such as roads, railway lines, airports, shops, factories or any other developments.

- Ensuring that all building permits and planning permissions are in order (e.g. building licence, water and electricity supply, sewage connection) and are genuine, and that a property was built in accordance with the plans. Any extensions or additions such as a swimming pool must be included on the plans and be authorised. A new building must have a habitation certificate (*cédula de habitação* or *licença de habitabilidade*) certifying it can be lived in, issued when a building conforms with the building standards and codes. If a building was constructed before 1951 the owner should have a certificate from the land registry verifying this.

  Before buying land for building you should obtain a certificate (*parecer camarário*) from the local town hall stating what can be built on it. Obtain a copy of the usage licence (*licença de utilização*) from the local town hall which shows what a property or land can be used for. A non-residential licence must also state the permitted commercial or industrial use of a property. It's important to check the size of dwelling that can be built on a plot or how far an existing building can be extended.

- Checking that there are no encumbrances, e.g. mortgages or loans, against a property or outstanding debts (see below). It's important to obtain a certificate (*certidão de registro*) from the local land registry confirming that the property is free from encumbrances, which is required by the notary (*notário*) when the deed is signed at the completion of the sale. You

<u>must</u> ensure that any debts against a property are cleared before you sign the deed of sale (*escritura*). There can be a delay of up to a year between charges being registered in the registry 'log' book and charges actually being entered into the main land registry (and showing up on the certificate). **It's therefore important for you or your lawyer to go to the land registry and check <u>all</u> entries <u>on the day of the completion</u> (this could be done a few days earlier and then you only need to examine entries since the last check on the day of completion).** Other checks include:

– enquiring at the town hall whether there are any unpaid taxes such as property tax (see page 109) or other charges outstanding against a property;

– checking that there are no outstanding community charges for the last five years (it may be possible for a vendor to pay the last year and ignore previous bills) and obtaining copies of the co-ownership rules and the latest accounts of the community of owners (which should state whether there are any impending expenses for which you would be liable);

– checking that all bills for electricity, water, telephone and gas have been paid for the last few years. Receipts should be provided by the vendor for all taxes and services.

If you buy a property on which there's an outstanding loan or taxes, the lender or local authority has first claim on the property and has the right to take possession and sell it to repay the debt. All unpaid debts on a property in Portugal are inherited by the buyer.

The cost of conveyancing for a property in Portugal depends on whether you employ a foreign or Portuguese lawyer or both. If you employ a foreign-based lawyer, you should expect to pay €150 or more per hour for his services plus additional fees for the work of his Portuguese partners or associates. The fees may be stated as a percentage of the purchase price, e.g. 1 to 2 per cent, with a minimum fee of around €1,000. Before hiring a lawyer, compare the fees charged by a number of practices and obtain quotations in writing. Check what's included in the fee and whether it's 'full and binding' or just an estimate (a low basic rate may be supplemented by much more expensive 'extras'). You should also employ a lawyer to check the contract (see below) before signing it to ensure that it's correct and includes everything necessary, particularly regarding any necessary conditional clauses.

In Portugal, the sales contract (*escritura pública de compra e venda*, commonly referred to simply as the *escritura*) is prepared by a public notary (*notário*), who's responsible for ensuring that it's drawn up correctly and that the purchase price is paid to the vendor. He also certifies the identity of the parties, witnesses the signing of the deed, arranges for its registration (in the name of the new owner) in the local property register and collects any fees or taxes due. The *notário* represents the state and <u>doesn't</u> protect the interests of the buyer or the seller and will rarely point out possible pitfalls in a contract, proffer advice or volunteer any information (as for example, an estate agent usually will). Don't expect a *notário* to speak English or any language other than Portuguese (although some do) or to explain the intricacies of Portuguese property law.

Anyone buying (or selling) property in Portugal shouldn't even think about doing it without taking expert, independent legal advice. You should certainly never sign anything or pay any money before engaging a lawyer. Your lawyer should also check that the notary does his job correctly, thus providing an extra safeguard. It isn't recommended to use the vendor's lawyer, even if this would save you money, as he's primarily concerned with protecting the interests of the vendor and not the buyer. See also **Avoiding Problems** on page 130.

PURCHASE CONTRACTS

The first stage in buying a property in Portugal is usually the signing of a promissory contract (*contrato de promessa de compra e venda*), which sets out the details of the contract such as the identity of the owner, a detailed description of the property and land boundaries, registration and tax numbers, purchase price, deposit and date of completion. It may be possible to obtain a draft in English. It's also possible to have a notary draw up the deed of sale (*escritura*) without having a promissory contract. However, when you're paying a deposit, which is usual, it's necessary to have a promissory contract drawn up.

Buying 'Off-plan': When buying an unbuilt property 'off-plan', i.e. a property still to be built or which is partly built only, it's usual to pay a small holding deposit, e.g. €750, to reserve a property until a promissory contract is signed (usually around four weeks later). When buying off-plan, payment is made in stages. Stage payments vary considerably and may consist of a 20 per cent deposit; 20 per cent on completion of the roof; 20 per cent on tiling the bathroom and kitchen (or when the doors and window frames are installed); 20 per cent when the building is complete; 10 per cent when the exterior work is completed (such as the patio, pool and landscaping); and the remaining 10 per cent on completion (which may be withheld for 6 or 12 months as an insurance against defects, provided you can get the builder to agree to this in the contract). An alternative may be 15 per cent on signing the contract, 20 per cent on the completion of the foundations, 20 per cent on completion of the walls, 30 per cent on the completion of the roof and 10 per cent at completion.

If a property is already partly built, the builder may expect a higher initial payment, depending on its stage of completion.

The contract must contain the timetable for the property's completion; stage payment dates; the completion date and penalties for non-completion; guarantees for building work; details of the builder's insurance policy (against non-completion); and a copy of the plans and drawings. The floor plan and technical specifications are signed by both parties to ensure that the standard and size of construction is adhered to. The contract should also contain a clause allowing you to withhold up to 10 per cent of the purchase price for 6 to 12 months as a guarantee against the builder not correcting any faults in the property. The completion of each stage should be certified in writing by your own architect before payments are made. It's important to ensure that payments are made on time, otherwise you could lose all previous payments and the property could be sold to another buyer. **It's important to verify that the builder or developer has an insurance policy (or 'termination' guarantee) to protect your investment in the event that he goes bust before completing the property and its infrastructure.** If he doesn't then you shouldn't buy from him!

Buying a New Completed Property or a Resale Property: When buying a resale or a new finished property (i.e. not off-plan) it's usual to sign a promissory contract (*contrato de promessa de compra e venda*) and pay a deposit (*sinal*). **Before signing a contract, it's important to have it checked by your lawyer.** One of the main reasons is to safeguard your interests by including any necessary conditional clauses (see below) in the contract. The deposit is usually equal to 10 to 20?? per cent of the agreed purchase price (the actual amount may be negotiable), the balance being paid at the completion when the deed of sale (*escritura*) is signed. A deposit is refundable under strict conditions only, notably relating to any conditional clauses such as failure to obtain a mortgage, although a deposit can be forfeited if you don't complete the transaction within the period specified in the contract. If you withdraw from a sale after all the conditions have been met, you will not only lose your deposit, but may also be required to pay the estate agent's commission. On the other hand, if the vendor withdraws he must repay you the amount of the deposit plus compensation, which is usually equal to the amount of the deposit (you therefore receive double the amount of the deposit). It's possible to include a clause in the contract for 'specific performance', which means that you can insist on a sale being completed rather than be compensated for breach of contract.

Make sure that you know exactly what the conditions are regarding the return or forfeiture of a deposit. Many Portuguese estate agents or lawyers don't have the legal authority to hold money on behalf of their clients and deposits should be deposited only in a separate (preferably bonded) account. **It isn't recommended to make out cheques for deposits or other**

monies in the name of an estate agent. Note that it's quite usual in Portugal for a deposit to be given to the vendor, although this should be avoided because if there's a dispute and the purchase isn't completed, it can take some time to get your deposit returned.

Conditional Clauses: All contracts, whether for new or resale properties, usually contain a number of conditional or annulling clauses (*cláusula de anulação*) that must be met to ensure the validity of the contract. Conditions usually apply to events out of the control of either the vendor or buyer, although almost anything the buyer agrees with the vendor can be included in a contract. If any of the conditions aren't met the contract can be suspended or declared null and void, and the deposit returned. However, if you fail to go through with a purchase and aren't covered by a clause in the contract, you will forfeit your deposit or could even be forced to go through with a purchase. If you're buying anything from the vendor such as carpets, curtains or furniture that are included in the purchase price, you should have them listed and attached as an addendum to the contract. Any fixtures and fittings present in a property when you view it (and agree to buy it) should still be there when you take possession, unless otherwise stated in the contract (see also **Completion** on page 173). There are many possible conditional clauses concerning a range of subjects, including the following, and you should discuss whether conditional clauses are necessary with your lawyer.

● being able to obtain a mortgage (although it's common in Portugal to have a mortgage approved before signing a contract);

● obtaining planning permission and building permits;

● plans to construct anything (e.g. roads, railways, etc.) which would adversely affect the enjoyment or use of a property;

● confirmation of the land area (by a surveyor) being purchased with a property;

● pre-emption rights or restrictive covenants over a property (such as rights of way);

● contingent on the sale of another property;

● subject to a satisfactory building survey or inspection.

Inheritance & Capital Gains Tax: Before registering the title deed, carefully consider the tax and inheritance consequences for those in whose name the deed will be registered. Property can be registered in a single name; both names of a couple or joint buyers' names; the name or names of children, giving the parents sole use during their lifetime (*usufruto/Interesse vitalício*) or in the name of a Portuguese or foreign company (see below). However you decide to buy a property, it should be done at the time of purchase, as it will be more expensive (or even impossible) to change it later. Discuss the matter with your lawyer before signing a contract. See also **Capital Gains Tax** on page 110 and **Inheritance & Gift Tax** on page 112.

Buying Through an Offshore Company: There are considerable advantages to owning a home in Portugal through an offshore company, particularly for non-residents, although the Portuguese tax authorities have recently introduced new tax measures designed to impose taxes on offshore companies. Under new legislation introduced in 2002 several restrictive measures were introduced meaning that it now isn't quite so advantageous to buy through an offshore company. Property tax is paid at a fixed rate of 2 per cent (normal rates are from 0.7 to 1.3 per cent – see page 109) and rental tax is also payable on all properties (see page 192) whether the property is rented or not. There are still advantages, however, and you should consult with a fiscal expert if you are considering this option. Owning a property through an offshore company is often an advantage when you're selling, as the sale can be effected much more easily, quickly and cheaply, and it may help to increase the asking price (although a prospective buyer may not appreciate or want the advantages). Some of the advantages include:

● Avoidance (in most cases) of SISA (transfer tax), and notarial and registry charges upon resale of a property. SISA, legal, notarial and registry fees can amount to as much as 15 per cent of the value of a property.

● Ease of the sale of the property, which simply involves transferring ownership of the company shares to the buyer. This also avoids the lengthy and protracted procedures which are necessary to register a title in Portugal, resulting in lower legal fees.

● Avoidance of local inheritance taxes on the property, including any potential liability to double taxation.

● Ease of transfer to heirs in the event of the owner's death and avoidance of local succession laws, which may stipulate to whom the property must pass. A number of people (e.g. in a family) can be part owners, each holding a number of shares, or a couple can own a property as a joint tenancy (which isn't recognised in Portugal) and on the death of either partner a simple transfer of his or her shares can be effected.

● The shares of an offshore company can be used to secure a loan for the purchase of the property. The shares are charged to the bank in return for a loan equal to a percentage of the value of the property.

● Confidentiality (the buyer can remain anonymous), asset protection and limited liability.

● By holding a property through an offshore company, the company shares can also be held on trust.

There are a few disadvantages in owning a Portuguese property through an offshore company, one of which is the cost of setting up the company and annual fees (although this is potentially less than the possible savings). The cost varies according to who establishes the company and where it's incorporated, but there's usually a set-up fee of between €1,050 and €3,240 plus an annual amount (from €800 to €2,450) for administration fees and taxes. Gibraltar is generally considered to be one of the least expensive and most reliable jurisdictions. Jersey and the Isle of Man are also popular jurisdictions for offshore companies in Portugal. If you own a property through an offshore company, you cannot claim remission from property tax (*contribuição autárquica*) for the first ten years of ownership as a 'normal' owner can (see page 172). There are a number of companies who can establish an offshore company, including International Company Services (Portugal) Limitada, Av. Denfensores de Chaves 15, 6th Floor, Suites F & G, 1000 Lisbon (☎ 213-142 030, ✉ port@ICSL.com).

Bear in mind that the laws regarding the ownership of Portuguese property through offshore companies <u>are currently in a state of change and all advantages may be annulled or further reduced in the future.</u>

COMPLETION

Completion (or closing) is the name for the signing of the final deed (*escritura de compra e venda*), the date of which is usually one or two months after signing the promissory contract, as stated in the contract (although it may be 'moveable'). Completion involves the signing of the deed of sale, transferring legal ownership of a property, the payment of the balance of the purchase price, plus other payments such as the *notário's* fees and the deed registration fee. SISA must be paid before the signing of the *escritura* and is usually paid a few days earlier. The receipt must be presented to the notary at the completion and is retained by him (so obtain a copy for your records).

Final Checks: Property is sold subject to the condition that it's in at the time of completion (not when first viewed) and therefore you should be aware of anything that occurs between signing the promissory contract and completion. Before signing the deed of sale, it's important to check that the property hasn't fallen down or been damaged in any way, e.g. by a storm, vandals or the previous owner. If you've employed a lawyer or are buying through an agent, he should accompany you on this visit. You should also do a final inventory immediately prior to completion (the previous owner should have already vacated the property) to ensure that the vendor hasn't absconded with anything that was included in the price.

You should have an inventory of the fixtures and fittings and anything that was included in the contract or purchased separately, e.g. carpets, light fittings, curtains or kitchen appliances, which should be present and in good working order. This is particularly important if furniture and furnishings (and major appliances) were included in the price. You should also ensure that expensive items (such as kitchen apparatus) haven't been substituted by inferior (possibly second-hand) brands. Any fixtures and fittings (and garden plants and shrubs) present in a property when you viewed it should still be there when you take possession, unless otherwise stated in the contract.

If you find anything is missing, damaged or isn't in working order you should make a note and insist on immediate restitution such as an appropriate reduction in the amount to be paid. In such cases it's normal for the *notário* to delay the signing of the deed until the matter is settled, although an appropriate amount could be withheld from the vendor's proceeds to pay for repairs or replacements. **You should refuse to go through with the purchase if you aren't completely satisfied, as it will be difficult or impossible to obtain redress later.** If it isn't possible to complete the sale, you should consult your lawyer about your rights and the return of your deposit and any other funds already paid.

N.B. It's also important to check that no charges have been registered against a property at the (*conservatória do registo predial*) that don't appear on the *certidão de registro* (see page 132). This must be done on the day of the completion.

Signing: The final act of the sale is the signing of the *escritura*, which takes place in the *notário's* office. Before the deed of sale is signed, the *notário* checks that all the conditions contained in the contract have been fulfilled. It's normal for all parties to be present when the deed of sale is read, signed and witnessed by the *notário*, although a party can give someone power of attorney (*procuração público*) to represent them. This is quite common among foreign buyers and sellers, and can be arranged by a notary in Portugal or at a Portuguese mission abroad (which is more expensive). If a couple buy a property in both their names, the wife can give the husband power of attorney (or vice versa). The *notário* reads the *escritura* aloud and both the vendor and buyer must sign it indicating that they have understood and accept the terms of the document. If you don't understand Portuguese you should take along an interpreter. It isn't necessary to have your lawyer present at the completion.

Payment: The balance of the price, after the deposit and any mortgages are subtracted, must be paid by banker's draft or bank transfer. For most people the most convenient way is by banker's draft, which also means that you will have the payment in your possession (a bank cannot lose it!) and the *notário* can confirm it immediately. It also allows you to withhold payment if there's a last minute problem that cannot be resolved. When the vendor and buyer are both foreigners, they can agree that the balance is paid in any currency and payment can also be made abroad. However, the deed of sale must state the sale price in euros and fees and taxes must be paid on this price.

At the time of signing, both the vendor and buyer declare that payment has been made in the agreed foreign currency. In this case the payment should be held by a lawyer or solicitor in the vendor's or buyer's home country.

Registration: After signing the *escritura* you should request a number of notarised copies for your records. The original deeds are stored in the notary's office and a certified copy is produced and registered at the land registry (*conservatória do registo predial*) by the *notário*. Note that it can take some months to complete the registration. It's important to send the certified copy of the *escritura* to the property registry as soon as possible, preferably the same day that it's signed. **Registering ownership of a property is the most important act of buying property in Portugal, because until the property is registered in your name, even after you've signed the contract before the notary, charges can be fraudulently registered against it without your knowledge.** The reason is that under Portuguese law, title is only enforceable against third parties after registration of the property at the land registry (not by signing the *escritura*). Only when the *escritura* has been registered at the land registry are you the legal owner of the property.

The purchase must also be registered with the tax office (*repartição de finanças*), who require the buyer's tax number and a copy of the initial pages of his passport. Don't forget to transfer all utilities into your name from the day of completion.

RENOVATION & RESTORATION

Many old country or village homes in Portugal are in need of restoration, renovation or modernisation. Before buying a property requiring total restoration or modernisation you should consider the alternatives, as it isn't for the faint-hearted. Spending extra on a purchase may represent better value for money than spending the money on building work. It's often cheaper to buy a restored or partly restored property rather than a ruin in need of total restoration, unless you're planning to do most of the work yourself. The price of most restored properties doesn't reflect the cost and amount of work that went into them and many people who have restored a 'ruin' would never do it again and advise others against it. In general the Portuguese don't care for old homes and much prefer modern apartments and villas with all mod cons.

Inspections: It's vital to check a property for any obvious faults, particularly an old property. Most importantly a building must have sound walls, without which it's cheaper to erect a new building! Almost any other problem can be fixed or overcome (at a price). A sound roof that doesn't leak is desirable, as ensuring that a building is waterproof is the most important priority if funds are scarce. Don't believe a vendor or agent who tells you that a roof or anything else can be repaired or patched up, but obtain expert advice from a local builder. Sound roof timbers are also important, as they can be expensive to replace. Old buildings often need a damp-proof course (condensation and damp can be a problem), timber treatment, new windows and doors, a new roof or extensive repairs, insulation, a modern kitchen and bathroom, re-wiring and central heating. In addition many older properties have iron or steel plumbing pipes, which are prone to leaks and corrosion and expensive to replace.

Mains water, sewerage, electricity, gas and telephones are still rare in many country areas, where generators, solar energy and wind power are fairly common. **If a house doesn't have electricity or mains water, it's important to check the cost of extending these services to it, which can be expensive.** Many rural properties get their water from a spring or well, which is usually fine, but you should check the reliability of the water supply, as wells can and do run dry! If you're planning to buy a waterside property, you should also check the frequency of floods. If they're commonplace, you should ensure that a building has been designed with floods in mind, e.g. with electrical installations above flood level and solid tiled floors.

Planning Permission & Building Permits: If modernisation of an old building involves making external alterations, such as building an extension or installing larger windows or new doorways, you will need planning permission and a building licence (*licença de obras*) from your local town hall. Even relatively minor changes may need planning permission and in many areas buildings must remain as single-floor dwellings. If you plan to do major restoration or building work, you should ensure that a conditional clause is included in the contract stating that the purchase is dependent on obtaining planning and building permission. **Never start any building work before you have official permission.**

DIY or Builders? One of the first decisions you need to make regarding restoration or modernisation is whether to do all or most of the work yourself or have it done by professional builders or local artisans. A working knowledge of Portuguese is essential for DIY, especially the words associated with building materials and measurements (renovating a house in Portugal will also greatly improve your ability to swear in Portuguese!). When restoring a period property it's imperative to have a sensitive approach to restoration. You shouldn't tackle jobs yourself or with friends unless you're sure you're doing them right. In general you should aim to retain as many of a property's original features as possible and stick to local building materials such as wood, stone and tiles, reflecting the style of the property. When renovations and 'improvements' have been botched, there's often little that can be done except to start again from scratch. It's important not to over-modernise an old property so that much of its natural rustic charm and attraction is lost. Bear in mind that even if you intend to do most of the work yourself, you will still need to hire local artisans for certain jobs.

Finding a Builder: When looking for a builder it's best to obtain recommendations from local people you can trust, e.g. an estate agent, *notário*, architect, neighbours and friends (although estate agents and other professionals aren't always the best people to ask, as they may receive commissions). It's also wise to obtain references from previous customers. It may be better to use a local building consortium or contractor rather than a number of independent tradesmen, particularly if you won't be around to supervise them (although it will cost you a bit more). On the other hand, if you supervise it 'yourself' using local hand-picked craftsmen you can save money and learn a great deal into the bargain.

Supervision: If you aren't on the spot and able to supervise work, you should hire a 'clerk of works' such as an architect or structural engineer to oversee a large job, otherwise it could drag on for months (or years) or be left half-finished. This will add around 5 or 10 per cent to the total bill, but it's usually worth every euro. Be extremely careful whom you employ if you have work done in your absence and ensure that your instructions are accurate in every detail. Make certain that you understand exactly what has been agreed and if necessary get it in writing (with drawings). It isn't unusual for foreign owners to receive huge bills for work done in their absence, which shouldn't have been done at all! **If you don't speak Portuguese it's even more important to employ someone to oversee building works. Progressing on sign language and a few words of Portuguese is a recipe for disaster!**

Quotations: Before buying a home in Portugal for restoration or modernisation, it's essential to get an accurate estimate of the work and costs involved. You should obtain written estimates (*estimativas*) or quotations (*orçamentos*) from at least two builders before employing anyone. For estimates to be accurate, you must detail exactly the work required, e.g. for electrical work this would include the number of points and switches, and the quality of materials to be used. If you have only a vague idea of what you want, you will receive a vague and unreliable estimate. Make sure that an estimate includes everything you want done and that you fully understand it (if you don't, get it translated). You should fix a date for the start and completion of work, and if you can get a builder to agree to it, include a penalty for failing to finish on time. After signing a contract it's usual to pay a deposit, the amount of which depends on the size and cost of a job.

Cost: All building work such as electrical work, masonry and plumbing is calculated by the square metre or metre. The cost of restoration depends on the type of work involved, the quality of materials used and the region. As a rough guide you should expect the cost of totally renovating an old 'habitable' building to be at least equal to its purchase price and possibly two to three times as much. How much you spend on restoring a property will depend on your purpose and the depth of your pockets. If you're restoring a property as an investment it's easy to spend more than you could ever hope to recoup when you sell it. On the other hand, if you're restoring a property as a holiday or permanent home there's no limit to what you can do and how much money you can spend. Keep an eye on your budget (which will inevitably be plus or minus 25 to 50 per cent – usually plus!) and don't be in too much of a hurry. Some people take many years to restore a holiday home, particularly when they're doing most of the work themselves. It isn't unusual for buyers to embark on a grandiose renovation scheme, only to run out of money before it's completed and be forced to sell at a huge loss. **Always bear in mind that dream ruins can easily become ruined dreams!**

Swimming Pools: It's common for foreign buyers to install a swimming pool at a home in Portugal, which if you're letting, will greatly increase your rental prospects and the rent you can charge. Many self-catering holiday companies won't take on properties without a pool. There are many swimming pool installation companies in Portugal or you can buy and install one yourself. If you're having a new home built in Portugal, you should employ a specialist pool company (who will provide a guarantee) to install it and not a general builder.

Above ground pools are the cheapest, but they're unsightly and are best only as a stop-gap or for those who really cannot afford anything better. Expect to pay around €3,000 for an 8 x 4 metre above ground pool. A better option is a liner pool, which can be installed by anyone with basic DIY skills. A liner pool measuring 8 x 4 metres costs around €12,500 fully installed, around the same price as a conventional pool. A saline water option costs a bit more, but gives a better quality of water and offers lower maintenance costs. A concrete fully-tiled pool of 8 x 4 metres costs from €13,000 to €20,000 installed, including filtration and heating, and can be almost any shape. You will need planning permission to install a pool and should apply a few months in advance. Pools require regular maintenance and cleaning. If you have a holiday home in Portugal or let a property, you will need to employ someone to maintain your pool (you may be able to get a local family to look after it in return for being able to use it).

See also **Buying a Resale Home** on page 152, **Inspections & Surveys** on page 164, **Water** on page 185 and **Heating & Air-conditioning** on page 189.

HOME SECURITY

When moving into a new home, it's often wise to replace the locks (or lock barrels) as soon as possible, as you have no idea how many keys are in circulation for the existing locks. This is true even for new homes, as builders often give keys to sub-contractors. In any case it's wise to change the external lock barrels regularly, particularly if you let a home. If they aren't already fitted, it's wise to fit high security (double cylinder or dead bolt) locks. Most modern apartments are fitted with an armoured door (*porta blindada*) with individually numbered, high security locks with three sets of levers. Extra keys for these locks cannot usually be cut at a local hardware store and you will need to obtain details from the previous owner or your landlord.

In areas with a high risk of theft (e.g. most resort areas and major cities), your insurance company may insist on extra security measures such as two locks on all external doors, internal locking shutters, and security bars or metal grilles (*grades de segurança*) on windows and patio doors on ground and lower floors, e.g. the first and second floors of high and low-rise buildings. Some grilles (e.g. on bedroom windows) should be hinged for emergency exit, particularly if you have only one external door to your home. Bars must be thick enough to prevent the use of rod cutters and strong enough that they cannot be forced apart by a car jack. Many people also wrap a chain around patio or main door security grilles and secure them with a padlock when a property is unoccupied, although a better solution is to fit a metal security bracket which cannot be cut with bolt-cutters. A policy may specify that all forms of protection on doors must be employed when a property is unoccupied and that all other forms (e.g. shutters) must also be used after 10pm and when a property is left empty for two or more days.

You may wish to have a security alarm fitted, which is usually the best way to deter thieves and may also reduce your household insurance (see page 61). It should include all external doors and windows, internal infra-red security beams, and may also include a coded entry keypad (which can be frequently changed and is useful for clients if you let) and 24-hour monitoring (with some systems it's even possible to monitor properties remotely from another country). With a monitored system, when a sensor (e.g. smoke or forced entry) detects an emergency or a panic button is pushed, a signal is sent to a 24-hour monitoring station. The person on duty will telephone to check whether it's a genuine alarm and if he cannot contact you someone will be sent to investigate. Some developments and urbanisations have security gates and are patrolled 24-hours a day by security guards.

You can deter thieves by ensuring that your house is well lit at night and not conspicuously unoccupied. External security 'motion detector' lights (that switch on automatically when someone approaches); random timed switches for internal lights, radios and TVs; dummy security cameras; and tapes that play barking dogs (etc.) triggered by a light or motion detector may all help deter burglars. In rural areas it's common for owners to fit two or three locks on external doors, alarm systems, grilles on doors and windows, window locks, security shutters and a safe for valuables. The advantage of grilles is that they allow you to leave windows open without inviting criminals in (unless they're <u>very</u> slim). You can fit UPVC (toughened clear plastic) security windows and doors, which can survive an attack with a sledgehammer without damage, and external steel security blinds (which can be electrically operated), although these are expensive. A dog can be useful to deter intruders, although it should be kept inside where it cannot be given poisoned food. Irrespective of whether you actually have a dog, a warning sign showing an image of a fierce dog may act as a deterrent. You should have the front door of an apartment fitted with a spy-hole and chain so that you can check the identity of visitors before opening the door. **Remember, prevention is better than cure, as stolen property is rarely recovered.**

Holiday homes are particularly vulnerable to thieves, especially in rural areas, and are often ransacked. No matter how secure your door and window locks, a thief can usually gain entry if he's sufficiently determined, often by simply smashing a window or even breaking in through the roof or by knocking a hole in a wall in a rural area! In isolated areas thieves can strip a house bare at their leisure and an unmonitored alarm won't be a deterrent if there's no-one around to hear it. If you have a holiday home in Portugal it's unwise to leave anything of real value (monetary or sentimental) there and best to have full insurance for your belongings (see page 61). One 'failsafe' way to protect a home when you're away is to employ a housesitter to look after it. This can be done for short periods or for six months (e.g. during the winter) or longer if you have a holiday home in Portugal. It isn't usually necessary to pay someone to housesit for a period of six months or more, when you can usually find someone to do it in return for free accommodation. However, you must take care whom you engage and obtain references.

An important aspect of home security is ensuring you have early warning of a fire, which is easily accomplished by installing smoke detectors. Battery-operated smoke detectors can be purchased for around €9 and should be tested periodically to ensure that the batteries aren't exhausted. You can also fit an electric-powered gas detector that activates an alarm when a gas leak is detected. When closing up a property for an extended period, e.g. over the winter, you should ensure that everything is switched off and that it's secure. If you vacate your home for an extended period, you may be obliged to notify a caretaker, landlord or insurance company, and to leave a key with a caretaker or landlord in case of emergencies. If you have a robbery, you should report it immediately to your local police station where you must make a statement (*denúncia*). You will receive a copy, which is required by your insurance company if you make a claim.

ELECTRICITY

Immediately after buying or renting a property (unless utilities are included in the rent), you must sign a contract at the local office of Electricidade de Portugal (EDP) (☎ freephone 800-505 505, 💻 www.edp.pt). You need to take with you some identification (passport or residence card), a copy of the deeds, the current electricity contract and a bill paid by the previous owner (and a good book, as queues can be long). If you've purchased a home in

Portugal, the estate agent may arrange for the utilities to be transferred to your name or go with you to the offices (no charge should be made for this service). Make sure all previous bills have been paid and that the contract is put into your name from the day you take over, otherwise you will be liable for debts left by the previous owner. If you're a non-resident owner, you should also give your foreign address or the address of your fiscal representative in Portugal, in case there are any problems requiring your attention, such as your bank refusing to pay the bills.

Wiring Standards & Connection: Most modern properties (e.g. less than 20 years old) in Portugal have good electrical installations. However, if you buy an old home you may be required to obtain a certificate from a qualified electrician stating that your electricity installation meets the required safety standards, even when the previous owner already had an electricity contract. You should ensure that the electricity installations are in a good condition well in advance of moving house, as it can take some time to have a new meter installed or get it reconnected. If you buy a rural property without electricity, you will need to pay to have the service extended to the property, which could be prohibitively expensive. In remote areas there may be no electricity supply at all and you will need to install a generator. When you buy a new community property (see page 153), the cost of connection to utility services is included in the price of the property.

Meters: In an old apartment block there may be a common meter, with the bill being shared among the apartment owners according to the size of their apartments. However, all new properties have their own meters, which for an apartment block or townhouse development may be installed in a basement in a special room or be housed in a meter 'cupboard' in a stair well or outside a group of properties. Meters should be positioned outside homes so that they can be read by the electricity company when you aren't at home.

Plugs: Depending on the country you've come from, you will need new plugs (*fichas* or *tomadas*) or a lot of adapters. Plug adapters for most foreign electrical apparatus can be purchased in Portugal, although it's wise to bring some adapters with you, plus extension cords and multi-plug extensions that can be fitted with Portuguese plugs. There's often a shortage of electricity points in Portuguese homes, with perhaps just one per room (including the kitchen), so multi-plug adapters may be essential. Most Portuguese plugs have two round pins, possibly with an earth built into the plug, although most sockets aren't fitted with earth contacts. Small low-wattage electrical appliances such as table lamps, small TVs and computers, don't require an earth. However, plugs with an earth must be used for high-wattage appliances such as fires, kettles, washing machines and refrigerators. These plugs must always be used with earthed sockets, although they will also fit non-earthed, two-pin sockets. Electrical appliances that are earthed have a three-core wire and must never be used with a two-pin plug without an earth socket. **Always**

make sure that a plug is correctly and securely wired, as bad wiring can be fatal.

Fuses: In modern properties, fuses (*fusívels*) are of the earth trip type. When there's a short circuit or the system has been overloaded, a circuit breaker is tripped and the power supply is cut. If your electricity fails, you should suspect a fuse of tripping off, particularly if you've just switched on an electrical appliance (usually you will hear the power switch off). Before reconnecting the power, switch off any high-power appliances such as a stove, washing machine or dishwasher. Make sure you know where the trip switches are located and keep a torch handy so you can find them in the dark (see also **Power Supply** below).

Bulbs: Electric light bulbs in Portugal are of the Edison type with a screw fitting. If you have lamps requiring bayonet bulbs you should bring some with you, as they cannot be readily purchased in Portugal. You can, however, buy adapters to convert from bayonet to screw fitting (or vice versa). Bulbs for non-standard electrical appliances (i.e. appliances that aren't made for the Portuguese market) such as refrigerators and sewing machines may not be available in Portugal, so bring some spares with you.

Power Supply: The electricity supply in Portugal is 220 volts AC with a frequency of 50 hertz (cycles) and either two or three phase. Not all appliances, e.g. TVs made for 240 volts, will function with a power supply of 220 volts. Power cuts are frequent in many areas of Portugal and when it rains heavily the electricity supply can become very unstable, with frequent power cuts lasting from a few micro seconds (just long enough to crash a computer) to a few hours. If you use a computer it's recommended to fit an uninterrupted power supply (UPS) with a battery backup, which allows you time to shut down your computer and save your work after a power failure. If you live in an area where cuts are frequent and rely on electricity for your livelihood, e.g. for operating a computer, fax machine and other equipment, you may need to install a backup generator. **Even more important than a battery backup is a power surge protector for appliances such as TVs, computers and fax machines, without which you risk having equipment damaged or destroyed.** In remote areas you must install a generator if you want electricity, as there's no mains electricity, although some people make do with gas and oil lamps (and without TVs and other modern conveniences). In some urbanisations, water is provided by electric pump and therefore if your electricity supply is cut off, so is your water supply.

If the power keeps tripping off when you attempt to use a number of high-power appliances simultaneously, e.g. an electric kettle and a heater, it means that the power rating (*potência*) of your property is too low. This is a common problem in Portugal. If this is the case, you may need to contact your electricity company and ask them to upgrade the power supply to your property (it can also be downgraded if the power supply is more than you require). The power supply increases by increments of 1.1kW, 2.2kW, 3.3kW, 6.6kW, 9.9kW, 13.2kW, 16.5kW and 19.8kW (usually indicated on your meter). Bear in mind that it can take some time to get your power supply changed. Your standing charge depends on the power rating of your supply, which is why owners tend to keep it as low as possible, e.g. most holiday homes have a power rating of just 3.3kW.

Converters & Transformers: If you have electrical equipment rated at 110 volts AC (for example, from the USA) you will require a converter or a step-down transformer to convert it to 220 volts. However, some electrical appliances are fitted with a 110/220 volt switch. Check for the switch, which may be inside the casing, and make sure it's switched to 220 volts before connecting it to the power supply. Converters can be used for heating appliances, but transformers are required for motorised appliances. Total the wattage of the devices you intend to connect to a transformer and make sure that its power rating exceeds this sum.

Generally all small, high-wattage, electrical appliances, such as kettles, toasters, heaters, and irons need large transformers. Motors in large appliances such as cookers, refrigerators, washing machines, dryers and dishwashers, will need replacing or fitting with a large transformer. In most cases it's simpler to buy new appliances in Portugal, which are of good quality and reasonably priced, and sell them when you leave if you cannot take them with you. The dimensions of cookers, microwave ovens, refrigerators, washing machines, dryers and dishwashers purchased abroad may differ from those in Portugal (and therefore may not fit into a Portuguese kitchen).

An additional problem with some electrical equipment is the frequency rating, which in some countries, e.g. the USA, is designed to run at 60Hertz (Hz) and not Europe's 50Hz. Electrical equipment without a motor is generally unaffected by the drop in frequency to 50Hz (except TVs). Equipment with a motor may run okay with a 20 per cent drop in speed; however, automatic washing machines, cookers, electric clocks, record players and tape recorders must be converted from the US 60Hz cycle to Portugal's 50Hz cycle. To find out, look at the label on the back of the equipment. If it says 50/60Hz it should be okay; if it says 60Hz you can try it, **but first ensure that the voltage is correct as outlined above.** Bear in mind that the transformers and motors of electrical devices designed to run at 60Hz will run hotter at 50Hz, so make sure that apparatus has sufficient space around it to allow for cooling.

Tariffs: The cost of electricity in Portugal is relatively high compared with many other EU countries. The tariff depends on your power rating (*potência*), which is used to calculate your monthly standing charge, which is payable irrespective of whether you use any electricity during the billing period. The actual consumption is charged per kwH, which in 2002 was around €0.05 per kwH at the lower rate (bi-hourly tariff) up to €0.09 per kwH at the higher rate.

There's a lower social tariff for clients whose annual consumption is less than 400kwH a year.

To save on electricity costs, you can switch to night tariff and run high-consumption appliances overnight, e.g. storage heaters, water heater, dishwasher and washing machine (which can be operated by a timer). If you use a lot of water, it's better to have a large water heater (e.g. 150 litres) and heat water overnight. If you use electricity for heating, you can install night storage heaters that run on the cheaper night tariff, which can save you up to 45 per cent. The night tariff has two cycles: a weekly cycle when the tariff operates for seven hours a night, 17 hours on Saturday and all day Sunday; and a daily cycle when the tariff operates for nine hours daily (ten hours daily in the summer). To qualify for the night tariff, your main switchboard must have circuit breakers (not fuses) and an earth trip, you must also have a special meter fitted and use over 400 units (400 kwH) a year.

Electricity Bills: Electricity bills (*facturas/recibos*) are sent out monthly and most show estimated (*estimativa*) rather than actual consumption (in kwH). You should learn to read your electricity bill and meter and check your consumption to ensure that you aren't being overcharged. If the estimated consumption is much higher than the actual consumption, you can telephone the reading to EDP (☎ freephone 800-505 505) and they will adjust your bill accordingly. EDP have a shortage of meter readers and meters are therefore read infrequently or even not at all! Bills also include an exploration charge (*Taxa RS*) and VAT/*IVA*.

It's best to pay all your utility bills by direct debit (*débito direto*) from a Portuguese bank account. Bills should then be paid automatically on presentation to your bank, although some banks cannot be relied on 100 per cent. Both the electricity company and your bank should notify you when they have sent or paid a bill. You can pay a fixed monthly amount based on what you paid in the previous year and pay by direct debit, called an 'EDP agreed account' (*conta certa EDP*). Your meter is read at the end of the year and the amount owing adjusted either way (if you owe EDP a large amount you're given up to three months to pay). You can also pay bills at a post office, local banks (listed on the bill), at an EDP office or at PayShops located in main towns and large shopping centres.

GAS

Mains gas is supplied by Gás de Portugal (now owned by Galp Energia) but is only available in Lisbon and nearby areas. In other regions, including the Algarve, bottled butane and propane gas is used and costs less than mains gas in most northern European countries, although the price has increased considerably in recent years. Some resorts have central gas tanks to which villas and apartments are connected. Many people use gas for cooking, hot water and heating (gas fires using gas bottles are popular in winter in the Algarve). You can have a combined gas hot water and heating system installed (providing background heat), which is relatively inexpensive to install and cheap to run. Cooking by bottled gas is cheaper than electricity and there's no standing charge. Cookers often have a combination of electric and (bottled) gas rings (you can choose the mix). If your gas rings are sparked by electricity, keep some matches handy for use during power cuts. **Bear in mind that old gas water heaters can leak carbon monoxide and have been the cause of fatal accidents in Portugal and a number of other countries, although this is unlikely with a modern installation.** Gas heaters must be regularly serviced and de-scaled annually. Before a property with a gas-fuelled water appliance can be let, it must be inspected by a licensed inspector and issued with a safety certificate.

Butane gas bottles (*garrafa de gas/butano*) weighing 11kg (costing around €8) or 45kg (cost from €30 to €35) are available from local stores and are also delivered to homes. The delivery service is generally very efficient in all areas except remote rural locations. You pay a deposit on the first bottle and thereafter exchange an empty bottle for a full one. Check when moving into a property that the gas bottle isn't empty, keep a spare bottle or two handy and make sure you know how to change bottles (if necessary, ask the previous owner or estate agent to show you). A bottle used just for cooking will last an average family around six weeks. Some rural homes use propane gas, which is supplied in large bottles that can be stored outside, as it can withstand a greater range of temperatures than butane (which is for internal use only). You can also have a large gas tank installed (underground or over ground) on your property, provided you have the space (tanks must be installed a certain distance from a house). Note, however, that gas tanks are expensive to install (along with all the necessary piping), systems need regular maintenance and having a gas tank on your property will increase your household insurance.

WATER

Water, or rather the lack of it, is a major concern in some regions of Portugal, particularly the Algarve, and is the price paid for all those sunny days. As in some other countries that experience regional water shortages, Portugal as a whole has sufficient water, but it isn't distributed evenly. There's surplus rainfall in the north and a deficiency in the south. Like most of southern Iberia, southern Portugal experienced a severe drought in the early 1990s (broken in the winter of 1995/96), when thousands of people had to endure water rationing. Water shortages are exacerbated in the Algarve where the local population swells by up to tenfold during the summer tourist season, the hottest and driest period of the year.

Water shortages are also aggravated by poor infrastructure (a lot of water is lost due to leaking pipes) and wastage due to poor irrigation methods. There's also surprisingly little emphasis on water conservation in Portugal, particularly considering the frequent droughts. Consumption is particularly high in the Algarve with its numerous swimming pools, lawns, gardens and golf courses. In rural areas a regular supply cannot be taken for granted and many rural homes have no running water, while farmers periodically face ruin due to the lack of water for irrigation. However, domestic consumption has reduced in many regions due to a sharp increase in cost in recent years, and the fact that people also learnt to use less water during the drought years. **In Portugal, water is a precious resource and not something simply to pour down the drain!**

Restrictions: During water shortages, local municipalities may restrict water consumption or cut off supplies altogether for long periods. Restrictions can be severe and you can forget about watering the garden or washing your car unless you have a private water supply. If a water company needs to cut your supply, e.g. to carry out maintenance work on pipes and other installations, they will usually notify you in advance so that you can store water for cooking. In some areas, water shortages can create low water pressure, resulting in insufficient water to take a bath or shower. In many developments, water is provided by electric pump and therefore if your electricity is cut off, so is your water supply. In urbanisations the tap to turn water on or off is usually located outside properties and therefore if your water goes off suddenly you should check that someone hasn't switched it off by mistake.

Check the Supply: One of the most important tasks before renting or buying a home in Portugal is to investigate the reliability of the local water supply (over a number of years) and the cost. Ask your prospective neighbours and other local residents for information. In most towns and cities supplies are adequate, although there may be cuts in summer. In rural areas it's common to have your own borehole (*furo*) or well (*poço*), which may need an electric pump to ensure sufficient pressure. On the Algarve, boreholes must be registered with the local town hall and a licence issued. Bear in mind that a well containing water in winter may be bone dry in summer and you may have no rights to extract water from a water channel running alongside your land. Dowsing (finding water by holding a piece of forked wood) is as accurate as anything devised by modern science (it has an 80 per cent success rate) and a good dowser can also estimate the water's yield and purity to within 10 or 20 per cent accuracy. Before buying land without a water supply, engage an experienced dowser with a successful track record to check it.

Storage Tanks: If you have a detached house or villa, you can reduce your water costs by collecting and storing rainwater and by having a storage tank (*depósito*) installed. Tanks can be either roof-mounted or installed underground; the latter are cheaper and can be any size, but require an electric pump. Check whether a property has a water storage tank or whether you can install one. A mains supply can be augmented with a large storage tank that refills itself automatically when the water supply is restored after having been cut off. In rural areas many properties don't have running water and obtain their water from a well or borehole, an underground cistern (*cisterna*) or a storage tank (*depósito*). A storage tank or cistern can be filled by tanker from a commercial supplier, by the local fire brigade or from a neighbour with a plentiful bore-hole supply. It's possible to use recycled water from baths, showers, kitchens and apparatus such as washing machines and dishwashers to flush toilets or water a garden.

Contracts: After buying a property you should arrange for the water contract to be registered in your name at the local town hall. Take along some identification (passport or residence card) and the previous contract and bills paid by the former owner. When registering, non-resident owners should also give their foreign address or the address of their Portuguese fiscal representative in case there are any problems requiring the owner's attention (such as your bank refusing to pay water bills). Check in advance that all water bills have been paid by the previous owner, otherwise you will be liable for any debts.

Hot Water: Water heating in apartments may be provided by a central heating source for the whole building or apartments may have their own water heaters. If you install your own water heater, it should have a capacity of at least 75 litres. Many holiday homes have quite small water boilers, which are often inadequate for more than two people. If you need to install a water heater (or fit a larger one), you should consider the merits of both electric and bottled gas heaters. An electric water boiler with a capacity of 75 litres (sufficient for two people) costs €150 to €300 and usually takes between 60 and 90 minutes to heat water to 40 degrees in winter.

A gas flow-through water heater is more expensive to purchase and install than an electric heater, but you get unlimited hot water immediately whenever you want it and there are no standing charges. Make sure that a gas heater has a capacity of 10 to 16 litres per minute if you want it for a shower. A gas heater costs from around €125 to €300 (although there's little difference in quality between the cheaper and more expensive heaters), plus installation costs. Note that a gas water heater with a permanent flame may use up to 50 per cent more gas than a model without one. A resident family with a constant consumption is better off with an electric heater operating on the night tariff, while non-residents using a property for short periods will find a self-igniting gas heater more economical. Solar energy can also be used to provide hot water (see page 190).

Costs: Water is a local matter in Portugal and is usually controlled by local municipalities, many of which have their own wells and reservoirs, although in some municipalities and urbanisations water distribution is the responsibility of a private company. The cost of connection to the local water supply for a new home varies considerably with the supplier and the property's location. In most municipalities there's a standing charge, which may include a minimum consumption, even if you don't use any water during the billing period. The cost of water has risen considerably in Portugal in recent years (as a result of drought) and in some towns, water bills have increased by up to 200 per cent or more. The cost in the Algarve is around €1 per m³, although costs vary with consumption. To save on water costs, you can buy a 'water-saver' which mixes air with water, thus reducing the amount of water used. The cost of fitting an apartment with water savers is around €40 only, which can be recouped in six months through lower water bills. In some community developments, the cost of water is included in community fees (see page 155).

Mains water is metered and you're usually billed every two months (bills include sewerage). Meters are usually read infrequently and usage is often estimated. You should learn to read your water bill and meter and check your consumption, to ensure that your water company isn't overcharging you. If the estimated consumption is much higher than the actual consumption, you can obtain a refund and have payments reduced (alternatively, if your estimated bills are low you could be hit with a very high bill when the meter is eventually read). Consumption is usually priced in three bands according to the amount consumed and rates rise considerably as consumption increases. If you use a lot of water (e.g. swimming pool, sprinklers, baths, etc.) the cost will be around ten times higher than someone who just uses water to shower and for drinking and cooking. Check your water bill carefully, as overcharging on bills is widespread. Sometimes water company meters show a huge disparity (increase!) in consumption compared with a privately installed meter. Keep an eye on consumption, as a leaking pipe can be very expensive. Bills can be paid in person at the town hall and by various other methods, although it's easiest to pay by direct debit (*débito direto*) from a Portuguese bank account.

Water Quality: Water is supposedly safe to drink in all urban areas, although it can be of poor quality (possibly brown or rust coloured), full of chemicals and taste awful. Many residents prefer to drink bottled water, of which millions of litres are consumed each year in Portugal. In rural areas water may be extracted from springs and taste excellent, although the quality standards applied in cities are usually absent and it may be of poor quality. Water in rural areas may also be contaminated by the fertilisers and nitrates used in farming, and by salt water in some coastal areas (which will kill your plants and lawns). If you're in any doubt about the quality of your water you should have it analysed. **Note that although boiling water will kill any bacteria, it won't remove any toxic substances contained in it.** You can install filtering, cleansing and softening equipment to improve its quality. You can also install a water purification unit to provide drinking water costing around €1,300. The main drawback is that purification systems operating on the reverse osmosis system waste three times as much water as they produce! Obtain expert advice before installing a system, as not all equipment is effective.

Many regions (e.g. the Algarve) have hard (*duro*) water, containing high concentrations of calcium and magnesium. You can install a water softener, which will prevent the build-up of scale in water heaters and water pipes (which increases heating costs and damages electric heaters and other appliances). An ion exchange magnetic or electronic (the best sort) water softener is recommended (a large softener isn't much more expensive than a small one and is cheaper to run). Costs vary and can run to tens of hundreds of euros for a sophisticated system, which also consumes large quantities of water for regeneration. It's necessary to have a separate drinking water supply if you have a water softener installed in your home (softened water is high in sodium from the sodium salts used in the softening process, and isn't suitable for drinking).

Septic Tanks: In rural areas there are no sewage plants and sewage is drained into septic tanks (*fosas sépticas*) which are emptied by tankers. The absence of a septic tank or other waste water system isn't usually a problem, provided the land size and elevation allows for its installation. If a property already has a septic tank, check that it's in good condition. An old style septic tank takes bathroom waste only, while new all-purpose septic tanks on a soak-away system cope with a wide range of waste products. Make sure that a tank is large enough for the property in question, e.g. 2,500 litres for two bedrooms and up to 4,000 litres for five bedrooms. You must never use certain cleaning agents such as ammonia in a septic tank, as it will destroy it. Specially formulated cleaners are available, including products that will extend its life.

HEATING & AIR-CONDITIONING

Central heating (*aquecimento*) is essential in winter in northern and central Portugal and isn't a luxury in the Algarve. If you're used to central heating and like a warm house in winter, you will almost certainly miss central heating, even in the Algarve. Central heating systems in Portugal may be powered by oil, gas, electricity, solid fuel (usually wood) or even solar power. Oil-fired central heating isn't common in Portugal due to the high cost of heating oil and the problems associated with storage and deliveries. Whatever form of heating you use, it's important to have good insulation, without which up to 60 per cent of the heat generated is lost through the walls and roof. Many (particularly older) properties in Portugal don't have good insulation and builders may not always adhere to current regulations, e.g. new homes must have double cavity walls and adequate damp proofing. Ceiling insulation is essential to prevent heat loss through the roof at night and can be difficult to install in existing properties.

Solid Fuel: Wood is the cheapest and most common heating fuel in Portugal, where many homes have wood-burning fireplaces and stoves (which may be combined with a central heating system). Open log fires are popular and efficient, although many chimneys in homes in resort areas are for decoration and aren't functional. Fireplaces should be located on an inside wall to reduce heat loss and must be properly designed and made of the correct bricks, otherwise the heat simply dissipates. Many modern homes use enclosed wood-burning stoves (costing from €1,300) for heating, although you should note that a chimney used with a wood-burning stove with doors must have chimney liners. Stock up on wood in summer when it's cheapest.

Electric Heating: Electric heating isn't common in Portugal, as it's too expensive and requires good insulation and a permanent system of ventilation. It's best to avoid totally electric apartments, as the bills can be astronomical although a system of night-storage heaters operating on the night tariff can be economical. Convection or panel-type heaters are useful for background heating, but running costs are high compared with gas heaters. There are special electric heaters for wardrobes to keep clothes free from damp and mould. If you rely on electricity for your heating, you should expect to pay at least €75 and €150 per month during the coldest months of the year, even in the Algarve. An air-conditioning system (see below) with a heat pump provides cooling in summer and economical heating in winter. Note that if you have electric central heating or air-conditioning, you may need to upgrade your power supply (see page 182).

Gas Heating: Portable gas heaters using standard gas bottles cost from around €70 to €150 and are an economical way of providing heating in areas that experience mild winters (such as the Algarve). Gas heaters must be used only in rooms with adequate ventilation and it can be dangerous to have too large a difference between indoor and outdoor temperatures. Gas poisoning due to faulty ventilation ducts in gas water heaters (e.g. in bathrooms) isn't uncommon in Portugal. It's possible to install a central heating system operating from standard gas bottles, which costs from €2,000 for a small home (Primus of Sweden is one of the leading manufacturers). If you have space for a large gas tank, then gas central heating is an option (the best systems are those which distribute gas-heated water through radiators). Under-floor heating is also popular, although it isn't so 'instantly' controllable as radiators.

Solar Energy: The use of solar energy to provide hot water and heating (with a hot-air solar radiator) is surprisingly uncommon in Portugal, where the amount of energy provided by the sun each year per square metre is equivalent to eleven gas bottles (the sun provides around 8,000 times the world's present energy requirements annually!). A solar power system can be used to supply all your energy needs, although it's usually combined with an electric or gas heating system, as it cannot usually be relied upon year-round for heating and hot water. If you own a home in Portugal, solar energy is a viable option and the authorities offer grants and tax allowances to encourage homeowners to install solar energy systems.

The main drawback is the high cost of installation, which varies considerably with the region and how much energy you require. A 400-litre hot-water system costs around €2,500 and must be installed by an expert. The advantages are no running costs, silent operation, it's maintenance-free and there are no (or very small) electricity bills. A system should last 30 years (it's usually guaranteed for ten years) and can be upgraded to provide additional power in the future. Solar power can also be used to heat a swimming pool. Continuous advances in solar cell and battery technology are expected to dramatically increase the efficiency and reduce the cost of solar power, which is forecast to become the main source of energy world-wide in the next century. A solar power system can also be used to provide electricity in a remote rural home, where the cost of extending mains electricity is prohibitive.

Air-conditioning: In some regions of Portugal, summer temperatures can reach over 40°C (104°F) and although properties are built to withstand the heat, you may wish to install air-conditioning (*ar condicionado*). Note, however, that there can be negative effects if you suffer from asthma or respiratory problems. You can choose between a huge variety of air-conditioners, fixed or moveable, indoor or outdoor installation, and high or low power. Air-conditioning units cost from around €600 (plus installation) for a unit that's sufficient to cool an average sized room. An air-conditioning system with a heat pump provides cooling in summer and economical heating in winter (and can also be used to heat a swimming pool). Some air-conditioners are noisy, so check the noise level before buying one. Many people fit ceiling fans for extra cooling in the summer (costing from around €50); these are standard fixtures in some new homes.

Humidifiers: Central heating dries the air and may cause your family to develop coughs and other ailments. If you find the dry air unpleasant it's possible to purchase a humidifier to add moisture to the air. These range from simple water containers hung from radiators to expensive electrical or battery-operated devices. Humidifiers that don't generate steam should be disinfected occasionally with a special liquid available from chemists (to prevent nasty diseases). Dehumidifiers are invaluable to ensure a damp-free atmosphere during the wet months (those with humidity settings and automatic switching are best).

PROPERTY INCOME

Many people planning to buy a holiday home in Portugal are interested in owning a property that will provide them with an income from letting to cover the running costs and offset the mortgage payments. **Note, however, that you're highly unlikely to meet all your mortgage payments and running costs from rental income.** Buyers who over-stretch their financial resources often find themselves on the rental treadmill, constantly struggling to earn sufficient income to cover their costs. In the early 1990s many foreign buyers lost their Portuguese homes after they defaulted on their mortgage payments, often because rental income failed to meet expectations. It's difficult to make a living providing holiday accommodation in most areas of Portugal, as the season is too short and there's simply too much competition. On the other hand, letting a home for just a few weeks in the summer can recoup your annual running costs and pay for your holidays.

If you're planning on holiday lets, don't overestimate the length of the season, which varies with the region. In some areas it's as long as 16 weeks, while in others it's ten weeks or less. The letting season is longest in Madeira (where properties have year-round letting potential) and the Algarve. Bear in mind that buying property in Portugal (and in most other countries) isn't a good investment compared with the return on income that can be achieved by investing elsewhere. **Most experts recommend that you shouldn't purchase a home in Portugal if you need to rely heavily on rental income to pay for it.**

Regulations & Restrictions: In order to do short-term lettings, properties must be inspected by local authorities and registered with the regional tourist authority. Owners must comply with certain safety regulations concerning gas appliances, fire prevention (e.g. chimney cleaning, smoke detectors and fire extinguishers or fire blankets), accidents (a first-aid kit must be provided), swimming pools and have public liability (*responsibilidade civil*) insurance. If you use a letting company they should apply for the necessary permit and may also pay taxes on your behalf. However, the authorities have a problem trying to get foreign, non-resident owners to comply and most simply turn a blind eye. Many companies and owners let properties illegally without registering with the local authorities, in order to avoid paying taxes on rental income, although there are large fines for offenders. In some developments, owners' letting rights are restricted and they may be required to let through a development's management company. Note also that some lenders' terms (such as offshore lenders) don't permit long-term or regular letting.

Tax on Rental Income: If you let your property in Portugal then you're liable for income tax, although many property owners let their properties illegally (note that there are large fines if you are caught). All rental properties are liable for income tax, either for individuals (IRS) or corporate income tax

(IRC) if the property is owned by an offshore company. If the property is owned by a resident, rental income is subject to the income tax (see page 102). If the property is owned by a non-resident or by an offshore company, rental income is subject to a fixed rate of 25 per cent. Note that as from 2002, all properties owned by offshore companies are subject to rental tax, whether the property is rented or not (see page 172).

Certain expenses such as maintenance (*manutenção*), repairs (*conservação*) and rates (*contribuição autarquica*) are deductible from the amount of rental tax due. Maintenance and repairs include work such as painting, plumbing and building insurance. In apartments that form part of a community property, expenses such as cleaning, security and community fees are also deductible. Work such as changes or additions to the structure of the building (e.g. extensions), the installation of heating or air-conditioning and the building of a swimming pool aren't considered deductible expenses. Note that all deductible expenses must be accompanied by an official receipt, which must state the name and fiscal number of the individual or company who provided the service, and must usually include VAT (*IVA*).

Location/Swimming Pools: If income from your Portuguese home has a high priority, you should buy a property with this in mind. To maximise rental income a property should be located as close as possible to the main attractions and/or a beach, be suitably furnished and professionally managed. A swimming pool is obligatory in most areas, as properties with pools are much easier to let than those without, unless a property is situated on a beach, lake or river. It's usually necessary to have a private pool with a single family home, although a shared pool is adequate for an apartment or townhouse. You can charge a higher rent for a property with a private pool and it may be possible to extend the letting season even further by installing a heated or indoor pool. Some private letting agencies won't handle properties without a pool.

Rents: Rental rates vary considerably with the season, the region, and the size and quality of a property. An average apartment or townhouse sleeping four in an average area can be let for between €500 to €1,000 per week, depending on the season, location and quality. At the other end of the scale, a luxury villa in a popular area with a pool and accommodation for six to eight can be let for €2,000 to €4,000 per week in the high season. The high season generally includes the months of July and August and possibly the first two weeks of September. The mid-season usually comprises May, June, late September and October (plus the Easter and Christmas periods), when rents are around 25 per cent lower than the high season; the rest of the year is the low season. During the low season, which may extend from October to April, rates are usually up to 50 per cent lower than the high season. In winter, rents may drop to as low as €500 per week for a two bedroom apartment on the Algarve, although there may be a minimum let of around two months. Rates usually include linen, gas and electricity, although heating in winter, e.g. gas or electric heaters, is charged extra.

Furnishings & Equipment: If you let a property, don't fill it with expensive furnishings or valuable personal belongings. While theft is rare, items will certainly get damaged or broken over a period of time. Store anything you don't wish to leave in your home when letting in a safe place, such as a lockable storage room or a garage. When furnishing a property that you plan to let, you should choose hard-wearing, dark coloured carpets which won't show the stains, and buy durable furniture and furnishings. Simple inexpensive furniture is best in a modest home, as it will need to stand up to hard wear. Small one or two bedroom properties usually have a settee in the living room, which converts into a double bed. Properties should be well equipped with cooking utensils, crockery and cutlery, and it's also usual to provide bed linen and towels. You may also need a cot or high chair for young children. Depending on the price and quality of a property, your guests may also expect central heating, a washing machine, dishwasher, microwave, covered parking, a barbecue, garden furniture and a TV. Some owners provide bicycles and badminton and table tennis equipment. It isn't usual to have a telephone in rental homes, although you could install a credit card telephone or one that will receive incoming calls only.

Keys: You will need several sets of spare keys, which will inevitably get lost at some time. If you employ a management company, their address should be on the key fob and not the address of the house. If you let a home yourself, you can use a 'key-finder' service, whereby lost keys can be returned to the key-finder company by anyone finding them. You should ensure that you get 'lost' keys returned, otherwise you may need to change the lock barrels (in any case it's wise to change them annually if you let a home). You don't need to provide clients with keys to all the external doors, only the front door (the others can be left in your home). If you arrange your own lets, you can mail keys to clients in your home country, otherwise they can be collected from a caretaker in Portugal. It's also possible to install a security key-pad entry system, the code of which can be changed after each let.

Letting Agents: If you're letting a second home, the most important decision is whether to let it yourself or use a letting agent (or agents). If you don't have much spare time then you're better off using an agent, who will take care of everything and save you the time and expense of advertising and finding clients. An agent will usually charge commission of between 10 and 30 per cent of gross rental income, some of which can be recouped through higher rents. If you want your property to appear in an agent's catalogue, you must contact him the summer before you wish to let it (the deadline is usually September). Although self-catering holiday companies may fall over themselves to take on a luxury property on the Algarve, the top letting agents turn down many of the properties they're offered.

Most agents don't permit owners to use a property during the peak letting season (July and August) and may also restrict their use at other times. There are numerous self-catering holiday companies operating in Portugal and many Portuguese estate agents also act as agents for holiday and long-term lets. **Take care when selecting an agent, as a number have gone bust in recent years owing customers hundreds of euros.** Make sure that your income is kept in a special 'escrow' account and paid regularly, or even better, choose an agent with a bonding scheme who pays you the rent <u>before</u> the arrival of guests (some do). It's absolutely essential to employ a reliable and honest (preferably long-established) company - anyone can set up a holiday letting agency and there are many 'cowboy' operators. Ask a management company to substantiate rental income claims and occupancy rates by showing you examples of actual income received from other properties. Ask for the names of satisfied customers and check with them.

Other things to ask a letting agent include: who they let to; where they advertise; whether they have contracts with holiday and travel companies; whether you're expected to contribute towards marketing costs; and whether you're free to let the property yourself and use it when you wish. The larger companies market homes via newspapers, magazines, the Internet, overseas agents and coloured brochures, and have representatives in a number of countries. Management contracts usually run for a year. A management company's services should include arranging routine and emergency repairs; reading meters (if electricity is charged extra); routine maintenance of house and garden, including lawn cutting and pool cleaning; arranging cleaning and linen changes between lets; advising guests on the use of equipment; and providing information and advice (24-hours a day for emergencies). Agents may also provide someone to meet and greet clients, hand over the keys and check that everything is in order. The actual services provided will usually depend on whether a property is a basic apartment or a luxury villa costing €4,000 or more a week. A letting agent's representative should also make periodic checks when a property is empty to ensure that it's secure and that everything is in order. When letting an apartment short-term, you must check that it's permitted under the community rules (*estatutos/regras*). You may also be required to notify your insurance company.

Doing Your Own Letting: Some owners prefer to let a property to family, friends, colleagues and acquaintances, which allows them more control (and <u>hopefully</u> the property will also be better looked after). In fact, the best way to get a high volume of lets is usually to do it yourself, although many owners use a letting agency in addition to doing their own marketing in their home country. If you wish to let a property yourself there's a wide range of Portuguese and foreign newspapers and magazines in which you can advertise, e.g. ***Dalton's Weekly*** and newspapers such as the ***Sunday Times*** in Britain. Many of the English-language newspapers and magazines listed in

Appendix A also include advertisements from property owners. You will need to experiment to find the best publications and days or months to advertise.

There are also companies producing directories of properties let directly by owners such as Private Villas (☎ 020-8329 0170, 🖳 www.privatevillas. co.uk) in Britain. You pay for the advertisement and handle bookings yourself. Portuguese regional tourist agencies can put you in touch with Portuguese letting agents. You can also advertise among friends and colleagues, in company and club magazines (which may even be free), and on notice boards in companies, stores and public places. The more marketing you do, the more income you're likely to earn. It also pays to work with other local people in the same business and send surplus guests to competitors (they will usually reciprocate). It isn't necessary to just advertise locally or stick to your home country, as you can also extend your marketing abroad (or advertise via the Internet). It's usually necessary to have a telephone answering machine and possibly a fax machine.

To get an idea of the rent you should charge simply ring a few letting agencies and ask them what it would cost to rent a property such as yours at the time of year you plan to let it. They're likely to quote the highest possible rent you can charge. You should also check the advertisements in newspapers and magazines. Set a realistic rent, as there's a lot of competition. Add a returnable deposit (e.g. €150) as security against loss (e.g. of keys) or breakages. A deposit should be refundable up to six weeks before the booking only. It's normal to have a minimum two-week rental period in July and August. You will need a simple agreement form, which includes the dates of arrival and departure and approximate times. If you intend to let to non-English speaking clients, you must have a letting agreement in Portuguese or other foreign languages.

If you plan to let a home yourself, you will need to decide how to handle enquiries about flights and car rentals. It's easier to let clients do it themselves, but you should be able to offer advice and put them in touch with airlines, ferry companies, travel agents and car rental companies. You will also need to decide whether you want to let to smokers or accept pets and young children (some people don't let to families with children under five years of age due to the risks of bed-wetting). It's usually best to provide linen (some agents provide a linen hire service), which is expected in Portugal, and electricity is also usually included in the rental fee.

It's recommended to produce a coloured brochure containing external/internal pictures (or a single colour brochure with coloured photographs affixed to it, although this doesn't look so professional), important details, the exact location, local attractions, details of how to get there (with a map), and the name, address and telephone number of your local caretaker or letting agent. You should enclose a stamped addressed envelope when sending out leaflets. It's necessary to make a home look as attractive as possible in a brochure without distorting the facts or misrepresentation. Advertise honestly and don't over-sell your property.

Local Information: You should also provide an information pack (in your home) for clients explaining how things work (such as heating and air-conditioning); **security measures**; what not to do; where to shop; recommended restaurants; local emergency numbers and health services such as doctors, hospitals and dentists; and assistance such as a general repairman, plumber, electrician and pool maintenance (which may be handled by a local representative). If you allow young children and pets, you should make a point of emphasising any dangers, such as falling into the pool. It's also beneficial to have a visitors' book where your clients can write their comments and recommendations. If you want to impress your guests you may wish to arrange for fresh flowers, fruit, a good bottle of wine and a grocery pack to greet them on their arrival. It's little touches like this that ensure repeat business and recommendations! If you go 'the extra mile' it will pay off and you may even find after the first year or two that you rarely need to advertise. Many people return to the same property each year and you should do an annual mail-shot to previous clients and send them some brochures. **Word-of-mouth advertising is the cheapest and always the best.**

Caretaker: If you own a second home in Portugal, you will find it beneficial or even essential to employ a local caretaker, irrespective of whether you let it. You may also need to employ a gardener. You can have your caretaker prepare the house for your family and guests as well as looking after it when it isn't in use. If you have a holiday home in Portugal it's best to have your caretaker check it periodically (e.g. weekly) and to give him authority to authorise minor repairs. If you let a property yourself, your caretaker can arrange for (or do) cleaning, linen changes, maintenance and repairs, gardening and pay bills. If you employ a caretaker or housekeeper you should expect to pay at least the minimum Portuguese wage of €348.01 per month (2001).

Increasing Rental Income: It's possible to increase rental income outside the high season by offering special interest or package holidays, which could be organised in conjunction with other local businesses in order to broaden the appeal and cater for larger parties. These may include activity holidays such as golf, tennis, cycling or hiking; cooking, gastronomy and wine tours/tasting; and arts and crafts such as painting, sculpture, photography and writing courses. You don't need to be an expert or conduct courses yourself, but can employ someone to do it for you.

Long-term Furnished Lets: As described here, long-term lets refer mainly to furnished lets of up to six months, usually outside the high season (although 'long-term' is often used to refer to lets of six months or longer). Bear in mind that tenants have considerable legal rights in Portugal, which discourages long-term lets. A short-term contract must clearly state the rental period and that it's for temporary occupation only. Although the law is on your side, you should be aware that if a tenant with a short-term rental contract refuses to leave it can take months to have him evicted (which is why many foreign home owners let to foreigners only, rather than to Portuguese families). Most people who let year round have low, medium and high season rates. Rates are naturally much lower for winter lets and may be less than half high season rates, with tenants paying for electricity and heating. Central heating is essential if you want to let long-term in some areas.

Closing a Property for the Winter: Before closing up a property for the winter, you should turn off the water at the mains (required by insurance companies) and drain all pipes, switch off fuses (except the one for a dehumidifier or air-conditioner if you leave it on while you're away), empty the food cupboards and the refrigerator/freezer, disconnect gas cylinders and empty dustbins. You should also leave the interior doors and a few small windows (with grilles or secure shutters) open to provide some ventilation. Lock all the doors and shutters and secure anything of value against theft or leave it with a neighbour or friend. Check whether any essential work needs to be done before you leave and if necessary arrange for it to be done in your absence. Most importantly leave a set of keys with a neighbour or have a caretaker check your home periodically.

SELLING A HOME

Although this book is primarily concerned with buying a home in Portugal, you may wish to sell your Portuguese home at some time in the future. Before offering a home for sale it's wise to investigate the state of the property market. For example, unless you're forced to sell, it definitely isn't recommended during a property slump when prices are depressed. It may be wiser to let your home long-term and wait until the market has recovered. It's also unwise to sell in the early years after purchase, when you will probably make a loss unless it was an absolute bargain. Having decided to sell, your first decision will be whether to sell it yourself (or try) or use the services of an estate agent. Although the majority of properties in Portugal are sold through estate agents, many people also sell their own homes. If you need to sell a property before buying a new one, this must be included as a conditional clause (see page 171) in the contract for a new home.

Price: It's important to bear in mind that (like everything) property has a market price and the best way of ensuring a quick sale (or any sale) is to ask a realistic price. In recent years prices have risen sharply and in 2002 the property market was experiencing a shortage of resale properties, particularly those on the Algarve and luxury villas anywhere. It's currently a seller's market and well-priced desirable properties are being snapped up like hot cakes. However, you should beware of trying to make a massive profit and over-pricing your property – buyers are also familiar with the market and generally know when a property isn't worth the asking price.

If your home's fairly standard for the area, you can find out its value by comparing the prices of other homes on the market, or those which have recently been sold. Most agents will provide a free appraisal of a home's value in the hope that you will sell it through them. However, don't believe everything they tell you, as they may over-price it simply to encourage you. You can also hire a professional valuer (e.g. a surveyor) to determine the market value. You should be prepared to drop the price slightly (e.g. 5 or 10 per cent) and should set it accordingly, but shouldn't grossly over-price a home, as it will deter buyers. Don't reject an offer out of hand unless it's ridiculously low, as you may be able to get a prospective buyer to raise his offer. When selling a second home in Portugal, you may wish to include the furnishings (plus major appliances) in the sale, which is a common practice in resort areas when selling a relatively inexpensive second home with modest furnishings. You should add an appropriate amount to the price to cover the value of the furnishings or alternatively you could use them as an inducement to a prospective buyer at a later stage, although this isn't normal practice.

Presentation: The secret to selling a home quickly lies in its presentation (always assuming that it's competitively priced). First impressions (both exterior and interior) are vital when marketing a property and it's important to present it in its best light and make it as attractive as possible to potential buyers. It may pay to invest in new interior decoration, new carpets, exterior paint and landscaping. A few plants and flowers can do wonders. When decorating a home for resale, it's important to be conservative and not to do anything radical (such as installing a red or black bathroom suite, or painting the walls purple). White is usually the best colour for walls, woodwork and porcelain.

It may also pay you to do some modernisation such as installing a new kitchen or bathroom, as these are of vital importance (particularly kitchens) when selling a home. However, although modernisation may be necessary to sell an old home, you shouldn't overdo it, as it's easy to spend more than you could ever hope to recoup on the sale price. If you're using an agent, you can ask him what you should do (or need to do) to help sell your home. If a home's in poor repair this must be reflected in the asking price and if major work is needed which you cannot afford, you should obtain a quotation (or two) and offer to knock this off the price. You have a duty under Portuguese law to inform a prospective buyer of any defects which aren't readily apparent and which materially affect the value of a property.

Selling Your Home Yourself: While certainly not for everyone, selling your own home is a viable option for many people and is particularly recommended when you're selling an attractive home at a realistic price in a favourable market. It may allow you to offer it at a more appealing price, which could be an important factor if you're seeking a quick sale. How you market your home will depend on the type of property, the price, and the country or area from where you expect your buyer to come. For example, if your property isn't of a type and style, or in an area, that's desirable to the Portuguese, it's usually a waste of time advertising it in the local Portuguese press.

Marketing: Marketing is the key to selling your home. The first step is to get a professional looking 'for sale' sign made (showing your telephone number) and erect it in the garden or place it in a window. Do some research into the best newspapers and magazines for advertising your property (see **Appendix A**), and place an advertisement in those that look most promising. You could also have a leaflet printed (with pictures) extolling the virtues of your property, which you could drop into local letter boxes or have distributed with a local newspaper (many people buy a new home in the immediate vicinity of their present home). You may also need a 'fact sheet' printed (if your home's vital statistics aren't included in the leaflet mentioned above) and could offer a finder's fee, e.g. €500, to anyone who finds you a buyer. Don't omit to market your home around local companies, schools and organisations, particularly if they have many itinerant employees. Finally, it may help to provide information about potential mortgage sources for buyers. With a bit of effort and practice you may even make a better job of marketing your home than an estate agent! Unless you're in a hurry to sell, set yourself a realistic time limit for success, after which you can try an agent. When selling a home yourself, you will need to engage a lawyer to draw up the sales contract.

Using an Agent: Most owners prefer to use the services of an agent or agents, either in Portugal or in their home country, e.g. when selling a second home in Portugal. If you purchased the property through an agent, it's often best to use the same agent when selling, as he will already be familiar with it and may still have the details on file. You should take particular care when selecting an agent, as they vary considerably in their professionalism, expertise and experience (the best way to investigate agents is by posing as a buyer). Many agents cover a relatively small area, so you should take care to choose one who regularly sells properties in your area and price range. If you own a property in an area popular with foreign buyers, it may be worthwhile using an overseas agent who advertises in foreign newspapers and magazines, such as the English-language publications listed in **Appendix A.**

Agents' Contracts: Before he can offer a property for sale, an agent must have a signed authorisation from the owner in the form of an exclusive or non-exclusive contract. An exclusive contract (*contrato de mediação*) gives a single agent the exclusive right to sell a property, while a non-exclusive contract allows you to deal with any number of agents and to negotiate directly with private individuals. Many people find that it's better to place a property with a number of agents under non-exclusive contracts. Exclusive contracts are for a limited period only, e.g. three to six months, and state the agent's commission and what it includes. Choose an agent who regularly sells properties in your price range and enquire how the property will be marketed and who will pay the costs.

Agents' Fees: When selling a property in Portugal, the agent's commission is usually paid by the vendor and included in the purchase price. Fees vary from around 5 to 10 per cent, depending on the price of a property, and are lower with an exclusive contract than with a non-exclusive contract. Shop around for the best deal, as there's fierce competition among agents to sell good properties (many 'tout' for properties to sell by advertising in the expatriate press in Portugal). **Note that if you sign a contract without reserving the right to find your own buyer, you must pay the agent's commission even if you sell your home yourself!** Make sure that you don't sign two or more exclusive contracts to sell your home. Check the contract and make sure you understand what you're signing. Contracts state the agent's commission, what it includes, and most importantly, who must pay it. Generally you shouldn't pay any fees unless you require extra services and you should never pay the agent's commission before a sale is completed and you've been paid.

Warning: As when buying a home in Portugal, you must be very, very careful who you deal with when selling a home. Make sure that you're paid with a certified banker's draft before signing over your property to a buyer, as once the deed of sale (*escritura*) has been signed the property belongs to the buyer, whether you've been paid or not. **Be extremely careful if you plan to use an intermediary, as it isn't uncommon for a 'middle man' to disappear with the proceeds!** Never agree to accept part of the sale price 'under the table'; if the buyer refuses to pay the extra money there's nothing you can do about it (at least legally). Although rare, sellers occasionally end up with no property and no money! All sales should be conducted through a lawyer. See also **Estate Agents** on page 162 and **Capital Gains Tax** on page 110.

5.

ARRIVAL & SETTLING IN

In addition to information about moving house, immigration and customs, this chapter also contains checklists of tasks to be completed before or soon after arrival in Portugal and when moving, plus suggestions for finding local help and information.

MOVING HOUSE

After finding a home in Portugal it usually takes just a few weeks to have your belongings shipped from within continental Europe. From anywhere else it varies considerably, e.g. around four weeks from the east coast of America, six weeks from the US west coast and the Far East, and around eight weeks from Australasia. Customs (*alfândega*) clearance is no longer necessary when shipping your household effects between EU countries. However, when shipping your effects from a non-EU country to Portugal you should enquire about customs' formalities in advance from a Portuguese mission. If you fail to follow the correct procedure you can encounter problems and delays, and may be erroneously charged duty or even fined. The relevant forms to be completed by non-EU citizens may depend on whether your Portuguese home will be your main residence or a second home. Removal companies usually take care of the paperwork and ensure that the correct documents are provided and properly completed (see **Customs** on page 207).

It's recommended to use a major shipping company with a good reputation. For international moves it's best to use a company that's a member of the International Federation of Furniture Removers (FIDI) or the Overseas Moving Network International (OMNI), with experience in Portugal. Members of FIDI and OMNI usually subscribe to an advance payment scheme providing a guarantee, whereby if a member company fails to fulfil its commitments to a client the removal is completed at the agreed cost by another company or your money is refunded. Some removal companies have subsidiaries or affiliates in Portugal, which may be more convenient if you encounter problems or need to make an insurance claim. If you engage a shipping company in Portugal, it's wise to avoid small unregistered companies ('man and van'), as some have been known to disappear with their client's worldly possessions (on the other hand, many are extremely reliable). A local shipping company should have a Portuguese business address, a registered licence number, a VAT (*IVA*) number and must be licensed to do removals in Portugal.

You should obtain at least three written quotations before choosing a company, as rates vary considerably. Removal companies should send a representative to provide a detailed quotation. Most companies will pack your belongings and provide packing cases and special containers, although this is naturally more expensive than packing them yourself. Ask a company how they pack fragile and valuable items, and whether the cost of packing cases, materials and insurance (see below) are included in a quotation. If you're doing your own packing, most shipping companies will provide packing crates and boxes. Shipments are charged by volume, e.g. the cubic metre in Europe and the cubic foot in the USA. You should expect to pay from €5,000 to €7,500 to move the contents of an average three to four bedroom house within western Europe, e.g. from London to the south of Portugal. If you're flexible about the delivery date, shipping companies will usually quote a lower fee based on a 'part load', where the cost is shared with other deliveries. This can result in savings of 50 per cent or more compared with a 'special' delivery. Whether you have an individual or shared delivery, obtain the maximum transit period in writing, otherwise you may need to wait months for delivery!

Be sure to fully insure your belongings during removal with a well-established insurance company. Don't insure with a shipping company that carries its own insurance, as they will usually fight every cent of a claim. Insurance premiums are usually 1 to 2 per cent of the declared value of your goods, depending on the type of cover chosen. It's prudent to make a photographic or video record of valuables for insurance purposes. Most insurance policies cover for 'all-risks' on a replacement value basis. Note, however, that china, glass and other breakables can usually be included in an 'all-risks' policy only when they're packed by the removal company. Insurance usually covers total loss or loss of a particular crate only, rather than individual items (unless they were packed by the shipping company). If you need to make a claim be sure to read the small print, as some companies require clients to make a claim within a few days, although seven is usual. Send a claim by registered mail. Some insurance companies apply an 'excess' (deductible) of around 1 per cent of the total shipment value when assessing claims. This means that if your shipment is valued at €25,000 and you make a claim for less than €250, you won't receive anything.

If you're unable to ship your belongings directly to Portugal, most shipping companies will put them into storage and some offer a limited free storage period prior to shipment, e.g. 14 days. **If you need to put your household effects into storage, it's imperative to have them fully insured, as warehouses have been known to burn down!** Make a complete list of everything to be moved and give a copy to the removal company. Don't include anything illegal (e.g. guns, bombs, drugs or pornography) with your belongings, as customs checks can be rigorous and penalties severe. Provide the shipping company with <u>detailed</u> instructions of how to find your Portuguese address from the nearest main road and a telephone number where you can be contacted.

After considering the shipping costs, you may decide to ship only selected items of furniture and personal effects to Portugal and buy new furniture locally. If you're importing household goods from another European country, it's possible to rent a self-drive van or truck. If you rent a vehicle outside Portugal you will usually need to return it to the country where it was hired. If you plan to transport your belongings to Portugal personally, check the customs requirements in the countries you must pass through. Most people find it isn't wise to do their own move unless it's a simple job, e.g. a few items of furniture and personal effects only. It's no fun heaving beds and wardrobes up stairs and squeezing them into impossible spaces! If you're taking pets with you, you may need to get your vet to tranquillise them, as many pets are frightened (even more than people) by the chaos and stress of moving house.

Bear in mind when moving home that everything that can go wrong often does, so allow plenty of time and try not to arrange your move to your new home on the same day as the previous owner is moving out. That's just asking for fate to intervene! **Last but not least, if your Portuguese home has poor or impossible access for a large truck you must inform the shipping company (the ground must also be firm enough to support a heavy vehicle).** Bear in mind that if large items of furniture need to be taken in through an upstairs window or balcony, you may need to pay extra. See also **Customs** on page 207 and the **Checklist** on page 213.

IMMIGRATION

On arrival in Portugal, your first task will be to negotiate immigration and customs. Fortunately this presents few problems for most people, particularly European Union (EU) nationals after the establishment of 'open' EU borders on 1st January 1993. However, non-EU nationals coming to Portugal for any purpose other than as a visitor usually require a visa (see page 18). Portugal is a signatory to the Schengen agreement (named after a Luxembourg village on the Moselle River) which came into effect in 1994 and was intended to introduce an open-border policy between member countries. Schengen members include Austria, Belgium, France, Germany, Italy, Luxembourg, the Netherlands, Portugal and Spain. Under the agreement, immigration checks and passport controls take place when you first arrive in a member country, after which you can travel freely between member countries without further checks.

When you arrive in Portugal from a country that's a signatory to the Schengen agreement, there are usually no immigration checks or passport controls. Officially, Portuguese immigration officials should check the passports of EU arrivals directly from non-Schengen countries (such as Britain and Ireland), although this doesn't always happen. If you're a non-EU national and arrive in Portugal by air or sea from outside the EU, you must go through immigration (*imigração*) for non-EU citizens. Non-EU citizens are required to complete an immigration registration card, which is provided on aircraft and ships. If you have a single-entry visa it will be cancelled by the immigration official. **If you require a visa to enter Portugal and attempt to enter without one, you will be refused entry.** Some people may wish to get a stamp in their passport as confirmation of their date of entry into Portugal.

If you're a non-EU national coming to Portugal to work, study or live, you may be asked to show documentary evidence. Immigration officials may also ask visitors to produce proof of their accommodation or financial resources, e.g. cash, travellers' cheques and credit cards. Visitors are supposed to have a minimum of €60 plus €12 for each day of their intended stay, although this isn't usually enforced. The onus is on visitors to show that they're genuine and that they don't intend to breach Portuguese immigration laws. Immigration officials aren't required to prove that you will break the law and can refuse you entry on the grounds of suspicion only.

CUSTOMS

The Single European Act, which came into effect on 1st January 1993, created a single trading market and changed the rules regarding customs (*alfândega*) for EU nationals. The shipment of personal (household) effects to Portugal from another EU country is no longer subject to customs' formalities. EU nationals planning to take up permanent or temporary residence in Portugal are permitted to import their furniture and personal effects free of duty or taxes, provided they were purchased tax-paid within the EU or have been owned for at least six months. A detailed inventory is recommended (although it's unlikely that anyone will check your belongings) and the shipping company should have a photocopy of the owner's passport notarised by a Portuguese consulate. There are no restrictions on the import or export of Portuguese or foreign banknotes or securities, although if you enter or leave Portugal with gold in any form, currency and travellers' or other bearer cheques exceeding €12,470 in value (see page 90), you must make a declaration to Portuguese customs.

Information about duty-free allowances can be found on page 72 and pets on page 73.

Visitors

Your belongings aren't subject to duty or VAT when you visit Portugal for up to six months (182 days). This applies to the import of private cars, camping vehicles (including trailers or caravans), motorcycles, aircraft, boats and personal effects. Goods may be imported without formality, provided their nature and quantity doesn't imply any commercial aim. All means of transport and personal effects imported duty-free mustn't be sold or given away in Portugal, and must be exported when a visitor leaves Portugal. If you cross into Portugal by road, you may drive through the border post without stopping (most are now unmanned). However, any goods and pets that you're carrying mustn't be subject to any prohibitions or restrictions (see page 209). Customs' officials can still stop anyone for a spot check, e.g. to check for drugs or illegal immigrants.

If you arrive at a seaport by private boat there are no particular customs' formalities, although you must show the boat's registration papers on request. A vessel registered outside the EU may remain in Portugal for a maximum of six months in any calendar year, after which it must be exported or imported (when duty and tax must be paid). Foreign-registered vehicles and boats mustn't be lent or rented to anyone while in Portugal.

Non-EU Residents

Non-EU nationals planning to take up permanent or temporary residence in Portugal are permitted to import their household goods and personal effects free of duty or taxes, provided they've owned them for at least one year. You require a baggage certificate (*certificado de bagagem*), which is available from Portuguese missions on production of the following documents:

- a notarised copy of the property deed (*escritura*) for your Portuguese home or a residence permit (*residência*);

- two copies of a detailed inventory (in Portuguese) listing the items to be imported and their estimated value in euros. All items to be imported should be included on the list, even if some are to be imported at a later date.

- two copies of a declaration (affidavit) in Portuguese that you have no other accommodation in Portugal and that you own the personal effects being imported and they have been in your possession for one year;

- your passport.

The baggage certificate must be used within 90 days of its issue. On arrival in Portugal you need to provide a declaration that you have no furnished accommodation there and that you're only importing the items listed on the inventory. There's a fee for clearance of your personal effects based on their weight and value. After arrival in Portugal a document must be drawn up by a local notary in which you undertake not to sell, rent or otherwise dispose of your household goods within one year of their official importation (which may be extended to ten years in the case of valuable items such as antiques and works of art).

Goods must be imported within one year of cancelling your previous residence and may be imported in a number of consignments, although it's best to have one consignment only (if there's more than one consignment, subsequent consignments should be cleared through the same customs' office). If you use a shipping company to transport your belongings to Portugal, they will usually provide all the necessary forms and take care of the paperwork. Keep a copy of all forms and communications with customs' officials, both with Portuguese customs' officials and customs' officials in your previous country of residence. If the paperwork isn't in order, your belongings may end up incarcerated in a Portuguese customs' storage depot for a number of months or could even be sold at auction by the authorities. If you personally import your belongings, you may need to employ an authorised customs' agent (*despachante*) to clear them. You should have an official record of the export of valuables from any country in case you wish to re-import them later.

Prohibited & Restricted Goods

Certain goods are subject to special regulations in Portugal and in some cases their import and export is prohibited or restricted. This particularly applies to the following:

- animal products;
- plants;
- wild fauna and flora and products derived from them;
- live animals;
- medicines and medical products (except for prescribed drugs and medicines);
- firearms and ammunition;
- certain goods and technologies with a dual civil/military purpose;
- works of art and collectors' items.

If you're unsure whether any goods you're importing fall into the above categories, you should check with Portuguese customs or a Portuguese mission. Visitors arriving in Portugal from 'exotic' regions, e.g. Africa, South America, and the Middle and Far East, may find themselves under close scrutiny from customs' and security officials looking for illegal drugs.

RESIDENCE CARD

A foreigner residing in Portugal for longer than six months must apply for a residence card (*autorização de residência*). If you come to Portugal with the intention of remaining longer than six months (e.g. as an employee, student or a non-employed resident), you must apply for a residence card on your arrival.

EU nationals who visit Portugal with the intention of finding employment or starting a business have up to six months to find a job and apply for a residence card. However, if you don't have a regular income or adequate financial resources your application will be refused. Failure to apply for a residence card within the specified time is a serious offence and can result in a heavy fine and even deportation.

FINDING HELP

One of the major problems facing new arrivals in Portugal is how and where to obtain help with day to day problems, for example, finding temporary accommodation, schooling, insurance and so on. Therefore in addition to the comprehensive information provided in this book, you will also need detailed local information. How successful you are at finding local help depends on your employer (if applicable), the town or area where you live (e.g. residents of resort areas are far better served than those living in rural areas), your nationality, Portuguese language proficiency and your sex (women are usually better catered for than men through women's clubs).

There's an abundance of information available in Portuguese, but not so much in English and other foreign languages. An additional problem is that much of the available information isn't intended for foreigners and their particular needs. You may find that your friends and colleagues can help, as they can often offer advice based on their own experiences and mistakes. **But take care!** Although they mean well, you're likely to receive as much false and conflicting information as accurate (it may not necessarily be wrong, but often won't apply to your particular situation).

Your local town hall (*câmara*) may be a good source of information, but you usually need to speak Portuguese to benefit and may still be sent on a wild goose chase from department to department. However, some town halls in areas where there are many foreign residents have a foreigners' department (*departamento de estrangeiros*) where staff speak English and other foreign languages (an advantage of living somewhere where there are many other foreigners). Apart from assisting with routine everyday matters, a foreigners' department can be helpful when applying for a resident card, social security membership or a Portuguese driving licence (and other formal applications), and they may save you the expense of employing a *despachante* to make these applications on your behalf.

A wealth of valuable information is available in major cities and resort towns, where foreigners are well served by English-speaking clubs and expatriate organisations. One organisation worthy of special mention is the Association of Foreign Property Owners in Portugal (AFPOP), Rua Infante D. Henrique 22-2°, 8500 Portimão (☎ 282-458 509, ✉ afpop@ip.pt). AFPOP publishes a newsletter; provides accountancy, building, investment and legal consultancies; maintains a list of recommended professionals; and offers advice on anything to do with buying, letting and maintaining a home in Portugal. Contacts can also be found through many expatriate magazines and newspapers (see **Appendix A**) in Portugal. Most consulates provide their nationals with local information, which may include details of lawyers, translators, doctors, dentists, schools, and social and expatriate organisations.

CHECKLISTS

Before Arrival

The checklists on the following pages include tasks which you need (or may need) to complete before and after arrival in Portugal, and when moving your home permanently to Portugal.

- **Check that your family's passports are valid.**
- Obtain a visa, if necessary, for all your family members (see page 18). Obviously this must be done before arrival in Portugal.
- Arrange health and travel insurance for yourself and your family (see pages 56 and 64). This is essential if you aren't covered by an international health insurance policy and won't be covered by Portuguese social security.
- Obtain an international driver's licence, if necessary (see page 41).
- Open a bank account in Portugal (see page 94) and transfer funds. You can open an account with many Portuguese banks while abroad, although it's best done in person in Portugal.
- It's wise to obtain some euros before arriving in Portugal, as this will save you having to change money on arrival (and you will probably receive a better exchange rate).
- If you don't already have one, it's recommended to obtain an international credit or charge card, which will prove particularly useful in Portugal.
- If you plan to become a permanent resident, you may also need to:
  - arrange schooling for your children.
  - organise the shipment of your personal and household effects.
  - obtain as many credit references as possible, for example from banks, mortgage companies, credit card companies, credit agencies, companies with which you've had accounts, and references from professionals such as lawyers and accountants. These will help you establish a credit rating in Portugal.

If you're planning to become a permanent resident in Portugal, don't forget to take all your family's official documents with you. These may include birth certificates; driving licences; marriage certificate, divorce papers or death certificate (if a widow or widower); educational diplomas and professional certificates; employment references and curriculum vitaes; school records and student ID cards; medical and dental records; bank account and credit card details; insurance policies (plus records of no-claims' allowances); and receipts for any valuables. You also need the documents necessary to obtain a residence card plus certified copies, official translations and numerous passport-size photographs (students should take at least a dozen).

After Arrival

The following checklist contains a summary of the tasks to be completed after arrival in Portugal (if not done before):

● On arrival at a Portuguese airport or port, have your visa cancelled and your passport stamped, as applicable.

● If you aren't taking a car with you, you may wish to rent (see page 46) or buy one locally. Note that it's practically impossible to get around in rural areas without a car.

● Open a cheque account (see page 94) at a local bank and give the details to any companies that you plan to pay by direct debit (such as utility companies).

● Arrange whatever insurance is necessary such as health, car, household and third party liability.

● Obtain local information (see page 210).

● Make courtesy calls on your neighbours and the local mayor within a few weeks of your arrival. This is particularly important in small villages and rural areas if you want to be accepted and become part of the local community.

● If you plan to become a permanent resident in Portugal, you will need to do the following within a few weeks (if not done before your arrival):

    – Apply for a residence permit at your local town hall as soon as possible after arrival.

    – Apply for a social security card from your local social security office.

    – Apply for a Portuguese driving licence if necessary (see page 40).

    – Find a local doctor and dentist.

    – Arrange schooling for your children.

Moving House

When moving permanently to Portugal there are many things to be considered and a 'million' people to be informed. Even if you plan to spend only a few months a year in Portugal, it may still be necessary to inform a number of people and companies in your home country. The checklists below are designed to make the task easier and help prevent an ulcer or a nervous breakdown (provided of course you don't leave everything to the last minute). See also **Moving House** on page 204.

● If you live in rented accommodation you will need to give your landlord notice (check your contract).

● Arrange to sell or dispose of anything you aren't taking with you (e.g. house, car and furniture). If you're selling a home or business, you should obtain expert legal advice, as you may be able to save tax by establishing a trust or other legal vehicle. If you own more than one property, you may need to pay capital gains tax on any profits from the sale of second and subsequent homes.

● Arrange shipment of your furniture and belongings by booking a shipping company well in advance (see page 204). Major international shipping companies usually provide a wealth of information and can advise on a wide range of matters concerning an international relocation. Find out the exact procedure for shipping your belongings to Portugal from your local Portuguese mission.

● If you're exporting a vehicle to Portugal, you will need to complete the relevant paperwork in your home country prior to leaving and re-register it in Portugal on arrival. Contact your local Portuguese embassy or consulate for information.

● Check whether you need an international driving licence or a translation of your foreign driving licence(s) for Portugal. Note that some foreigners are required to take a driving test before they can buy and register a car in Portugal.

● Check whether you're entitled to a rebate on your road tax, car and other insurance. Obtain a letter from your motor insurance company stating your no-claims' discount.

● Arrange inoculations and shipment for any pets that you're taking with you (see page 73).

● You may qualify for a rebate on your tax and social security contributions. If you're leaving a country permanently and have been a member of a company or state pension scheme, you may be entitled to a refund or may be able to continue payments to qualify for a full (or larger) pension when you retire. Contact your company personnel office, local tax office or pension company for information.

- It's best to have health, dental and optical check-ups for all your family before leaving your home country. Obtain a copy of all health records and a statement from your private health insurance company stating your present level of cover.

- Terminate any outstanding loan, lease or hire purchase contracts and pay all bills (allow plenty of time, as some companies are slow to respond).

- Return any library books or anything borrowed.

- Inform the following:
    - your employers (e.g. give notice or arrange leave of absence) or clients (if you're self-employed);
    - your local town hall or municipality. You may be entitled to a refund of your local property or income taxes.
    - If it was necessary to register with the police in your home country (or present country of residence), you should inform them that you're moving abroad.
    - your electricity, gas, water and telephone companies. Contact companies well in advance, particularly if you need to get a deposit refunded.
    - your insurance companies (for example health, car, home contents and private pension); banks, post office (if you have a post office account), stockbroker and other financial institutions; credit card, charge card and hire purchase companies; lawyer and accountant; and local businesses where you have accounts.
    - your family doctor, dentist and other health practitioners. Health records should be transferred to your new doctor and dentist in Portugal, if applicable.
    - your children's schools. Try to give a term's notice and obtain a copy of any relevant school reports or records from your children's current schools.
    - all regular correspondents, subscriptions, social and sports clubs, professional and trade journals, and friends and relatives. Give them your new address and telephone number in Portugal and arrange to have your post redirected by the post office or a friend. Give close friends, relatives and business associates a telephone number where you can be contacted in Portugal.

- If you have a driving licence or car you will need to give the local vehicle registration office your new address in Portugal and, in some countries, return your car's registration plates.

● If you will be living in Portugal for an extended period (but not permanently), you may wish to give someone 'power of attorney' over your financial affairs in your home country so that they can act for you in your absence. This can be for a fixed period or open-ended and can be for a specific purpose only. **However, you should always take expert legal advice before doing this!**

● Finally, allow plenty of time to get to the airport, register your luggage, and clear security and immigration.

Have a safe journey! (*¡Bom viagem!*)

APPENDICES

APPENDIX A: USEFUL ADDRESSES

Embassies & Consulates

Embassies are located in the capital Lisbon and many countries also have consulates in other cities (British consulates are listed on page 220). Embassies and consulates are listed in the yellow pages under *Embaixadas*. Note that some countries have more than one office in Lisbon and therefore before writing or calling in person you should telephone to confirm that you have the correct office. The address and telephone numbers for embassies in Portugal are listed below:

Algeria: Rua Duarte P. Pereira, 58, 1400 Lisbon (☎ 213-016 356, 🖳 www.emb-argelia.pt).

Angola: Av. da República, 68, 1050 Lisbon (☎ 217-967 041).

Argentina: Av. João Crisóstomo, 8 r/c esq, 1000 Lisbon (☎ 217-977 311).

Austria: Av. Infante Santo, 43-4°, 1350 Lisbon (☎ 213-858 220-2).

Belgium: Pr. Marqués de Pombal, 14-6°, 1250 Lisbon (☎ 213-549 263).

Brazil: Estrada das Laranjeiras, 144, 1600 Lisbon (☎ 217-267 777).

Bulgaria: Rua do Sacramento a Lapa, 31, 1200 Lisbon (☎ 216-766 364).

Canada: Av. da Liberdade, 198/200, 3rd Floor, 1269 Lisbon (☎ 213-164 600).

Cape Verde: Av. do Restelo, 33, 1400 Lisbon (☎ 213-015 271).

Chile: Av. Miguel Bombarda, 5-1°, 1000 Lisbon (☎ 213-148 054, 🖳 www.emb-chile.pt).

China: Rua de S. Caetano, 2 (à Lapa), 1200 Lisbon (☎ 213-961 882).

Colombia: Praça José Fontana, 10-5°D, 1050 Lisbon (☎ 213-557 096).

Congo: Av. Fontes Pereira de Melo, 31-8°, 1050 Lisbon (☎ 213-523 127).

Costa Rica: Av. Columbano Bordalo Pinheiro, 93, 6°E, 1070 Lisbon (☎ 217-272 297).

Croatia: Rua D. Lourenço de Almeida, 24, 1400 Lisbon (☎ 213-021 033).

Cuba: Rua Pero da Covilhã, 14, 1400 Lisbon (☎ 213-015 317-8).

Cyprus: Av. Liberdade, 49, 6°E, 1250 Lisbon (☎ 213-194 180).

Czech Republic: Rua Pêro de Alenquer, 14, 1400 Lisbon (☎ 213-010 487).

Denmark: Ria Castilho, 14-C, 3°, 1296 Lisbon (☎ 213-541 250).

Egypt: Av. D. Vasco da Gama, 8, 1400 Lisbon (☎ 213-018 301).

Finland: Rua Miguel Lupi, 12, 5°, 1249 Lisbon (☎ 213-933 040, 💻 www. finlandia.pt).

France: Rua de Santos-o-Velho, 5, 1200 Lisbon (☎ 213-972 652, 💻 www. ambafrance-pt.org).

Germany: Campo dos Mártires da Pátria, 38, 1169 Lisbon (☎ 218-810 210, 💻 www.embaixada-alemanha.pt).

Greece: Rua do Alto do Duque, 13, 1400 Lisbon (☎ 213-016 991).

Guinea-Bissau: Rua de Alcolena, 17, 1400 Lisbon (☎ 213-030 440).

Hungary: Calçada de Santo Amaro, 85, 1300 Lisbon (☎ 213-645 929).

Iraq: Rua Arriaga, 9, (Alapa), 1200 Lisbon (☎ 213-960 944).

Ireland: Rua da Imprensa à Estrela, 1-4°, 1200 Lisbon (☎ 213-929 440).

Israel: Rua António Enes, 16-4°, 1000 Lisbon (☎ 213-570 251).

Italy: Largo de Conde Pombeiro, 6, 1150 Lisbon (☎ 213-515 320, 💻 www. embital.pt).

Japan: Av. Liberdade, 245-6°, 1269 Lisbon (☎ 213-110 560, 💻 www.pt. emb-japan.go.ip).

Korea (South): Av. 5 de Outubro, 68, 7°, 1050 Lisbon (☎ 217-974 032).

Libya: Av. das Descobertas, 24, 1400 Lisbon (☎ 213-016 301).

Luxembourg: Rua das Junelas Verdes, 43, 1200 Lisbon (☎ 213-962 781).

Mexico: Rua Braancamp, 40, 9°Esq., 1250 Lisbon (☎ 213-839 680, 💻 www. sre.gob.mx/portugal).

Morocco: Rua Alto do Duque, 21, 1400 Lisbon (☎ 213-020 842).

Mozambique: Av. de Berna, 7, 1050 Lisbon (☎ 217-971 994).

The Netherlands: Av. Infante Santo, 43-5°, 1350 Lisbon (☎ 213-961 163, 💻 www.emb-paisesbaixos.pt).

New Zealand: Av. Antonio Augusta de Aguilar, 9th Floor, 1097 Lisbon (☎ 213-509 690).

Nigeria: Rua Fernão Mendes Pinto, 50, 1400 Lisbon (☎ 213-016 191).

Norway: Av. Vasco da Gama, 1, 1400 Lisbon (☎ 213-015 344).

Pakistan: Av. da República, 20-1°, 1050 Lisbon (☎ 213-538 446).

Panama: Rua Pedro Sintra, 15, 1400 Lisbon (☎ 213-019 046).

Paraguay: Campo Grande, 4, 7°, 1700 Lisbon (☎ 217-965 907).

Peru: Rua Castilho, 50-4°, Dt°, 1250 Lisbon (☎ 213-861 552).

Poland: Av. das Descobertas, 2, 1400 Lisbon (☎ 213-012 350).

Romania: Rua de São Caetana, 5, 1200 Lisbon (☎ 213-960 866).

Russia: Rua Visconde de Santarém, 59, 1000 Lisbon (☎ 218-462 424).

S. Tomé Príncipe: Rua de Junqueira, 2, 1300 Lisbon (☎ 213-638 242).

Saudi Arabia: Av. Restelo 42, 1400 Lisbon (☎ 213-010 317).

Slovakia: Av. Fontes Pereira de Melo, 19, 7°-Dt°, 1050 Lisbon (☎ 213-549 838).

Slovenia: Av. Liberdade, 49, 6°E, 1250 Lisbon (☎ 213-423 301).

South Africa: Av. Luís Bivar, 10, 1050 Lisbon Codex (☎ 213-535 041).

Spain: Rua do Salitre, 1, 1250 Lisbon (☎ 213-472 382-3).

Sweden: Rua Miguel Lupi, 12-2°D, 1249 Lisbon (☎ 213-942 260, 💻 www.embsuecia.pt).

Switzerland: Travessa do Patricínio, 1, 1350 Lisbon Codex (☎ 213-973 121/2).

Thailand: Rua de Alcolena, 12-12A, 1400 Lisbon (☎ 213-014 848).

Tunisia: Rua de Alcolena, 35, 1400 Lisbon (☎ 213-010 330).

Turkey: Av. das Descobertas, 22, 1400 Lisbon (☎ 213-014 275).

United Kingdom: Rua de São Bernardo, 33, 1249 Lisbon (☎ 213-914 000, 💻 www.uk-embassy.pt).

United States of America: Av. das Forças Armadas, 1600 Lisbon (☎ 217-273 300, 💻 www.american-embassy.pt).

Uruguay: Rua Sampaio E Pina, 16-2°, 1000 Lisbon (☎ 213-889 265).

Venezuela: Rua Rodrigo Fonseca, 82, 1°E, 1250 Lisbon (☎ 213-861 567).

Yugoslavia: Av. das Descobertas, 12, 1400 Lisbon (☎ 213-015 311).

British Consulates in Portugal

Lisbon: Rua de São Bernardo, 33, 1249 Lisbon (☎ 213-924 159).

Madeira: Av. de Zarco 2, PO Box 417, 9001 Funchal (☎ 091-221 221).

Portimão: Largo Francisco A. Maurício 7-1°, 8500 Portimão (☎ 282-417 800).

Porto: Av. da Boavista, 3072, 4100 Porto (☎ 226-184 789).

English-Language Newspapers & Magazines

Algarve Property Advertiser, VIP, Largo 5 de Outubro, 28, 8400 Lagoa (Algarve), Portugal (☎ 282-340 660, ✉ vistaiberica@vistaiberica.com). Bimonthly property magazine available on subscription only.

Algarve Resident Magazine, Urbanização Lagoa-Sol, Lote 1B, 8400 Lagoa, Portugal (☎ 282-342 936, 🖳 www.algarveresident.com). Weekly newspaper issued on Friday.

Anglo-Portuguese News (APN), Apartado 113, 2766 Monte Estoril, Portugal (☎ 214-661 431, ✉ apn@mail.telepac.pt). Weekly newspaper issued on Thursday.

Essential Algarve, HDP Algarve, Parque Empresarial Algarve 7, EN 125, Apartado 59, 8400 Lagoa, Portugal (☎ 282-341 333, 🖳 www.essential-algarve.com). Monthly magazine.

Homes Overseas, Blendon Communications Ltd., 207 Providence Square, Mill Street, London SE1 2EW, UK (☎ 020-7939 9888, 🖳 www.homes overseas.co.uk). Bimonthly international property magazine.

International Homes, 3 St. Johns Court, Moulsham Street, Chelmsford, Essex CM2 0JD, UK (☎ 01245-358877, 🖳 www.international-homes.com). Bimonthly magazine.

Madeira News Magazine, Apt 621, 9008 Funchal, Madeira, Portugal (🖳 www.soft-madeira-news.com). Monthly magazine available by subscription only.

The News (🖳 http://the-news.pt, ✉ editor@the-news.pt). Weekly newspaper in English published at weekends.

The Portuguese Property Journal, Apartado 118, Santa Barbera de Nexe, 8001 Faro, Portugal (☎ 289-999706, ✉ von.hafe@netc.pt).

Private Villas, C I Tower, St George's Square, New Malden, Surrey KT3 4JA, UK (☎ 020-8329 0170, 🖳 www.privatevillas.co.uk). Annual catalogue of properties to let in Portugal and other countries.

World of Property, Outbound Publishing, 1 Commercial Road, Eastbourne, East Sussex BN21 3XQ, UK (☎ 01323-726040, 🖳 www.outboundnews papers.com). Bimonthly property magazine.

Miscellaneous

The Anglo-Portuguese Society, Canning House, 2 Belgrave Square, London SW1X 8PJ, UK (☎ 020-7245 9738).

The Association of Foreign Property Owners in Portugal (AFPOP), Rua Infante D. Henrique 22-2°, 8500 Portimão, Portugal (☎ 282-458 509, ✉ af pop@ip.pt).

Portuguese-British Chamber of Commerce (*Câmara de Comércio Luso-Britânica*), Rua da Estrela, 8, 1200 Lisbon (☎ 213-961 351).

Portuguese Embassy, 2125 Kalorama Rd., NW, Washington, DC 20008, USA (☎ 202-328 8610).

Portuguese Embassy, 11 Belgrave Square, London SW1X 8PP, UK (☎ 020-7235 5331).

Portuguese National Tourist Office, 2nd Floor, 22-25a Sackville Street, London W1X 1DE, UK (☎ 0906-364 0610 (cost 60p per minute), 🖥 www.portugalinsite.pt).

Portuguese National Tourist Office, 590 Fifth Ave., 4th Floor, New York, NY 10036-4702 (☎ 212-354-4403/4).

Portuguese-UK Chamber of Commerce, 4th Floor, 22/25a Sackville Street, London W1X 1DE (☎ 020-7494 1844, 🖥 www.portuguese-chamber.org.uk).

APPENDIX B: FURTHER READING

The books listed below are just a small selection of the many written for those planning to buy a home or work in Portugal. Note that some titles may be out of print, but may still be obtainable from book shops and libraries. Books prefixed with an asterisk (*) are recommended by the author.

General Tourist Guides

*AA Baedeker's Portugal, Mark Turner (AA Publishing)

AA Essential Algarve, Christopher Catling (AA Publishing)

AA Essential Portugal (AA Publishing)

AA Spiral Guide: Algarve, Paul Murphy, Susie Boulton (AA Publishing)

Berlitz Portugal (Berlitz Pocket Guides)

*Blue Guide: Portugal, Ian Robertson (A&C Black)

Collins Independent Travellers Guide Portugal, Martha de la Cal (Collins)

*DK Eyewitness Travel Guides: Portugal, Martin Symington (Dorling Kindersley)

*Exploring Rural Portugal, Joe Staines & Lia Duarte (Christopher Helm)

Fielding's Paradors, Pousadas and Charming Villas (Fielding)

Fielding's Portugal (Fielding)

Fodor's Exploring Portugal (Fodor's)

*Fodor's Portugal (Fodor's)

*Frommer's Portugal, Darwin Porter & Danforth Prince (Macmillan)

Insider's Guide to Portugal, Harry Blutstein (Insider's Guides)

*Insight Guides: Portugal (APA Publications)

Karen Brown's Portugal: Charming Inns & Itineraries (Karen Brown Guides)

Landscapes of Algarve, B. & E. Anderson (Sunflower Books)

*Let's Go 2002: Spain & Portugal (Macmillan)

*Lisbon, Manfredd Hamm & Werner Radasewsky (Nicolai)

*Lonely Planet: Portugal (Lonely Planet)

Madeira, Rodney Bolt (Cadogan)

Madeira & Porto Santo, Gravette (Windrush Press)

*Michelin Red Guide: Spain - Portugal (Michelin)

*Michelin Green Guide Portugal (Michelin)

Off the Beaten Track: Portugal, N. Timmonds (Moorland)

Portugal, David J. Evans (Cadogan)

Portugal: Nelles Guides (Nelles Verlag)

*Portugal: The Rough Guide, Mark Ellingham, John Fisher & Graham Kenyon (Rough Guides)

Portugal: A Traveller's Guide, Ian Robertson (John Murray)

Portugal Guide, Ron Charles (Open Road Publishing)

Portuguese Traveller: Great Sights and Hidden Treasures, B. Rogers (Mills & Sanderson)

Rivages Hotels and Country Inns of Character and Charm in Portugal (Fodor's)

The Rough Guide to the Algarve, Matthew Hancock (Rough Guides)

The Rough Guide to Lisbon, Matthew Hancock (Rough Guides)

*The Rough Guide to Portugal, Mark Ellingham (Rough Guides)

A Short Trip in the Alentejo, Robert & Jane Wilson

*Special Places to Stay: Portugal, Alistair Sawday (Alistair Sawday Publications)

Time Off in Spain and Portugal, Teresa Tinsley (Horizon)

Timeout Guide to Lisbon (Penguin Books)

Visitor's Guide to Portugal, Barbara Mandell (Moorland)

Living, Working & Doing Business

Blackstone Franks Guide to Living In Portugal (Kogan Page)

Business Portugal, Peter Daughtrey (Vista Ibérica Publicações)

Doing Business in Portugal (Price Waterhouse)

How To Live & Work in Portugal, Sue Tyson-Ward (How To Books)

*Living in Portugal, Anne de Stoop (Flammarion)

Living in Portugal, Susan Thackeray (Robert Hale)

Live & Work in Spain & Portugal, Jonathan Packer (Vacation Work)

Portugal's Bureau Jungle Book, Edward Eves (Vista Ibérica Publicações)

Food & Wine

The Food of Portugal, Jean E. Anderson (Hearst)

*Gastronomy of Spain and Portugal, Maite Manjón (Garamond)

How to Eat Out in Portugal, Maria Martinelli (Gremese International)

The Port Companion: A Connoisseur's Guide, Godfrey Spence

Portugal's Wines and Winemakers, R. Mayson (Century Wine Library)

Portuguese Cooking: The Authentic and Robust Cuisine of Portugal, Caro Robertson (North Atlantic)

*The Taste of Portugal, Edite Viera (Grub Street)

The Traveller's Food and Wine Guide: Spain and Portugal, Christine Boyle & Chris Nawrat (Carbury)

*The Wines of Portugal, Jan Read (Faber)

Miscellaneous

*A Concise History of Portugal, David Birmingham (Cambridge University Press)

A Cottage in Portugal, Richard Hewitt

*Country Manors of Portugal, Marcus Binney (Scala)

Golf's Golden Coast, John Russell & Nuno Campos (Vista Ibérica Publicações)

A History of Spain & Portugal, William Atkinson (Penguin)

Houses and Gardens of Portugal, Patrick Bowe

Houses with Tradition in Portugal, Jorge Pereira da Sampaio

Journey to Portugal, Jose Saramago (The Harvill Press)

Landscapes of Portugal, Brian & Eileen Anderson

*On Foot Through Europe: A Trail Guide to Spain and Portugal, Craig Evans (Quill)

Portugal 1001 Sights: An Archaeological and Historical Guide, James M Anderson & M Sheridan Lea (Robert Hale)

*Portugal: A Book of Folk-Ways, Rodney Gallop

Portugal's Pousada Route, Stuart Ross (Vista Ibérica Publicações)

Portuguese Gardens, Helder Carita & Homem Cardoso (Antique Collector's Club)

*The Portuguese: The Land and Its People, Marion Kaplan (Penguin)

*Pousadas of Portugal, Sam & Jane Ballard

*Southern Portugal: Its People, Traditions & Wildlife, John & Madge Measures

*Spain and Portugal by Rail, Norman Renouf (Bradt Publications)

*They Went to Portugal, Rose Macaulay (Penguin)

*Walking in Portugal, Bethan Davies & Ben Cole (Footprint)

APPENDIX C: USEFUL WEBSITES

There are many websites of interest to homeowners and visitors to Portugal, and as the Internet increases in popularity the number grows daily. Most provide useful information and generally offer free access, although some require a subscription or payment for services. Listed below are some of the best websites for Portugal (the list is by no means definitive).

All Travel Portugal: a comprehensive travel website with useful information (🖳 www.alltravelportugal.com).

Castles and Palaces: an interesting site with information about Portugal's castles and palaces (🖳 www.castelos.org).

General Information: good general information about Portugal (🖳 www. portugal-info.net).

General Tourist Information: comprehensive general information about Portugal (🖳 www.portugal-web.com and 🖳 www.portugal-live.net).

Portugal Insite: the official tourism website with a wealth of information about Portugal and what's on around the country available in English, German and Spanish (🖳 www.portugal-insite.pt).

Portugal Trade & Tourism: the official investment site with comprehensive information about doing business in Portugal as well as tourist information (🖳 www.portugal.org).

Portugal Travel Information: good general travel information for visitors (🖳 www.portugal.com).

Portuguese Cookery: an attractive site including recipes - a 'must' for gourmets (🖳 www.gastronomias.com - in Portuguese only).

Pousadas: the official website for Portugal's network of pousadas including online reservations (🖳 www.pousadas.pt).

Virtual Portugal: general tourist and travel information (🖳 www.portugal virtual.pt).

The Algarve

Algarve Golf: comprehensive guides to the Algarve golf courses including course prices and accommodation information (🖳 www.algarvegold. com/golf and 🖳 www.algarve-golf.com).

Algarve Information: the following sites all provide good general information, mostly aimed at holidaymakers and homebuyers (🖳 www. algarve-information.com, 🖳 www.algarve-web.com, 🖳 www.algarve.org).

Algarve Net: comprehensive information about visiting and living in the Algarve, including business listings (💻 www.algarvenet.com).

The Azores

Azores Islands: general information on all the islands (💻 www.multi. pt/azores).

Azores Tourist Information: the official tourism website (💻 www. drtazores.pt).

Madeira

Madeira Information: a wealth of information about the island as well as new items and events listings (💻 www.madeira-island.com).

Madeira Web: general tourism guide to the island (💻 www.madeira-web.com).

APPENDIX D: WEIGHTS & MEASURES

Portugal uses the metric system of measurement. Nationals of a few countries (including the Americans and British) who are more familiar with the imperial system of measurement will find the tables on the following pages useful. Some comparisons shown are only approximate, but are close enough for most everyday uses. In addition to the variety of measurement systems used, clothes sizes often vary considerably with the manufacturer (as we all know only too well). Try all clothes on before buying and don't be afraid to return something if, when you try it on at home, you decide it doesn't fit (most shops will exchange goods or give a refund).

Women's Clothes

Continental	34 36 38 40 42 44 46 48 50 52
UK	8 10 12 14 16 18 20 22 24 26
USA	6 8 10 12 14 16 18 20 22 24

Pullovers

	Women's	Men's
Continental	40 42 44 46 48 50	44 46 48 50 52 54
UK	34 36 38 40 42 44	34 36 38 40 42 44
USA	34 36 38 40 42 44	sm medium large xl

Note: sm = small, xl = extra large

Men's Shirts

Continental	36 37 38 39 40 41 42 43 44 46
UK/USA	14 14 15 15 16 16 17 17 18 -

Men's Underwear

Continental	5	6	7	8	9	10
UK	34	36	38	40	42	44
USA	small	medium		large	extra large	

Children's Clothes

Continental	92	104	116	128	140	152
UK	16/18	20/22	24/26	28/30	32/34	36/38
USA	2	4	6	8	10	12

Children's Shoes

Continental	18	19	20	21	22	23	24	25	26	27	28	29	30	31	32
UK/USA	2	3	4	4	5	6	7	7	8	9	10	11	11	12	13

Continental	33	34	35	36	37	38
UK/USA	1	2	2	3	4	5

Shoes (Women's and Men's)

Continental	35	35	36	37	37	38	39	39	40	40	41	42	42	43	44	44
UK	2	3	3	4	4	5	5	6	6	7	7	8	8	9	9	10
USA	4	4	5	5	6	6	7	7	8	8	9	9	10	10	11	11

Weight

Avoirdupois	Metric	Metric	Avoirdupois
1 oz	28.35 g	1 g	0.035 oz
1 pound*	454 g	100 g	3.5 oz
1 cwt	50.8 kg	250 g	9 oz
1 ton	1,016 kg	500 g	18 oz
1 tonne	2,205 pounds	1 kg	2.2 pounds

* A metric 'pound' is 500g, g = gramme, kg = kilogramme

Length

British/US	Metric	Metric	British/US
1 inch	2.54 cm	1 cm	0.39 inch
1 foot	30.48 cm	1 m	3 feet 3.25 inches
1 yard	91.44 cm	1 km	0.62 mile
1 mile	1.6 km	8 km	5 miles

Note: cm = centimetre, m = metre, km = kilometre

Capacity

Imperial	Metric	Metric	Imperial
1 pint (USA)	0.47 litre	1 litre	1.76 UK pints
1 pint (UK)	0.57 litre	1 litre	0.26 US gallons
1 gallon (USA)	3.78 litre	1 litre	0.22 UK gallon
1 gallon (UK)	4.54 litre	1 litre	35.21 fluid oz

Square Measure

British/US	Metric	Metric	British/US
1 square inch	0.45 sq. cm	1 sq. cm	0.15 sq. inches
1 square foot	0.09 sq. m	1 sq. m	10.76 sq. feet
1 square yard	0.84 sq. m	1 sq. m	1.2 sq. yards
1 acre	0.4 hectares	1 hectare	2.47 acres
1 square mile	259 hectares	1 sq. km	0.39 sq. mile

Temperature

° Celsius	° Fahrenheit	
0	32	freezing point of water
5	41	
10	50	
15	59	
20	68	
25	77	
30	86	
35	95	
40	104	

Note: The boiling point of water is 100°C / 212°F.

Oven Temperature

Gas	Electric	
	°F	°C
-	225–250	110–120
1	275	140
2	300	150
3	325	160
4	350	180
5	375	190
6	400	200
7	425	220
8	450	230
9	475	240

For a quick conversion, the Celsius temperature is approximately half the Fahrenheit temperature.

Temperature Conversion

Celsius to Fahrenheit: multiply by 9, divide by 5 and add 32.

Fahrenheit to Celsius: subtract 32, multiply by 5 and divide by 9.

Body Temperature

Normal body temperature (if you're alive and well) is 98.4° Fahrenheit, which equals 37° Celsius.

APPENDIX E: GLOSSARY

Abrigo para carro: Car port.

Adega: Wine cellar or vat room.

Administrador: Administrator, e.g. of a community of property owners in a community development.

Advogado: Lawyer or solicitor.

Agrimensor: Surveyor.

Água: Water.

Água da rede: Mains water.

Aldeia (branca): (White) village.

Alfândega: Customs.

Alpendre: Porch.

Alta qualidade: Top quality.

Alugar-se: For rent or to let.

Aluguel: Rent.

Aluguel de carro: Car rental.

Armário embutido: Built-in wardrobe.

Amortização: Instalments. The gradual process of systematically reducing debt in equal payments (as in a mortgage) comprising both principal and interest, until the debt is paid in full.

Andar: Floor, storey.

Andar térreo (Brazil) (rés-do-chão (Portugal), 1° Andar): ground floor (British) or first floor (American).

Anexo: Annexe or outbuilding.

Antena parabólica: Satellite dish.

Apartamento: Apartment, flat.

Apartamento conjugado: Studio apartment.

Apartamento com cozinha: Self-catering apartment.

Apartamento separado/independente: Separate apartment, e.g. with a villa.

Apliques/Acessórios de casa: Fittings.

Aquecedor de água: Water heater.

Aquecimento: Heating.

Aquecimento central: Central heating.

Aquecimento de água a gas: Gas water heating.

Aquecimento eléctrico: Electric heating/radiator.

Ar condicionado: Air-conditioning.

Arco: Arch.

Área coberta: Covered area.

Área de construção: Constructed area.

Área de habitação: Built/internal area.

Área de lote: Plot size.

Arrendamento: Lease.

Armário: Cupboard, wardrobe.

Armário embutido na parede: Fitted (built-in) wardrobe.

Arquiteto: Architect.

Arrecadação: Storeroom.

Arrecadação na cave: Basement storage cage.

Arrumo: Storage.

Artigo matricial: The article number under which property is filed at the tax office (according to the municipality in which it's situated).

Árvores: Trees.

Ascensor/Elevador: Lift, elevator.

Aspirador: Vacuum cleaner.

Assoalho: floor.

Associação dos Mediadores do Algarve (AMA): Association of Algarve estate agents.

Associação de Mediadores Imobiliários (AMI): Association of estate agents.

Associação de proprietários ou condónimos: Community of owners in a community development.

Autorização de residência: Residence card/permit.

Avenida: Avenue, usually abbreviated *Av.* or *Av^a*.

Azulejos: Tiles, often blue and white, used to decorate buildings.

Banho: Bath.

Bairro: Town district, quarter (*alto* is upper and *baixo* lower).

Balcão: Balcony.

Balde do lixo: Dustbin or trash can.

(em) Boas condições: In good condition.

Boletim/Certidão oficial: Official bulletin or certificate.

(em) Bom estado: In good condition.

Cabana: Hut.

Caderneta predial (rustica): Property registration document (rural).

Caderneta predial (urbana): Property registration document (urban).

Caixa (de Previdência): Social security.

Caixa-d'água: Water tank.

Calçado(a): Paved.

Câmara municipal: Town hall.

Câmbio: Exchange. Also the currency exchange rate.

Campestre: Rural, rustic.

Campo: Countryside, ground, field.

Canalização: Plumbing, sewage system.

Carpete: Fitted carpet.

Carpintaria: Woodwork, carpentry.

Cartão de contribuinte: Tax card.

Casa: House.

Casa de aldeia: Village house.

Casa antiga: Old house.

Casa de banho (completo): (Full) bathroom.

Casa de banho com chuveiro: Bathroom with shower.

Casa de banho privativa: En suite bathroom.

Casa de campo/Casa campestre: Country house or chalet.

Casa de fazenda: Farmhouse or house on a farm.

Casa de férias: Holiday or second home.

Casa de hóspedes ou visitas: Guest house.

Casa independente/separada: Detached villa.

Casa modelo: Show house.

Casa modesta: Modest or basic villa.

Casa renovada: Renovated house, e.g. old village house or cottage.

Casa rústica: Rustic or simple country house.

Casa senhorial: Manor.

Casa subsidiária: Subsidised housing.

Castelo: Castle.

Cave: Wine cellar, basement.

Cédula de habitação: A certificate certifying that a property can be lived in, which is issued when a building conforms with the building standards and codes.

Celeiro: Barn.

Censo electoral: Electoral roll.

Centro de saúde: State-administered medical centre.

Centro de jardinagem: Garden centre.

Cerâmica: Ceramic (e.g. tiles).

Cercado: Fenced.

Certidão de registro: Property certificate of registration.

Certificado/Certidão: Certificate.

Chão de madeira: Wooden floor.

Chão de mármore: Marble floor.

Chalé: Detached villa.

Chaminé: Chimney.

Chave no mão: Ready to occupy, i.e. a fully built and decorated property.

Cheque de viagem: Traveller's cheque.

Churrasco: Barbecue.

Cidade: Town or city.

Cisterna: Water tank/cistern.

Citação: Quotation.

Cláusula de anulação: Annulling or conditional clause (e.g. in a promissory contract).

Código postal: Postal code.

Cofre: Safe.

Compra: Purchase.

Comprador(a): Purchaser, buyer.

Compropriedade: Co-ownership.

Comunidade: Community.

Comunidade de proprietários: Community of owners in a community development such as an apartment block or townhouse development.

Condomínio: Condominium, service charges (community fees).

Condomínio fechado: Condominium in secure building.

Congelador: Freezer.

Conserto: Repair.

Conservatória do registro predial: Land registry.

Conservatório: Conservatory.

Construtor: Builder.

Consultor financeiro: Financial or tax consultant.

Conta: Bill.

Conta bancária: Bank account.

Contabilista: Accountant.

Contador (electricidada, gás, água): Meter (electricity, gas, water).

Contentor de lixo: Dustbin/trash can.

Conto: Popular term for 1,000 escudos (around €5).

Contrato/Acordo: Contract.

Contrato de arrendamento: Rental contract, lease.

Contrato de mediação: An exclusive contract between a vendor and an estate agent to sell a property.

Contrato de promessa de compra e venda: Promissory contract.

Contrato de venda: Sales contract.

Contribuição autártica: Property tax, rates.

Cópia certificada/legalizada: Authorised or certified copy.

Correio: Post office.

Costa: Coast.

Cozinha: Kitchen.

Cozinha aberta: Open plan kitchen with breakfast bar/dining area.

Cozinha (embutida) americana: American (fitted) kitchen.

Cozinha cantina: Eat-in kitchen.

Custos/Gastos: Costs or charges.

Débito directo: Direct debit.

Departamento de estrangeiros: Foreign residents' department, e.g. at a town hall.

Dependência/Anexo: Outbuilding, annexe.

Depósito: Deposit (down payment).

Depósito de água: Water tank.

Depósito de garantía/segurança: Guarantee or security deposit.

Desmobiliado: Unfurnished.

Despachante: An official agent licensed by the government to act as a middleman between members of the public and the bureaucracy.

Despensa: Pantry, larder.

Dinheiro na mão/pronto pagamento: Cash.

Direito de passagem: Right of way.

Direitos reais de propriedade: Real property rights.

Domiciliación de pagos: Standing order, e.g. for payment of utility bills.

Domicílio: Home, residence.

Domicílio fiscal: Main residence for tax purposes.

Ducha: Shower.

Dúplex: Duplex, maisonette, two-storey building.

Duplo: Double.

Edifício: Building.

Eletricidade: Electricity.

Elevador: Elevator/lift; also a funicular railway.

Emolumento: Arrangement fee.

Empréstimo: Loan.

Empreteiro: Builder, contractor.

Endereço: Address.

Energia: Energy, electricity supply.

Entrada: Hallway.

Equipado(a): Equipped.

Escada/Escadaria: Stairway, staircase.

Escritório: Office/study.

Escritório imobiliário/Escritório de mediador: Estate agent's office.

Escritório de vendas e de Aluguer: Sales and rental office.

Escritura pública de compra e venda: Notarised deed of sale.

Esgoto: Drain, sewer.

Espaço para a piscina: Room for a pool.

Espaçoso(a): Spacious.

Esquentador: Water heater.

Estábulo: Stable.

Estacionamento (privativo): Parking (private).

Estado: State, condition.

Estalagem: Inn.

Estatutos/Regras: Statutes, rules or by-laws, e.g. of a community development.

Estimativa: Estimate.

Estores: Blinds, shutters.

Estrada: Road.

Estrada nacional: Main road designated EN on maps.

Estragado: Dilapidated, run down.

Estúdio: Studio apartment.

Estudo: Study.

Estufa (para plantas): Greenhouse.

Factura: Bill.

Feira: Outdoor market or fair.

Fiança: Security deposit, surety.

Fogareiro: Cooker, stove.

Fonte: Spring.

Forno: Oven.

Fossa séptica: Septic tank.

Fosso: Ditch or water channel.

Freguesia: Parish.

Frigorífico: Refrigerator.

Furo: Borehole.

Garagem (dupla): Garage (double).

Garantia: Guarantee, warranty.

Garrafa de gás: Gas bottle.

Gastos/Despesas: Fees or expenses.

Gastos de comunidade: Community fees.

Geminada: Semi-detached (usually refers to terraced townhouses).

Gerador: Generator (for electricity).

Gradeado: Fenced, e.g. garden.

Grades de segurança em ferro: Iron security grilles.

Guarda: Keeper or guard.

Habitação: Dwelling, residence.

Hall de entrada: Entrance hall.

Hectar: Hectare or 10,000 square metres (2.471 acres).

Herdade: Large farm.

Hipermercado: Hypermarket.

Hipoteca: Mortgage.

Honorários: Fees.

Imposto: Tax.

Imposto de automoveis: Car tax.

Imposto comercial: Company or corporation tax.

Imposto de mais valias: Capital gains tax.

Imposto de selo: Stamp tax.

Imposto sobre o Rendimento das pessoas Singulares (IRS): Personal income tax.

Imposto sobre as Sucessões e Doações: Inheritance and gift tax.

Imposto sobre o Valor Acrescentado (IVA): Value added tax.

Imposto sucessório: Inheritance tax.

Inquilino: Tenant.

Inspeção/Vistoria/Revista: Property inspection or survey.

Interior: Hinterland, i.e. not on the coast (also the interior of a house).

Inventário: Inventory.

Invernadero: Conservatory or greenhouse.

IRS: Personal income tax.

IVA (Imposto sobre o Valor Acrescentado): Value added tax (VAT).

Janela: Window.

Janela com batente: French window.

Jardim (comunais): Garden (communal).

Ladrilho: Tiles, tiled floor.

Lago: Lake.

Lar: Home.

Lareira: Fireplace.

Largo: Small square, plaza.

Lavabo: Toilet.

Lavadora: Washing machine.

Lavanderia: Laundry or utility room.

Lei: Law.

Lei de arrendamentos urbanos: Law governing property rentals.

Lei de propiedade horizontal: Law of horizontal division of a community development defining the legal rights and obligations of owners.

Leilão: Auction.

Licença: Licence.

Licença de abertura: Opening licence (for a business).

Licença fiscal/Alvará: Business licence or permit.

Licença de habitabilidade: A certificate certifying that a property can be lived in, which is issued when a building conforms with the building standards and codes.

Licença de obras: Building licence.

Licença de primeira ocupação/ Licença de habitação: Licence required for the first occupation of a building, necessary to have an electricity meter installed.

Licença de utilização: A licence issued by a town hall stating what a property or land can be used for, e.g. residential, commercial or industrial use.

Ligação (de electricidade ou água): Connection (of electricity or water).

Lista de habitantes: List of inhabitants, e.g. of a town.

Lixo: Rubbish, garbage.

Localidade: Locality.

Localização: Location.

Loja: Shop or store.

Loja de ferragens: Ironmonger's.

Lote (de terreno): Plot (of land).

Lote para construção: Building plot.

Luxo/luxuoso: Luxury/luxurious.

Manutenção/Sustento: Maintenance.

Máquina de lavar (roupa): Washing machine.

Mármore: Marble.

(em) Mau estado: In poor condition, dilapidated.

Mediador autorizado/imobiliária: Estate agent.

Memória descritiva: List of building materials and specifications for a new property.

Mercado: Market.

Metros (quadrados): (Square) metres.

Mobilado/Mobiliado: Furnished.

(Sem mobília: Unfurnished.)

Mobília: Furniture.

Modernizado: Modernised.

Moradia: Dwelling, home.

Móveis/com Móveis: Furniture/ furnished.

Mudança: Move house.

Multipropriedades: Timeshare.

Município: Municipality, local authority.

Muro: Wall.

Muro refratário: Heat reflecting wall for a fireplace.

Notário: Notary public. The legal professional who handles the conveyancing for all property sales in Portugal (similar to a British solicitor or an American property lawyer).

Nova(o)/Recente: New.

Número de identificação fiscal (NIF): Fiscal number.

Obra em alvenaria: Brickwork.

Oferta especial/Oferta de ocasião: Special offer.

Ordem de despejo: Eviction order.

Paço: Palace or large country house.

Pagamento mensal: Monthly payment.

Palácio: Palace.

Parabólica: Satellite dish. For community properties it usually refers to a development or urbanisation with communal satellite TV.

Parcela para construão: Building plot.

Parcialmente construída: Partially constructed or completed.

Parecer camarário: A certificate from the local town hall stating what can be built on a plot of land.

Parede: Wall.

Parede divisória/medianero: Partition/party wall.

Parque: Park.

Parque de estacionamento: Parking.

Pátio de fazenda: Farmyard.

Pedreiro: Bricklayer or stonemason.

Pensão: Boarding house/ Bed and breakfast accommodation.

Perigo: Danger.

Permuta: A contract whereby two parties agree to exchange properties, usually with one party paying the other a sum to compensate for the difference in the properties' values.

Persianas: Blinds, shutters.

Piscina: Swimming pool.

Piscina aquecida: Heated swimming pool.

Piscina com aquecimento solar: Solar heated swimming pool.

Piscina comunitária: Communal (shared) swimming pool.

Piso: Floor (of a multi-storey building).

Plano da Ordem Costeira (POC): Coastal building law.

Planta de construção: Plan of building plots.

Poço: Well.

Poder limitado na Procuração: Limited power of attorney.

Poder geral na Procuração: General power of attorney.

Polícia municipal/local: Municipal or local police.

Pomar: Orchard.

Pombal: Dovecote (structure for housing pigeons).

Porta: Door, gate or portal.

Porta blindada: Armoured door, e.g. a high security front door of an apartment.

Porta corrediça: Sliding door.

Porta janela: French window.

Portão: Gate.

Porteiro: Caretaker or doorman, e.g. of an apartment block.

Potência (électrica): Power rating (electricity) of a property's electricity supply.

Pousada: Lodging or inn. Also the name of Portugal's luxury chain of state-run hotels, many of which are located in former castles, monasteries, palaces, convents and manor houses, and/or in outstanding settings.

Praça: Main square.

Praia: Beach.

Preço: Price.

Prédio: Building.

Prédio de apartamentos: Block of flats/apartments.

Prédios rustica: Rural or rustic property.

Prédios urbanos: Urban property.

Presidente: President or chairman, e.g. of a community development.

Presidente da Câmara: Mayor.

Primeira linha junto ao mar: Front line sea position, e.g. on the beach.

Processo/Ação judicial: Lawsuit.

Procuração: Power of attorney or proxy.

Procurador: Attorney, proxy or holder of a power of attorney.

Promotor/Promovedor: Developer, e.g. of an urbanisation.

Propriedade: Property.

Propriedade agrícola: Agricultural property.

Propriedade rural: Country property.

Propriedade urbana: Town property.

Província: Province, e.g. Algarve.

Provisão de vinho: Wine cellar or vat room.

Qualidade: Quality.

Quarteirão/Bairro: Neighbourhood or city quarter.

Quarto: Room, bedroom.

Quarto de casal: Room with a double bed.

Quarto duplo (com dois camas): Double bedroom (with two beds).

Quarto de empregada: Maid's room.

Quarto grande: Large room.

Quarto individual/simple: Single room.

Quarto principal: Master bedroom.

Quinta: Farmhouse or house on a farm.

Quota/Ação (de proprietário): An owner's share (expressed as a percentage) of a community development, used to calculate his percentage of community fees.

(em) Razoável estado: In reasonable condition.

Recente: Recent, new.

Recibo: Receipt.

Recolha de lixo: Rubbish collection.

Reformado: Renovated, reformed, modernised. Also retired (pensioner).

Registo de propriedade: Property registry.

Relatório: Report.

Relvado: Lawn.

Renda: Income.

Renovação: Renovation.

Renovado: Renovated.

Reparação: Repair.

Repartião de finanças: Tax office.

Reposição bancária: Bank repossession.

Representante fiscal: Fiscal representative.

Rés-do-chão (R/C): Ground floor.

Residência: Residence, address.

Residência fiscal: Main residence for tax purposes.

Residência habitual/principal: Main or primary residence.

Residente: Resident.

Restauração: Restoration.

Ribeiro: Stream.

Rio: River.

Rossio: Main square.

Roupeiro: Fitted (built-in) wardrobe.

Rua: Street.

(em) Ruínas: In ruins.

Sala: Room.

Sala comun: Living-dining room.

Sala de estar/visitas: Living room, lounge.

Sala de inverno: Conservatory (literally 'winter room').

Sala de jantar: Dining room.

Sala de jogos: Entertainment room.

Salão: Large room, salon.

Sanitários: Public toilets.

Segunda casa/residência: Second or holiday home.

Segurança social: Social security.

Seguro: Insurance.

Seguro de bens domésticos: Household insurance.

Seguro civil contra terceiros: Third party or public liability insurance.

Seguro de viagem: Travel insurance.

Seguro-saúde: Health insurance.

Selo fiscal: Official stamp (on a document).

Serviço de Estrangeiros e Fronteiras (SEF): Foreigners' department.

Sinal: Deposit.

SISA: Property transfer tax.

Sistema de esgotos: Sewage system.

Sistema de segurança: Security system (e.g. an alarm).

Situado(a): Situated.

Soalho (de madeira): Floor (wooden).

Sobrecarga/Sobretaxa: Surcharge.

Sociedade de Mediação Imobiliária: Society of Estate Agents.

Solar: Manor house or important town mansion.

Solário: Solarium, sun roof.

Solicitador: Solicitor.

Solo: Land, ground.

Soma: Amount.

Sossegado(a)/Sossego: Peaceful, quiet.

Sótão: Attic, loft.

Sótão de luxo: Penthouse.

Taxa: Tax.

Taxa de juro: Interest rate.

Taxa rodoviária: Road tax.

Taxas comunitárias: Community fees.

Telhado: Roof.

Telhado plano/Açoteia: Flat roof.

Temporário(a): Temporary or short-term.

Ténis: Tennis.

Terra/Terreno: Land, plot.

Terraço: Terrace.

Terraço coberto: Covered terrace.

Terraço fechado: Terrace with windows.

Terreno: Plot of land.

Terreno agrícola: Agricultural land.

Terreno para construção: Building land.

Terreno rural: Rural land.

Terreno urbanizável: Agricultural land that can be changed to building land.

Testamento: Will.

Tijoleira: Floor tiles.

Tijolo: Brick, brickwork.

Todos os gastos/despesas: All fees or charges/expenses.

Torre: Tower.

Tranqüilo: Quiet, peaceful.

Transferência: Banker's order.

Transferência de propriedade: Transfer of property, conveyancing.

Traspasse/ Trespasse: Lease or transfer of property.

Trave de madeira: Wooden beam.

Tribunal de expropriaçães: Special court to decide disputes over expropriation of property.

Turismo: Tourist office.

Último piso: Top floor.

Urbanização: Urbanisation or housing estate. A community development.

Urbano: Urban.

Urgente: Urgent.

Usufruto/Interesse vitalício: A life interest, e.g. in a property.

Valor tributável: The fiscal or rateable value of a property fixed by the local municipality, on which property taxes are calculated.

Varanda: Verandah, balcony.

Varanda envidraçada: Conservatory.

Velho: Old.

Vende-se/à Venda: For sale.

Vendedor(a): Vendor or seller.

Vestiário: Changing room.

Vestíbulo: Entrance hall.

Vidrado duplamente: Double glazed.

Vidro/Cristal: Glass.

Viga: Beams.

Vigas de madeira: Wooden beams, beamed ceiling.

Vila: Town, villa.

Vista: View.

Vista da costa: Coastal views.

Vista do campo: Country views.

Vista do mar: Sea views.

Vista panorâmica: Panoramic views.

Vivenda: Residence, dwelling.

Vizinhança: Neighbourhood.

APPENDIX F: MAPS OF REGIONS & PROVINCES

The maps of Portugal below and opposite show the 6 'tourist' regions and 11 provinces, plus the Portuguese island of Madeira (shown approximately two-and-a-half times larger). A map of Portugal showing the major cities and geographical features is shown on page 6.

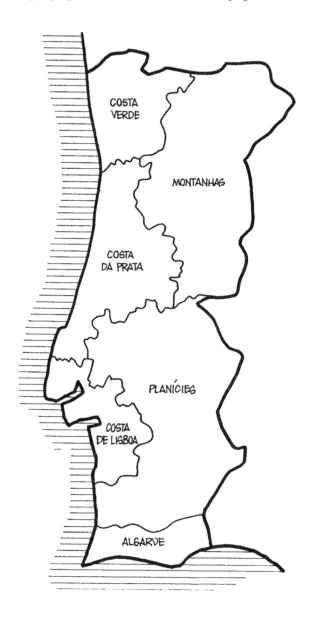

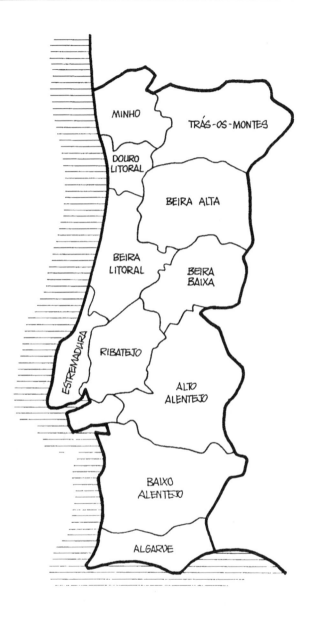

INDEX

BUYING A HOME IN SPAIN

Buying a Home in Spain is essential reading for anyone planning to purchase property in Spain and is designed to guide you through the jungle and make it a pleasant and enjoyable experience. Most importantly, it's packed with vital information to help you avoid the sort of disasters that can turn your dream home into a nightmare! Topics covered include:

- Avoiding problems
- Choosing the region
- Finding the right home & location
- Estate agents
- Finance, mortgages & taxes
- Home security
- Utilities, heating & air-conditioning
- Moving house & settling in
- Renting & letting
- Permits & visas
- Travelling & communications
- Health & insurance
- Renting a car & driving
- Retirement & starting a business
- And much, much more!

Buying a Home in Spain is the most comprehensive and up-to-date source of information available about buying property in Spain. Whether you want a detached house, townhouse or apartment, a holiday or a permanent home, this book will help make your dreams come true.

Buy this book and save yourself time, trouble and money!

Order your copies today by phone, fax, mail or e-mail from: Survival Books, PO Box 146, Wetherby, West Yorks. LS23 6XZ, United Kingdom (☎/▤ +44 (0)1937-843523, ✉ orders@ survivalbooks.net, 💻 www.survivalbooks.net).

ORDER FORM

ALIEN'S GUIDES / BEST PLACES / BUYING A HOME / WINES

Qty.	Title	Price (incl. p&p)*			Total
		UK	Europe	World	
	The Alien's Guide to Britain	£5.95	£6.95	£8.45	
	The Alien's Guide to France	£5.95	£6.95	£8.45	
	The Best Places to Buy a Home in France	Winter 2002			
	The Best Places to Buy a Home in Spain	£13.45	£14.95	£16.95	
	Buying a Home Abroad	£13.45	£14.95	£16.95	
	Buying a Home in Britain	£11.45	£12.95	£14.95	
	Buying a Home in Florida	£13.45	£14.95	£16.95	
	Buying a Home in France	£13.45	£14.95	£16.95	
	Buying a Home in Greece & Cyprus	£13.45	£14.95	£16.95	
	Buying a Home in Ireland	£11.45	£12.95	£14.95	
	Buying a Home in Italy	£13.45	£14.95	£16.95	
	Buying a Home in Portugal	£13.45	£14.95	£16.95	
	Buying a Home in Spain	£13.45	£14.95	£16.95	
	How to Avoid Holiday & Travel Disasters	£13.45	£14.95	£16.95	
	Rioja and its Wines	£11.45	£12.95	£14.95	
	The Wines of Spain	£15.95	£18.45	£21.95	
				Total	

Order your copies today by phone, fax, mail or e-mail from: Survival Books, PO Box 146, Wetherby, West Yorks. LS23 6XZ, UK (☎/▤ +44 (0)1937-843523, ✉ orders@survivalbooks.net, 🖳 www.survivalbooks.net). If you aren't entirely satisfied, simply return them to us within 14 days for a full and unconditional refund.

Cheque enclosed/please charge my Delta/Mastercard/Switch/Visa* card

Card No. __ __ __ __ __ __ __ __ __ __ __ __ __ __ __ __

Expiry date _____ **Issue number (Switch only)** _____

Signature _____ **Tel. No.** _____

NAME _____

ADDRESS _____

_____

_____

* Delete as applicable (price includes postage – airmail for Europe/world).

LIVING AND WORKING IN SPAIN

Living and Working in Spain is essential reading for anyone planning to spend some time in Spain including holiday-home owners, retirees, visitors, business people, migrants, students and even extraterrestrials! It's packed with over 400 pages of important and useful information designed to help you **avoid costly mistakes and save both time and money.** Topics covered include how to:

- Find a job with a good salary & conditions
- Obtain a residence permit
- Avoid and overcome problems
- Find your dream home
- Get the best education for your family
- Make the best use of public transport
- Endure motoring in Spain
- Obtain the best health treatment
- Stretch your euros further
- Make the most of your leisure time
- Enjoy the Spanish sporting life
- Find the best shopping bargains
- Insure yourself against most eventualities
- Use post office and telephone services
- Do numerous other things not listed above

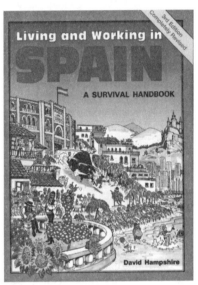

Living and Working in Spain is the most comprehensive and up-to-date source of practical information available about everyday life in Spain. It isn't, however, a boring text book, but an interesting and entertaining guide written in a highly readable style.

Buy this book and discover what it's *really* like to live and work in Spain.

Order your copies today by phone, fax, mail or e-mail from: Survival Books, PO Box 146, Wetherby, West Yorks. LS23 6XZ, United Kingdom (☎/▤ +44 (0)1937-843523, ✉ orders@ survivalbooks.net, ▱ www.survivalbooks.net).

ORDER FORM

LIVING & WORKING SERIES / RETIRING ABROAD

Qty.	Title	Price (incl. p&p)*			Total
		UK	Europe	World	
	Living & Working Abroad	£14.95	£16.95	£20.45	
	Living & Working in America	£14.95	£16.95	£20.45	
	Living & Working in Australia	£14.95	£16.95	£20.45	
	Living & Working in Britain	£14.95	£16.95	£20.45	
	Living & Working in Canada	£14.95	£16.95	£20.45	
	Living & Working in France	£14.95	£16.95	£20.45	
	Living & Working in Germany	£14.95	£16.95	£20.45	
	Living & Working in the Gulf States & Saudi Arabia	Winter 2002			
	Living & Working in Holland, Belgium & Luxembourg	£14.95	£16.95	£20.45	
	Living & Working in Ireland	£14.95	£16.95	£20.45	
	Living & Working in Italy	£14.95	£16.95	£20.45	
	Living & Working in London	£11.45	£12.95	£14.95	
	Living & Working in New Zealand	£14.95	£16.95	£20.45	
	Living & Working in Spain	£14.95	£16.95	£20.45	
	Living & Working in Switzerland	£14.95	£16.95	£20.45	
	Retiring Abroad	£14.95	£16.95	£20.45	
				Total	

Order your copies today by phone, fax, mail or e-mail from: Survival Books, PO Box 146, Wetherby, West Yorks. LS23 6XZ, UK (☎/▤ +44 (0)1937-843523, ⊠ orders@survivalbooks.net, ▄ www.survivalbooks.net). If you aren't entirely satisfied, simply return them to us within 14 days for a full and unconditional refund.

Cheque enclosed/please charge my Delta/Mastercard/Switch/Visa* card

Card No. __ __ __ __   __ __ __ __   __ __ __ __   __ __ __ __

Expiry date_____   **Issue number (Switch only)** _____

Signature _____   **Tel. No.** _____

NAME _____

ADDRESS _____

_____

_____

* Delete as applicable (price includes postage – airmail for Europe/world).

NOTES

NOTES

NOTES

NOTES